The Elusive What and the Problematic How: The Essential
Leadership Questions for School Leaders and Educational
Researchers

Th

EDUCATIONAL LEADERSHIP AND LEADERS IN CONTEXTS
Volume 3

Series Editor
Tony Townsend and Ira Bogotch
Florida Atlantic University, Boca Raton, FL, USA

Scope

The series, *Educational Leadership and Leaders in Contexts,* emphasizes how historical and contextual assumptions shape the meanings and values assigned to the term leadership. The series includes books along four distinct threads:

- *Reconsidering the role of social justice within the contexts of educational leadership*
- *Promoting a community of leadership: Reaching out and involving stakeholders and the public*
- *Connecting the professional and personal dimensions of educational leadership*
- *Reconceptualizing educational leadership as a global profession*

Perhaps to a greater extent than ever before, today's educational leaders find themselves living in a world that is substantially different from what it was just a decade ago. The threads of social justice, community leadership, professional and personal dimensions, and globalism have added contextual dimensions to educational leaders that are often not reflected in their local job descriptions. This book series will focus on how these changing contexts affect the theory and practice of educational leaders.

Similarly, the professional lives of educational leaders has increasingly impinged upon their personal well-being, such that it now takes a certain type of individual to be able to put others before self for extended periods of their working life. This series will explore the dynamic relationship between the personal and the professional lives of school leaders.

With respect to communities, recent educational reforms have created a need for communities to know more about what is happening inside of classrooms and schools. While education is blamed for many of the ills identified in societies, school leaders and school communities are generally ignored or excluded from the processes related to social development. The challenge facing school leaders is to work with and build community support through the notion of community leadership. Thus, leadership itself involves working with teachers, students, parents and the wider community in order to improve schools.

As for the fourth thread, globalism, school leaders must now work with multiple languages, cultures, and perspectives reflecting the rapid shift of people from one part of the world to another. Educational leaders now need to be educated to understand global perspectives and react to a world where a single way of *thinking and doing* no longer applies.

The Elusive What and the Problematic How:
The Essential Leadership Questions for
School Leaders and Educational Researchers

Tony Townsend
Florida Atlantic University

Ira Bogotch
Florida Atlantic University

SENSE PUBLISHERS
ROTTERDAM / TAIPEI

A C.I.P. record for this book is available from the Library of Congress.

ISBN 978-90-8790-568-2 (paperback)
ISBN 978-90-8790-569-9 (hardback)
ISBN 978-90-8790-570-5 (e-book)

Published by: Sense Publishers,
P.O. Box 21858, 3001 AW
Rotterdam, The Netherlands

Printed on acid-free paper

PREFACE

For some time the editors of this book have been discussing issues related to improving the quality of education as it relates to student outcomes in schools. The editors come from two different education backgrounds, one (Ira) where educational leadership traditionally has been developed through masters or other certification programs offered by universities that were obliged to follow the various certification rules set down by their associated US state departments of education and the other (Tony) where leaders in most Australian schools were traditionally appointed to leadership positions before they had any training on how to become a leader. These two very diverse backgrounds, the first where self-selection into a program is later followed by further training at the district level, with the possible eventual selection as a school leader on the one hand, and the second where the individual is identified as being a potential leader and then undergoes departmental led training as a leader which may or may not be done in conjunction with university credits, led to some interesting conversations.

The 2006 International Congress for School Effectiveness and Improvement, which was hosted by the College of Education at FAU, provided the opportunity for people from many parts of the world to contribute to the interaction and a number of the people who presented at the conference were able to reshape their papers, which looked at various aspects of leadership research, into chapters that considered both the 'what' of educational leadership and the 'how' we come to know this through educational research.

The current book is an attempt to analyze these factors to try and establish a way forward for the future of leadership research. We would like to thank the authors for their contributions and look forward to hearing from readers that might wish to respond to the contents.

Tony Townsend and Ira Bogotch
Boca Raton, Florida
May 2008

TABLE OF CONTENTS

Section One: The What of School Leadership

IRA BOGOTCH AND TONY TOWNSEND

1. WHAT ARE THE ESSENTIAL LEADERSHIP QUESTIONS IN A RAPIDLY CHANGING WORLD?

INTRODUCTION

Educational leadership, like many other facets of human life, can be looked at from two different points of view. We have chosen to call these points of view the 'what' and the 'how'. The 'what' in this instance is the knowledge required to do the job well. It is 'knowing' about curriculum, about management, about human relations and about the various factors, both inside and outside the school, that are required to keep those within the school, students, teachers and others, safe and productive. However, it is only when this 'knowing' is joined by the 'how' that school leadership is successful. The 'how' in this instance is the set of processes used by the school leader to communicate, implement, evaluate and relate the knowledge base to those with whom the leader interacts, together with the attitudes and values that are shared between both leader and followers. We would argue that the practice of educational leadership is artistry, when these two factors come together in a way that promotes both simultaneously.

If leadership is artistry, then we can make some comparisons to other types of artistry. A person may know how to mix paint, how to prepare a canvas and how to apply paint to the canvas (the what), but it is only when this knowledge interacts with the ideas and values that lead to judgments about how and where to apply that paint, that the painter moves from being a dabbler to being an artist. Likewise a person with great ideas but no knowledge on how to apply them becomes a talent unfulfilled. So too, with the actor, where a person may know the lines and where on stage to move, but without the flair required to convince us that the circumstances are real rather then playacting, the master becomes a ham. A doctor may know Grey's Anatomy from front to back, but without 'bedside manner' his patients may desert whereas a doctor with great patient rapport but little knowledge becomes a danger and a teacher may be able to recite all the necessary information for students to pass their tests, but unless the presentation is delivered in a way that engages, the students will not succeed. On the other hand a teacher with flair but no knowledge may be entertaining, but won't help students to achieve their dreams.

T. Townsend and I. Bogotch (eds.), The Elusive What and the Problematic How: The Essential Leadership Questions for School Leaders and Educational Researchers, 3–15.

It is where knowledge and performance meet that artistry lies. Where the 'what' and the 'how' become the 'whow'. It is this area that this book chooses to explore, by using chapters from all over the world. We have deliberately asked our writers to separate the 'what' from the 'how' to provide a better understanding of the importance of the 'praxis' effect, where theory and practice meet.

Most nonfiction books, especially those on the subject of education, are written to combat specific ignorances. In education, a subject that the late North American social critic Neil Postman "claims dominion over the widest possible territory," we are immediately confronted by two sets of ignorance, the "what" and the "how." In Postman's words:

> [Education] purports to tell us not only what intelligence is but how it may be nurtured; not only what is worthwhile knowledge but how it may be gained; not only what is the good life but how one may prepare for it. There is no other subject—not even philosophy itself—that casts so wide a net, and therefore no other subject that requires of its professors so much genius and wisdom. (Postman, 1988)

By highlighting the "what" and "how" of education, the authors of this book are reaffirming our faith in both theory [the purposes and ends of education] and practice [the processes of preparation and nurturing]. We do so not in the traditional sense of applying prior theories to practice, but rather as a mutual relationship between educational thoughts and educational actions. On this stage, we are happy to be in the company of such theorists as John Dewey (1904; 1920/62; 1916/63), Gilbert Ryle (1949), Chris Argyris and Donald Schon (1975), etc. Whether called re-constructivism, knowing-how, double-loop learning, reflective practice, pedagogical content or, most recently, the instructional dynamic, (Ball and Forzani, 2007), the essays in this book make both the ends and the means of education visible. "To profess to have an aim and then neglect the means of its execution is self-delusion of the most dangerous sort" (Dewey, 1920/1962, p. 75). We believe this is necessary pedagogically for advancing knowledge and improving practice, including the practices of educational research.

Although we assert that knowledge of the "what" and the "how" are necessarily connected, perhaps even as being one thing as Ryle (1949) indicated, we do so in the context of differences. No two people or settings or interactions over time are ever the same. Thus, our discussions of the "what" and the "how" have three objectives: (1) we must account for contextual differences; (2) we must account for unanticipated knowledge and skills related to educational leadership and school improvement; and (3) we must make these processes, in terms of the ends and the means, completely visible to students of education. In so doing, we highlight systematic thinking, careful analysis, issues of validity, and practicality. Whether the professional objective involves the replication of research or the implementation of research-based programs, it is necessary that educators understand how ideas and actions together lead us toward new ideas and new actions – what we call generically educational leadership and school improvement. Conversely, we want to avoid, or at least limit as much as possible, ready made answers [i.e., miseducative what's] as well as haphazard and irrelevant actions [i.e., miseducative how's].

For the authors in this book, there can be no valid excuses for ignorance in any aspect of education as theory/practice. For example,
- If we come to learn that all educational problems involve knowledge of complex systems and processes, then quick, simple solutions should not be an educator's first or only expedient option.
- If all education requires a measure of cultural and contextual under-standings, then uniform, standardized programs and lessons will not meet the needs of all children or communities.
- If educational change takes time and strenuous efforts to take hold, then why do we abandon and restart reforms efforts year after year?
- If educational practices are best performed by those closest to the problems, then why do we not prepare and continuously develop teachers and administrators to grow intellectually and politically to make wise decisions?
- If who a person is culturally and intellectually shapes who they are as educators, then why are our recruitment, selection, induction, and retention policies not influenced by this assumption?
- If today's best practices have not taken careful note of successes in the past, then how do we validly measure best practices in use today?
- If one-time, standardized test scores are not adequate measures of a person's worth, a teacher's competency, or a schools' value to its community, then why do our policies and practices say otherwise?

Unfortunately, our ignorance of the "what" and the "how" has persisted across contexts and history. Why? In part, we believe that our strengths as educators have contributed to our problems. That is, our strength comes from our can-do, problem-solving, activist, desire to make a difference as teachers and school leaders. We as educators are pragmatic, political and ethical. At the same time, the demands that we place on ourselves and allow others to place on us have made us a vulnerable profession (Callahan, 1962, Lagemann, 2000). Constant busy-ness prevents any one from being at her/his intellectual, reflective, and critical best. Without study, discussion and debate, decisions are not well thought out and therefore susceptible to political pressures and popular opinions. We may, unintentionally perhaps, cut corners or act expediently just to survive. We may, deliberately perhaps, resort to a form of leadership language, with such words as strength, decisiveness, community, involvement, etc.; but such words only mask our ignorance; they are not educational nor can the words themselves bring about school improvement. For too long we have hidden behind the mantel of leadership instead of practicing real educational leadership.

It would be dishonest for us to deny the above realities. It would be also disingenuous to deny a theory-practice gap within education. There is empirical evidence that indicates that practitioners find educational theory impractical and irrelevant. Likewise, we have evidence that academicians find classroom and administrative practices, including the many so-called best practices, far short of the purposes and ideals of education. This has been so throughout history: Greek students were more attracted to the teachings of the sophists in order to learn how to sway their fellow citizens than they were to the intellectual critiques of Socrates. Not surprisingly, Socrates' student Plato took choice away from citizens and replaced it with a pre-set educational system functioning coherently in the service of society as a whole. He called this the Republic. It was not until the 20th Century and John Dewey that a philosopher once again asserted just how difficult education, teaching, learning, and leading, really is under any and all circumstances.

Over the centuries, social forces of modernization and progress should have elevated the status of education in societies. Instead, social forces have had the opposite effects, keeping educators and education vulnerable to centers of power, whether government, business, or military (Callahan, 1962). To some educationists, for example Bowles and Gintis (1976), the schools' functional role was designed in order to slot individuals into different social positions with respect to labor and service so as to sustain and maintain societies. In many instances, the real powers of education as intellect and vision, would be selectively reserved for those attending elite and often inaccessible schools and universities.

With new laws for universal and compulsory education, however, a place called school (Goodlad, 1984) evolved to deliver prescribed lessons to the masses. In rare instances only, a place called school allowed both educators and their students to reconstruct knowledge through educative experiences, human capital, and moral practices (Dewey, 1904/1965). Today, such places are rarer still. In this era of national educational policies that impose accountability onto local constituencies, a place called school does not allow for professional decision-making or professional judgments. Separating educators from theory; separating practice from reconstructive theory has disenfranchised educators who – by themselves at least – cannot be expected to reform the educational establishments around the world. All of us today must become even more aware of how professional judgments have been systematically erased in educational practice, especially in this current era of accountability. Professional judgments are not viewed by those in power as scientific, legitimate, research-based or theory. Instead, educational practices, limited by measurements, have supplanted the role of professional judgment. For Postman and us, this is ignorance.

It was out of this critical analysis that the idea for this book was born. We wanted to bring pedagogical knowledge of theory and practice together as a collective discussion of the "what" of education to be followed and explained in terms of the "how" of education. The authors of this book tell you why and how they arrived at the "what" of school leadership and school improvement. As you will see in the subsequent sections, their interpretations of the "how" differ greatly. Nevertheless, our message is that without an integrated understanding of both the "what" and the "how," we will not advance the ideals of education and consequently we will remain vulnerable.

Education is contextual and temporal in theory and practice. In other words, what we are experiencing today was not always the case in education, nor is it the case in many international settings. There are school, states, communities, and nations that combine innovative thinking and with innovative practices. Education has suffered most in countries where national, bureaucratic systems have standardized and mandated practices limited to behaviors/outcomes that are easily measured. Fortunately, education comes armed with inherent powers that resist monolithic enterprises, powers that are able to keep the ideals of education alive around the world, even in difficult circumstances. Thus, Nieto (2003) reminds us that educators have a resilience to keep going because of who we are; at times, it is our love of others that sustain us; and at other times, it is our anger at central authorities; or, it is our optimism and hope in the present and for the future; and, of course, there is our exercising of intelligence as educators.

Thus, we must all strive to bring professional knowledge to ourselves and others, even to those held hostage by oppressive and monopolistic systems. We all know that national and state educational policies, district and school educational decisions, educational programs, and local educational judgments all compete for the mantel of legitimacy. Those of us who work inside universities have argued that educational research – our research questions, methods, and findings should be at the top of the list when searching for educational solutions. Such a view reflects this book's overt bias. We believe, however, that when readers from all levels of education see the "what" and the "how" explained and demonstrated, then they, too, will embrace the legitimate meaning of research-based – as not only understanding for competency, but also being prepared for unanticipated contingencies (Ryle, 1949).

John Dewey (1904) pointedly asked why educators were constantly coming to new reforms, jumping onto bandwagons, and not distinguishing between substance and appearance. He believed that we as educators had not nurtured our own intellectual cores, and as a result we have been swayed to do this or that depending upon the political reform current of the day. He devoted his entire career to bringing knowledge through systematic experiments and laboratory learning to his audiences. His faith in the power of education as a profession never wavered. That same faith is reflected in this book.

THE WHAT OF SCHOOL LEADERSHIP

The first section of the book, chapters two through seven, looks at the question of 'what is school leadership?' from various perspectives. These perspectives range from a general understanding of the purposes and ends of education to what school leadership should look like within and across different settings and under different cultural conditions. Collectively, the 'what' of school leadership provides a strong foundation for school improvement efforts around the world.

In chapter two, John MacBeath argues the case that the notion of 'superleader' as the person who takes charge and can turn schools around by him or herself is no longer viable. He argues that when schools do succeed the leader is applauded, but if they fail the leader is criticized, sanctioned or dismissed. This is a simplistic view of a very complex organization and that if schools are to really become places of learning in the future then a different understanding of leadership is required. He argues that servant leadership, where the role of the leader is to bring out the best in others, together with an understanding that all people in the school, including teachers, administrative assistants and students need to be able to demonstrate leadership given appropriate circumstances, while the leader should be prepared to be the follower when these circumstances arise. As Townsend and Otero (1999) indicate, in a good school, everyone is a learner, a teacher and a leader.

In chapter three, Sharmistha Das provides an overview of the way in which school culture impacts on learning and the issues that leaders must consider in developing a school culture. She discusses the importance of considering the impact of values and the various roles people play in developing a school culture and outlines how short term efficiency-based values may impact on the longer term desire to provide students with a quality education. She provides an example to show how similar statements of value might create different outcomes in practice. The chapter then identifies the connections between school ethos and school effectiveness and how history, people and context of the school are critical factors in building a school culture. Her review of the literature demonstrates the complexity of the various terms associated with school culture and how different terms might be used in different contexts, countries and disciplines. She defines an effective school culture as one where there is a sense of

– belonging to an organization with a unique history,
– where people follow a certain code of practice,
– share a particular set of values, and
– respect a specific way of communication in pursuing a common goal towards children's learning.

The absence of some of these things might be considered as less effective and the absence of all of them is a toxic school culture, one that reinforces negative values. The chapter provides an overview of some of the typologies associated with school culture and the roles that school leaders might play in these.

In chapter four Lejf Moos, John Krejsler and Klaus Kasper Kofod consider what successful leadership means, based on the data collected during the International Successful School Principalship Project (ISSP). The data collected from the USA, UK, Australia, China, Canada, Sweden, Norway and Denmark suggest that although there are common directions undertaken by the nations involved in terms of movement towards decentralized aspects leading to school-site management, coupled with more centralized approaches to curriculum and assessment, there are many different approaches adopted at the local level, which makes any global statements of what makes successful school leadership problematic. They use the case of two schools in Denmark to demonstrate how the concept of success in these schools is interpreted and created in different ways as a means of demonstrating how at the local level what seems to be the same can be very different. One important outcome of the study, however, was that in both countries where the accountability movement has been in place for some years and in countries where it is comparatively new, principals agree that education is more than simply attending to the basic of literacy and numeracy. For schools to be successful, students must become good citizens.

In chapter five, Alma Harris and Pat Thompson focus their attention on the issue of leadership in schools that work under challenging circumstances.

First, they identify why the demographic, social, health and safety issues that exist in such schools might suggest that schools facing such circumstances might always struggle to perform as well as schools in much better areas, with much healthier, supported and protected children. Rather than indicating that this might be a reason why we need not aspire to improve student performance in these schools, they argue that the research does indicate that it is possible for such schools to substantially increase student achievement and that one of the main factors in doing this is the leadership that exists in these schools. They identify a series of common factors that characterize leaders that have been successful in challenged schools. At the center is the vision and values that arise from the underlying belief that all children can learn and then enabling the whole school community to align to these values and vision. Essentially these values could be identified as moral, focusing on the welfare of the people involved, rather than instrumental or custodial. Added to this was a firmness that enabled principals to ensure that the vision was followed and that hard decisions would be made when some teachers failed to do this. Always the focus was on improved teaching and learning. Underlying this was a structured plan of professional development, distributed leadership, community building and relationship building. These supported the twin activities of promoting both structural and cultural change within the school. This focus on capacity building, necessary for all schools, is essential for schools in challenging circumstances.

In chapter six Ira Bogotch, Luis Miron and Gert Biesta consider the specific case of the Algiers Charter School District Association's attempts to rebuild a school system in post-Katrina New Orleans. They consider this development from the viewpoint of a critical review of the school effectiveness and school improvement research, which they argue has gained a privileged status (particularly from politicians and government) when it comes to characterizing good schools, good teachers and good student outcomes. They suggest that the managerialist approaches that have been proposed and developed by education systems to improve student outcomes, have been based on SESI research that ignores the underlying conditions and values that reside in the schools themselves. In short the SESI research is accused of ignoring the contextual issues that are attached to schools by culture, race and socio-economic conditions. The chapter reports on the creation and progress of a new charter school district, one among other charter school systems, that seeks to transform the educational provision for students in a way that supports all those involved, through strong focused relationships with their teachers. They report that, at the early stages of this transformation, the new ethos has been promoted and supported. The fear, however, is twofold: first, the demands from further afield, related to accountability requirements associated with the SESI perspective might disrupt any attempts to build a new way of recreating a city through education; and, secondly, the entrepreneurialism inherent in the charter schools in Algiers and throughout New Orleans will not serve the city as a whole, but rather reinforce the cultural privileges inherent in the pre-Katrina public schools.

In chapter seven Charles Duke and Kavin Ming discuss what it means to be culturally competent, where educators and school leaders have to bring the complexity of cultural differences in society together with national mandates such the *No Child Left Behind Act* (NCLB) and the *Individuals with Disabilities Education Improvement Act* (IDEIA). They argue that cultural competence is more than just sensitivity, but a real awareness of both the richness and limitations brought about by working in a diverse setting. They indicate that cultural competence is part of multicultural education, but indicate that multicultural education still suffers from being seen as content rather than process. Teachers have a tendency to see multicultural education as a course, rather than something that should be understood by all teachers. Rather multicultural education is the knowledge base that generates the sets of skills that lead to cultural competence. They make the point that although current classrooms are now much more diverse and complex places, as integration of students with various differences (language, disabilities, color), that were previously taught in other places has occurred in recent times, the training necessary to support the skills required by the regular teacher to teach these children has not kept pace, leading to a mismatch between the needs of the students and the abilities of the teachers to serve them. The chapter considers some of the issues that need to be considered if cultural competence is to be promoted in pre-service teacher education programs and through professional development of teachers in the field.

THE HOW OF SCHOOL LEADERSHIP AND SCHOOL LEADERSHIP RESEARCH

The second section of the book considers the various research activities that have generated the positions held in the first section. Essentially the question here is 'How do we know what good leadership is?' These chapters consider the research from a number of countries and across countries in an effort to answer this question.

In chapter eight MacBeath describes the learning developed through the Carpe Vitam project, a multi-country study that looked at the linkages between learning and leadership. Five principles of practice are identified if leadership within the school would lead to learning. The first and most important of these is that leadership should focus on learning, and the other

11

four principles followed on from this one. They were that leadership needs to create and sustain the conditions for learning, that it must make learning visible and discussable, that it needs to be undertaken by all in the school, not just those in positions of leadership and finally that leadership for learning must practice accountability. For MacBeath, leadership is essentially subversive as it fails to accept what is currently offered and always seeks to improve the status quo.

In chapter nine Das provides data from four case study schools in Scotland to demonstrate that, although every school may have common factors related to school culture in play, it is how these factors are combined or handled that makes each school culture unique. The case studies demonstrate clearly how school culture reshapes and reorganizes itself based on the people and processes that are in play in the school. This reinforces the critical role that school leaders play in shaping school culture. The leadership shown in each of the case study schools is analyzed using Bush's (1995) models of educational management and Bolman and Deal's (1991) organizational frames.

In chapter ten Moos, Krejsler and Kofod consider the nature of the changing leadership interactions in schools in Denmark, arguing that the meeting of some of the newer international trends towards testing, accountability and decentralization with the more traditional understanding of the relations in the school that lead to a 'democratic community' has led to new interpretations of leadership in ways that are complex and not always accepted. They argue that the loose couplings that exist between semiautonomous departments and self-governing teams, a product of the move towards greater decentralization, is matched by tight couplings brought about by leadership teams maintaining control over many of the important decisions by structuring the school in a way that only the leaders have the overall knowledge required to make important decisions. So while the schools display many of the signs of democratic communities in many cases people seek out the leader's reassurance to ensure that they are on the right track. Although people are actively involved in the decision making process, there is also the social mechanism that wants them to make decisions that will be acceptable to the leader.

In chapter eleven Harris and Thompson identify the research underlying the arguments developed in chapter four. They identify four major strands of research that has helped to explain the development of this perception of leadership. These strands are identified as 'what works?' or accounts of research that led to generalizable understandings of practice, 'I did it my way', the stories of successful leaders, either written by themselves or others, 'what is going on here?' or ethnographic studies of either schools or leaders that help to enlighten us about the circumstances in which they operate, and 'what might schools/leaders do to help all children succeed?' where alternative approaches to leading schools in challenging circumstances, and critical, feminist and post-modern theories are considered. The authors also identify the importance of what they call 'How can we find out how to do better for all students and in so doing, make it happen?', where schools, sometimes in conjunction with universities, undertake action research projects that are often unpublished or only available to a small audience. They argue that although each method is important, that the true way forward for research of schools in challenging circumstances lies in the more comprehensive multi-method and multi-disciplinary approaches of studying leadership in these schools. Finally they identify what they see as being significant gaps in the research and challenge future leadership researchers to be more multi-disciplined and comprehensive in their approach.

In chapter twelve Bogotch and Miron consider the unique position they experienced as "native" son researchers into the educational system rebuilding that occurred in New Orleans post Katrina. They describe how the role of the researcher in circumstances such as these changes from being an observer to being an observant participant. They identify their concern that the political moves towards marketization and accountability, observable in the rest of the country may curtail the opportunity for real educational reform to take place. They make a plea that the role of research in the process of redevelopment on this scale cannot rely on what we previously knew about research. New research methods and new theories of education will have to be generated in such circumstances, but for this to happen more resources and time than are usually given to schools (and to researchers) must be provided.

In chapter thirteen Duke and Ming consider three necessary steps for school leaders to support their schools and teachers to become culturally competent. The first step in the process is for school leaders to become knowledgeable about today's society, in all its diversity and how in turn, this impacts schools, families and students. The second is that issues of cultural diversity should be systematically embedded in the professional development undertaken by people working in the school setting. The third step is to provide teachers with support to change the way in which they teach by either recruiting or training teachers or other professionals who are skilled in multiculturalism to provide advice and train teachers in these skills. The chapter provides some strategies for school leaders to use to increase the dialogue about cultural competence within schools and strategies

for teachers to use to improve their own cultural competence in the classroom. The strategies discussed are:
- take an introspective look at your own culture along with your feelings toward culturally diverse students,
- classroom meetings,
- arrange classroom discussions that highlight cultural diversity,
- engage in one-on-one conversations with students from diverse backgrounds,
- use multicultural literature for personal and professional development,
- use multicultural literature in the classroom,
- use culturally responsive classroom management strategies
- seek the guidance of a mentor, and
- establish sound parent relationships

In the final chapter of the book Tony Townsend and Ira Bogotch consider how the chapters contained in the two sections of the book demonstrate that understanding school leadership is not only a matter of knowing the what, but also knowing how to bring school leadership into practice. For the authors the two objectives merited distinct analyses. Identifying the 'what' as vision, cultural competence, servant leadership, distributed leadership, world class standards, communities of learners, etc. represents one phase of school improvement. By itself, this knowledge of school leadership is incomplete and illegitimate. They argue, we must marry the ends of education to the knowledge of how we make change, improve schools, initiate structures, evolve into new mindsets, reflect on practices in action, and manage processes that sustain, succeed, and regenerate learning. It is here that the 'what' and the 'how' become the 'whow', where artistry starts to take place. They consider two schools systems, Victoria, Australia and Florida, USA, to demonstrate how some parts of the world focus mostly on the what but others are starting to consider the how as well. However, they recognize (as does Richard Elmore, 2007) that there is still a long way to go before we get it right.

REFERENCES

Argyris, C., & Schon, D. (1975). *Theory into practice: Increasing professional effectiveness.* San Francisco: Jossey-Bass.
Ball, D. L., & Forzani, F. (2007). What makes education research "educational"? *The Educational Researcher, 36*(9), 529–540.
Bolman, L., & Deal, T. (1991). *Reframing organizations: Artistry, choices, and leadership.* San Francisco: Jossey Bass.
Bowles, S., & Gintis (1976). *Schooling in Capitalist America: Educational reform and the contradictions of economic life.* New York: Basic Books.
Bush, T. (1995). *Theories of educational management.* London: Paul Chapman Publishing.
Callahan, R. (1962). *Education and the cult of efficiency.* Chicago: University of Chicago Press.
Dewey, J. (1920/1962). *Reconstruction in philosophy.* New York: Mentor Books.

Dewey, J. (1916/1963). *Democracy and education*. New York: Macmillan Publishing USA.

Dewey, J. (1904). The relation of theory to practice in education. In: C. A. McMurray (Ed.), *The third NSSE yearbook*. University of Chicago Press.

Elmore, R. (2007). *Educational improvement in Victoria*. Melbourne, Victoria: Office for Government School Education, Department of Education.

Goodlad, J. (1984). *A place called school*. New York: McGraw-Hill.

Lagemann, E. (2000). *An elusive science: The troubling history of educational research*. Chicago: University of Chicago Press.

Nieto, S. (2003). *What keeps teachers going?* New York: Teachers College Press.

Neil Postman. (1988). *Conscientious objections: Stirring up trouble about language, technology, and education*. New York: Alfred A. Knopt.

Ryle, G. (1949). *Concept of mind*. New York: Barnes and Noble, Inc.

Townsend, T., & Otero, G. (1999). *The global classroom: Engaging students in third millennium schools*. Melbourne: Hawker Brownlow.

JOHN MACBEATH

2. WHAT IS LEADERSHIP?

Leadership is a word that invites immediate associations, with authority, conviction and with larger than life figures striding through corridors of power, making decisions that will impact on the lives of acquiescent followers. Leadership is a generic notion and one that is carelessly applied across differing institutional and political contexts.

Researchers have, for decades, looked for the common qualities of leaders that span the military, corporate business, public service agencies and the world of education. Such studies have appeal for governments always eager for templates that bridge description and prescription. In one of the early cross disciplinary forays in 1975 Lyle Spencer identified a range of common 'soft skill competences' that distinguished successful leaders in a number of different spheres of work. His findings were the spur for numerous successors, confirming the McBer division of leadership skills into 'soft' and 'hard', the people oriented qualities as against those more concerned with the technical or managerial aspects of the job. Each successive study offered new definitive, lists of key competencies of 'new leaders' (Goleman, 2002). These competency catalogues have been highly influential in proliferating self-assessment protocols (many available from the internet) and in recruitment of new leaders in the business world as well as in education.

'New leaders' are distinguished by their emotional intelligence, says Goleman, whose publications and empirical work at Harvard's Center for Creative Leadership have arrived at 23 competencies. These are, in alphabetical order, analytical problem solving, conflict management, continuous learning, creativity/innovation, customer service, decision making, diplomacy, empathy, employee development/coaching, flexibility, futuristic thinking, goal orientation, interpersonal skills, leadership, management, negotiation, personal effectiveness, persuasion, planning/organizing, presenting, self-management (time and priorities), teamwork and written communication.

It is a formidable list and presupposes superleaders whose personal qualities and range of skills is such that they will not only inspire followership but transform their places of work (be they businesses, hospitals or schools) into effective high performing, high reliability organizations.

T. Townsend and I. Bogotch (eds.), The Elusive What and the Problematic How: The Essential Leadership Questions for School Leaders and Educational Researchers, 17–32.

There is, however, sparse empirical evidence to connect individual leadership with high performing schools' qualities. This is because in good schools leadership is mediated and distributed across the organization and it is the industry of teachers in classrooms who make the difference (Mulford, 2003, Spillane, 2006).

In search of the 'what' of leadership we have to look not only at those who lead from the apex of the organizational pyramid but also those who exercise leadership at lower levels of organizational hierarchies and, at a deeper level still, leadership which is often imperceptible, subtle in its effects and expressed neither in status nor position but in activity.

THE FALLACY OF HEROIC LEADERSHIP

Advocacy of 'strong' leadership runs through much of the corporate and educational literature and is international in its scope. It is the foundation stone of accountability, as Elmore remarks:

> Accountability systems, and American views of leadership, tend to treat school leaders or principals as the primary agents of accountability in schools. The mythology of American education is heavily tilted in the direction of "strong leaders make good schools". (Elmore, 2005, p. 11)

Something of the fallacy of heroic leadership is portrayed in Norman Dixon's study of Military Incompetence (1994) in which the myths of the heroic leaders are exposed. From analysis of major wars in a number of different countries he adduces 15 incompetences. Among the 15 are:
– An inability to profit from past experience
– A resistance to exploiting available technology and novel tactics
– An aversion to reconnaissance, coupled with a dislike of intelligence (in both senses of the word)
– An apparent imperviousness to loss of life and human suffering amongst the rank and file
– A tendency to lay the blame on others
– A love of bull, smartness, precision and strict preservation of the military pecking order
– A high regard for tradition and other aspects of conservatism
– A lack of creativity, improvisation, inventiveness and open-mindedness

Asked to choose those that resonate most with their own workplaces, business leaders and school principals have no trouble in providing anecdotes in which these routinely play out in practice.[1] Incomptencies (the dark corollary to competences) may be seen as individual human frailties but, like their positive counterpart, they deserve a more systemic analysis.

Their very commonality and recurrence across time and place point to something deeply institutionalized in assumptions about leadership. In her book Longitude Dava Sobel (1997, pp. 12-13) recounts the story of *the Association*, a British warship sailing towards home shores along with four others. An intrepid Midshipman warned the captain that they were approaching the treacherous pinnacle rocks of the Scilly Isles. For his insuborindination the young sailor was hung from the yardarm. Not much later the ship ran aground on the pinnacle rocks leaving only two survivors to tell the tale. In modern guise the engineers who warned the NASA high command of the imminent disaster of the Challenger space shuttle launch were rewarded by the contemporary equivalent – losing their jobs.

Dissent and departure from the norm is intolerable in institutions built on strict hierarchy, and tall poppies are soon cut down to regulation size. Describing Major-General Damien-Smith, Dixon writes that the military had 'never forgiven him his brilliance and unorthodoxy' (p. 162). A 'dislike of intelligence (in both senses of the word)' is not restricted to the military or business world. An example of the latter comes from Judi Bevan's study of The Rise and Fall of Marks and Spencer (2002). Explaining its decline in the late 1990's she attributes this in large part to a leadership incapable of listening to divergent views, together with a sycophantic followership, too timid to confront hierarchical authority. Similar examples are all too easy to find in the world of educational leadership.

The construction of what it means to be a strong leader finds little endorsement in Collins and Porras' studies (1994, 2001) of successful corporations in the U.S. The leaders of those successful companies were described as modest and self-effacing, surprised to be singled out as effective leaders, building the leadership capacities of their colleagues. They recognized that self-aggrandizement and holding onto power actually diminishes the social and intellectual capital of the organization. There are echoes of this in Hesselbein et al's 1996 characterization of great leaders.

The most notable trait of great leaders, certainly of great change leaders, however, is their quest for learning. They show an exceptional willingness to push themselves out of their own comfort zones, even after they have achieved a great deal. They continue to take risks, even when there is no obvious reason for them to do so. And they are open to people and ideas even at a time in life when they might reasonably think—because of their success—that they know everything. (Hesselbein et al., 1996, p. 78) There are resonances of this in De Veer's (2004), characterization of leaders as:
– seeking opportunities to learn and act with integrity
– adapting to differences
– committed to making a difference

- seek broad based knowledge
- bringing out the best in people
- insightful-seeing things from new angles
- have courage to take risks
- seeking out and using feedback to learn from mistakes
- open to criticism.

These qualities provide an antithesis to the heroism of strong leaders single-handedly turning round a school before moving on, leaving an imprint behind so deep as to defy meaningful succession. As has been pointed out by numerous commentators (Argyris and Schon, 1978, Senge, 1990, Hargreaves and Fink, 2005) leadership conceived in this mould is more likely to destroy than to enhance the capacity of schools for self improvement.

By restraining the exercise of leadership to legitimate authority, we also leave no room for leadership that challenges the legitimacy of authority or the "system of authorization itself" (Heifetz, 1994, p. 21).

ORGANIZATIONAL LEARNING DISABILITIES

As Senge (1990) argues, disempowering disabilities are not restricted to the military but are found deeply embedded in organizations that lack the resilience and creative energy to challenge authority. First in his list of organizational learning disabilities is the stance 'I am my position'. This is all too familiar in the world of schools where principals and headteachers are their position and sometimes little else. The corollary to this is for others in the organization to define themselves in terms of their position - 'I am just a classroom teacher', 'I am only a classroom assistant', 'I'm only a student'.

Very often teachers and students are happy to collude with this definition of roles. On the one hand it offers the security that comes from well-defined parameters, and on the other from a reluctance to assume responsibility for anything that exceeds the prescribed institutional remit. Martin (2002) terms this the 'responsibility virus', evidence of which was found in abundance in English schools which took part in a study for the National College of School Leadership (MacBeath, Oduro and Waterhouse, 2004).

Teachers too often shared in leadership but without consciously recognizing the leadership roles they were performing, tending not to 'leadership' with themselves even when holding a designated promoted role. Where 'distributed leadership' was more explicit it ended to be seen in terms of subject leadership and referred to formal structures. Casting leadership exclusively in these terms, however, inhibits others in non-promoted roles to see leadership as their province, deprives the school of vital social capital and allows the 'responsibility virus' to multiply. (Martin, 2002, p. 25)

This study also furnished evidence of teachers' welcome for prescription and ready packaged teaching materials, not because they lacked professional will or autonomy but because in a high pressure, high stakes climate it reduced the hours in an already extended workload. In two successive studies conducted in English primary and secondary schools (Galton and MacBeath, 2002, MacBeath and Galton, 2004) teachers reported no longer feeling in control of their teaching, while principals expressed similar levels of frustration at the lack of latitude for professional initiative and the lack of professional trust accorded to them by 'nannying' government bodies.

Reviewing a large body of evidence Roger Martin (1997) found that the feelings of being out of control of your own work was significantly correlated with chronic illness (physical and psychological) and reduced life expectancy. The individual disabling of teachers and senior leaders from without is compounded by an institutional response which reaffirms hierarchical responsibilities and stifles potential exercise of leadership at every level of a school.

Mlgram's (see for example Milgram, 1964) famous experiments in conformity demonstrate how easily personal authority can be ceded as a result of acquiescent followership being persistently reinforced. Helplessness, it is now widely accepted, is learned (Garber and Seligman, 1980). The puzzle is to know how much of this is a human weakness, a consequence of social conditioning or a product of schooling. Institutions, said Ivan Illich (1971) are designed to frustrate their own goals and, in respect of leadership and learning, schools seem by design to successfully frustrate both. The logic of deschooling was to remove the institutional constraints and 'free the children' (Graubard, 1971). In common with school effects studies, however, the problem and the solution are seen as located within the school, and removing hampering conventions will not of itself restore a natural order of spontaneous learning and democratic leadership. What has been, often painfully, learned by freedom of schools is that conventions cannot be removed, only rethought.

THE END OF PRINCIPALSHIP?

The image of the lone star principal directing, shaping and 'running' the school may be one that has now outlived its usefulness. It is a world view so deeply entrenched that it may take a long time to shift. However, notions of highly talented individuals being sought out to transform practice is no longer a tenable proposition says Southworth (2002), a view which receives widespread endorsement, (Fullan, 1991, Hargreaves, 2004, Cheng, 2005).

The scale and nature of change is such that we have to rethink what it means to lead schools in the twenty-first century.

'Unrelenting change' is a story told in many different places as policy initiatives flow across the principal's desk in a seemingly endless stream (Mulford, 2003). The multiplicity and simultaneity of initiatives have become not only too pressing, argues Mulford, but external drivers undermine the power and discretion of school principals to exercise the leadership talents for which they were recruited. Instead they find themselves in compliant managerial roles, delivering agendas decided elsewhere and yet for which they are held to account.

The task of leading schools in the twenty first century can no longer be carried out by the heroic individual leader single handedly turning schools around, writes Gronn (2003). Schools are 'greedy institutions' and individual leadership is 'greedy work'. It is all consuming, demanding unrelenting peak performance from superleaders and, Gronn concludes, no longer a sustainable notion.

The end of principalship as we have known it may be impelled, however, by what has been loosely but widely termed as a recruitment 'crisis'. The crisis is common to many English speaking countries in which government policy shares uncannily similar demands, perhaps because policy borrowing is now so integral to the globalization agenda and susceptibility by policy makers and politicians to international league tables emanating from the OECD.

In 2003 Thomson and colleagues in Australia analyzed media reports on the recruitment crisis and identified two prevalent narratives, one of 'sleepless nights, heart attacks and sudden death accountabilities', the other of the 'savior principal... who is able to create happy teams of teachers, students and parents for whom all reform is possible' (2003:128). This duality needs to be understood, Thomson and colleagues argue, within a policy rhetoric of failing schools and 'best' practice. Where schools fail it is due to lack of leadership and when they succeed it is attributed to the savior principal. The policy logic that follows is to emulate what the best leaders do or have done. Unfortunately, this rarely works because this belief rests on a very shaky foundation, one which assumes that knowledge and skills transfer across contexts as if one school was simply like any other. Schools are not only greedy places but they are complex places too.

The following eight factors that recur most frequently in the 'crisis' literature focus on what happens to individual leaders to wear them down and sap their abilities to manage creatively. It has led many commentators to suggest alternative ways of thinking about and practising school leadership. The eight 'dissatisfiers' are:

1. Stress

The increase in stress reported by principals and headteachers in a number of countries is attributed to the competitive nature of a market economy, bringing with it a need to work harder, more demanding hours and in face of progressively higher stakes. Principals/headteachers carry on their own shoulders liability for the success or failure of their schools but with more responsibility and accountability than real power (Thomson et al., 2003). In a study of 266 schools in the UK (Boyland, 2002 quoted in Mulford 2003), 71 per cent of long term absences for men over 45 were attributed to stress, while the figure was 58 per cent for women in the same age range.

2. Workload

Workload is closely related to reports of stress and appears to be common to many countries. In the US it has been a continuing source of concern for half a decade (Hertling, 2002, Lovely, 2004). Jones' 1999 study of headteachers in the UK found close parallels with Livingstone's study of primary school heads in the same year in New Zealand and Louden and Wildy's 1999 study in Australia. One effect they report is for school leaders to devote less time to the core business of teaching and learning and more time to administrative tasks. Time, it is argued, has become fragmented, the demands of the urgent leaving inadequate space for the important while time for reflection and discussion with colleagues has shrunk commensurately.

In a 1998 UK Parliamentary report the Deputy General Secretary of the National Union of Teachers (NUT) claimed that:

> The reason why people are not applying for headteacher posts is that it is an enormously high-stakes, high-risk job without an understanding of their professional responsibilities or the fact that they may face a snowball of additional professional responsibilities in the future. Basically no one knows what the ground rules are when they apply for a headteacher post. That is the big issue.

(9th Parliamentary report on education & employment, 1998, item 166).

3. Accountability and bureaucracy

While principals/headteachers widely recognized the importance of accountability it was the bureaucratic aspects that demotivated them (Livingstone, 1999). Excessive paperwork combined with a constant pressure to justify actions taken and the 'blame and shame' attended with it is compounded, in the US at least, with threat of exposure and closure. Accountability has acquired negative connotations, researchers conclude, because it is not only highly demanding but often directed at the wrong things and located in the person of the individual leader where the buck is seen to stop.

4. Personal and domestic concerns

A frequently cited inhibitor among teaching staff to apply for principalship was 'crossing the professional border' into school leadership (Tucker and Codding, 1999) For many of those teachers unwilling to take that step 'the burden of headship' (James and Whiting, 1998) threatened to destroy the balance between school and family life. In Australia, Dorman and d'Arbon (2003) reported similar disinclination among staff for whom principalship implied not only longer hours but impacted profoundly 'on the balance of lifestyle'.

5. Salary

Salary rarely tops the list of dissatisfiers but it has to be weighed against the intensive demands and thanklessness of the job. Comparison between levels of responsibility of school leadership with leadership in other occupations are invidious. In an Australian study by Dorman and d'Arbon, (2003) principals commented on comparisons with similar positions of responsibility in industry or commerce 'where the management of human and material resources was seen as equivalent but not as highly recompensed' Principals, they claimed, earned less per hour than their staff although they worked thirty per cent longer hours in a week.

6. Social Factors

We are, argue other social commentators, living in a society where social relationships, parenting and attitudes of young people are experiencing dramatic and often unforeseen changes. The increasing diversity of the student population, multiplicity of language and ethnic backgrounds, short term refugeeism, the casualties of war, transience of the student body, concentrations of poverty in inner cities and depopulated rural areas, all bring their own, often formidable, challenges. Problems such as drug abuse, intimidation and violence create dilemmas which are often beyond the power of leadership to resolve but have repercussions within the school walls.

7. The teacher supply line

An OECD Education Policy Analysis in 2001 warned of a 'meltdown scenario' caused by a growing teacher exodus from the profession, positing widespread public dissatisfaction with the state of education in the face of a deep teacher-recruitment crisis and a growing sense of declining standards, especially in the worst affected areas. The 'crisis' in teacher recruitment impacts directly on recruitment for principalship which has to understand and accommodate to a changing profile of the profession and the nature of teachers' career paths. Those who came from industry looked for opportunities to work in teams and to have expanded influence. For example, new recruits with a background in industry, argues Susan Moore Johnson (2005), expect to work in teams and to share leadership responsibility but find themselves working in isolated classrooms, robbed of the initiative and latitude of decision-making they previously enjoyed.

8. Lack of succession

The 'hole in the bucket' inflow and outflow of staff, creates new kinds of challenges for sustainability and capacity building. A US study by Ingersoll (2003) reported 30 per cent of teachers leaving within three years, while 50 per cent are no longer in post after five years. This is a reflection of a shifting socio-economic situation in which job portfolios assume new shapes making it easier to cross professional demarcations. New recruits from other sectors of the economy bring to teaching changing expectations of the job, while others leave teaching as no longer the job they signed up to. This 'revolving door' syndrome, means there is a lack of flexibility for leadership in addressing issues creatively and with confidence in a minimal threshold of stability.

A FACTOR OF EIGHT

When these eight factors are taken together they depict something of the challenge facing the principalship in the new millennium. They suggest the need either for superleaders able to rise above the constraints and dissatisfiers, or a fundamental recasting of how we think about and practice school leadership. One variant, practised on a limited scale in the U.S. is dual leadership in which there are two incumbents in the job, sharing duties and carrying joint accountability. This is not too dissimilar from the Danish tradition in the Folkeskole in which there is no internal hierarchy and the school is led by a senior team of two. Although designated as principal and vice-principal they tend to work as a democratic leadership team.

When there is dual leadership or a principal and vice principal working closely together there may be a fluid and flexible interchange of roles, or alternatively leadership and management may be clearly demarcated, playing to the strengths of the respective individuals. One may be an inspirational leader but an ineffective manager, while the manager may possess of a high level organizational skill but lack leadership qualities.

THE WAR FOR TALENT

The search for the super leader who both leads and manages and fulfils all of the 23 Goleman criteria helps to explain why there is a recruitment crisis, seen to apply not only in schools but in the business world too. In 2001 McKinsey published a book entitled *The War for Talent* (Michaels et al., 2001) describing the search for that rare species of transformational being. In riposte Malcom Gladwell (2002) offered an alternative construction of the issue. While the Mckinsey thesis was that talented individuals create great organizations, Gladwell proposed a counterpoint – great organizations create talented individuals.

If Gladwell's analysis is preferred over the Mckinsey thesis the task of the principal is to let go rather than to hold on to power, to recognize and nurture incipient leadership and to spread it out. Perceiving and nurturing expertise enhances personal and professional authority rather than formal or institutional authority.

Improvement requires a relatively complex kind of cooperation among people in diverse roles performing diverse functions. This kind of cooperation requires understanding that learning grows out of differences in expertise rather than differences in formal authority. If collective learning is the goal, my authority to command you to do something doesn't mean much if it is not complemented by some level of knowledge and skill which, when joined with yours, makes us both more effective. Similarly, if we have the same roles, I have little incentive to cooperate with you unless we can jointly produce something that we could not produce individually. In both instances the value of direction, guidance, and co-operation stems from acknowledging and making use of differences in expertise. (Elmore, 2000)

Much of the terminology in the alphabet soup of leadership contains heroic connotations – charismatic, transformational, inspirational, visionary, leadership. One variant that stands out from the imperious crowd is 'servant leadership'. The originator of the term was Robert Greenleaf (1977) who developed his theory after reading Herman Hesse's (1957) *Journey to the East*. In that book the author describes a group of men on a journey to the East in which they are sustained by a servant who not only does the menial chores but keep up their spirits through his stories, songs and his very presence. When he suddenly disappears the group falls into disarray and abandons its journey.

The defining character of the servant leader is subjugation of the self, born not from low self-esteem but from a highly developed sense of self which is strong enough to feel no need for deference, adulation or reinforcement. This is the very antithesis of charismatic and narcissistic leadership, although it might be argued that by the very qualities that define service to others it conveys a powerful charismatic authority.

Greenleaf makes the following comparisons between the traditional leader and the servant leader (Figure 1).

Servant leadership presupposes a culture in which senior leaders are able to operate in the fashion described by the right hand column rather than the left. In a study for the National College of School Leadership in England (MacBeath, Waterhouse and Oduro, 2004) we found that the ability and confidence to 'let go' of authority and upset traditional expectations of headship required a slow burn. Like the teacher who takes over an unruly class, stamps her authority on the situation, and follows the maxim 'don't smile until Christmas' (Canfield and Ryan, 1970), English headteachers found they had to fit the mould before they could break it or even begin to fray it at the edges.

The traditional leader	The servant leader
- asks subordinates questions such as "did you do this? What is the status of…?"	- asks "How might I be of help?", "What is it that you need from me?"
- measures productivity and outcomes using quantitative indicators.	- expects people to do the right things because they understand what needs to be done and will do those things without being instructed.
- sees people as a valuable resource and himself as chief	- believes that people come first and that his role is facilitating and fostering the leadership capabilities of others
- is seen as a stern taskmaster often driven by a self-serving ethic	- models and lays stress on ethical behaviour and is trusting, accepting and open to new ideas
- promotes internal competition	- believes that service and competition are antithetical
- mediates disputes	- notices those whose views are not being heard and takes time to listen, to offer supportive coaching in order to help the individual and to strengthen the team
- demands compliance and seeks to recruit people in his own image	- empathises and accepts the person as they are but refuses to accept performance as less than the best that individual can offer.

Figure 1: The traditional leader and the servant leader

Authentic leaders breathe the life force into the workplace and keep the people feeling energized and focused. As stewards and guides they build people and their self-esteem. They derive their credibility from personal integrity and 'walking' their values. (Bhindi and Duignan, 1996, p. 29)

It is only when the culture is characterized by mutual trust and a willingness to cope with uncertainty and flux that leadership and followership can become interchangeable rather than fixed and immutable roles. In such a culture leaders find occasion to follow and followers discover occasions to lead as the occasion demands.

LEADERSHIP AS DISTRIBUTED

The term 'distributed leadership' is now widely used as an antithesis to heroic or charismatic leadership. It tends, however, to be interpreted as a conscious and deliberative act by those in positions of power, giving away tiny morsels of power, selecting out and appointing people to roles within the school. To think of leadership this way, as design, says Jim Spillane (2005), is problematic. Describing principals who have told him they plan to distribute leadership in their schools he points out to them that, if they have eyes to see it, leadership is already distributed. 'It bubbles up' and can either be blocked by institutional artifacts or allowed to rise freely.

Leadership is inherent in what Spillane et al calls 'reciprocal inter-dependencies' (2001, p. 34). Whether taking action, innovating or creating knowledge, individuals play off one another. What A does can only be fully understood by taking into account what B does, and vice versa, each bringing differing resources - skills, knowledge, and perspectives to bear.

We contend, in other words, that the collective cognitive properties of a group of leaders working together to enact a particular task leads to the evolution of a leadership practice that is potentially more than the sum of each individual's practice. Consequently, to understand the knowledge needed for leadership practice in such situations, one has to move beyond an analysis of individual knowledge and consider what these leaders know and do together. Depending on the particular leadership task, the knowledge and expertise of school leaders may be best explored at the group or collective level rather than at the individual leader level. (Spillane et al., 2001, p. 12)

Distributed leadership is made manifest in 'negotiated order' between leaders and followers. While leaders can often draw on their positional authority to support the beliefs and actions they advocate, followers can influence leaders by drawing on personal characteristics, access to information, their special knowledge or expertise and so may influence leadership strategies through subtle forms of manipulation, subversion and 'creative insubordination'. In other words, followers are an essential element of leadership activity. Nor, might we add, that those roles are static. Those who lead may also follow, while those who follow may also lead, depending on context and the task at hand

This is akin to what Sergiovanni terms leadership 'density'. (2001) Inserting a dipstick into the culture of a school can provide a reading of how far leadership penetrates into the 'way we do things round here'. Much of the incipient leadership is dormant, unrealized, and, says Ann Liebermann (video, 2005), 'many of the pedagogical and leadership secrets are ones which teachers take with them to the grave'.

The foremost task of leadership is to 'awaken the sleeping giant of teacher leadership' (Katzenmeyer and Moller, 2001). It is an apt metaphor to capture the dormant qualities of an underestimated and undervalued profession and the massive potential for leadership which lies often unexplored and unexploited. Why, asks Argyris (1993) are organizations generally less intelligent than their individual members? It is because they do not have, or have not found, ways to bring to fruition the hidden capital of their people.

This principle extends beyond teachers, to classroom assistants, to support staff of all kinds and to students, the school's largest untapped knowledge source, 'the treasure in our very own backyard' (SooHoo, 1993). If self-efficacy and emotional intelligence are essential allies of leadership then passivity and dependency are its adversaries (Dweck, 1986). Students will encounter few occasions in life after school when they are not required to take the initiative on behalf of others. There are few occupations that do not require some form of leadership and informed self conscious followership.

Schools which overlook these intelligence sources are inevitably poorer as a consequence. There is a danger of student voice and student leadership at one extreme being merely tokenistic and, at the other, enjoying a privileged status as against the voices of teachers or others with an equal right to be heard and to enjoy opportunities to make a difference.

Like teacher leadership, student leadership is there to see for those who have eyes to see it. Much of student leadership is exercised in the underlife of schools, often in anti-educational and anti-social activity. The power of the peer group has long been recognized as a key, and often insidious, determinant of learning (Hargreaves, 1967, Harris, 1998, Thrupp, 1999) and leadership often assumes insidious forms such as bullying and intimidation. In recognition of this, third millennium schools are increasing opportunities for young people to lead in pro-social ways and to lead the learning of others. Peer mentoring is one such example. There is also increasing scope, particularly in ICT, for students, even very young children and children with special needs, to lead their teachers' learning. Likewise through projects, sport, music, creative and performing arts and through extra-curricular activities young people have opportunities to lead their peers and often their teachers too. Leadership is to be found in the flow of learning activities in which students are engaged.

LEADERSHIP AS ACTIVITY

These insights lead us to a view of leadership, less as roles and more as activity. Because leadership is often so deeply buried within school life and invisible except to the enlightened eye (Eisner, 1991) we need a new frame, or new lens, through which to perceive it. To make leadership visible and bring it self consciously to the surface, one has to detect it in the minutiae of activity, often simply taken as read or, as was often said to us, 'it's just the way things are'. Yet when we examine micro activity within the school we can begin to detect situations in which leadership is informal and intuitive but often highly influential. In situations such as the following a school may ask itself 'Who singly or jointly exercises leadership?'

– A newly qualified teacher in the staffroom is showing signs of distress.
– A senior colleague has acted unjustly but no one is willing to challenge the decision.
– A parent is waiting outside the office looking lost.
– A fight has broken out among a group of students in the school yard.
– Students are complaining about boredom and passivity in their learning.

Making small acts of leadership visible broadens understanding and smooths the path to distributed leadership. It demystifies leadership and furthers student, professional and organizational learning.

Making leadership and learning visible is not simply an academic exercise for schools in the current policy climate. It is implicit in school self-evaluation, in school improvement, in schools as centers of inquiry, and as teachers as researchers. 'Know thyself' was a Socratic first principle of education. Without that self-knowledge schools simply become pieces to be moved in someone else's game plan. With self-knowledge the connective 'and' takes on new meaning.

Social capital flows from the endowment of mutually respecting and trusting relationships which enable a group to pursue its shared goals more effectively than would otherwise be possible. It can never be reduced to the mere possession or attribute of an individual. It results from the communicative capacity of a group. (Simon Szreter, 2000)

NOTES

[1]   Workshop run over a period of two years for Newcastle Talent Group

REFERENCES

Argyris, C. (1993). *Knowledge for action: A guide to overcoming barriers to organizational change*. San Franciso: Jossey-Bass.

Argyris, C., & Schön, D. (1978). *Organizational learning: A theory of action perspective*. Reading, MA: Addison Wesley.

Bevan, J. (2002). *The rise and fall of Marks and Spencer*. London: Profile Books.

Bhindi, N., & Duignan, P. (1996). *Leadership 2020: A visionary paradigm*. Paper presented at the Commonwealth Council for Educational Administration International Conference, Kuala Lumpur.

Boyland, R. (2002). Why the age of anxiety is 45 and beyond. *Times Educational Supplement*, 4 October, 2.

Canfield, J., & Ryan, K. (1970). *Don't smile until christmas*. Chicago: University of Chicago Press.

Castells, M. (2000). *End of millennium*. Oxford: Blackwell.

Cheng, Y. C. (2005). *Multiple thinking and multiple creativity in organization learning*. Hong Kong: Institute of Education.

Collins, J., & Porras, I. J. (1994). *Built to last*. New York: Harper Collins.

Collins, J., & Porras, I. J. (2001). *Good to great*. New York: Harper Collins.

Dixon, N. (1994). *On the psychology of military incompetence*. London: Pimplico.

Dweck, C. S. (1986). Motivational processes affecting learning. *American Psychologist, 41*(10), 1040–1048.

Dorman, J., & d'Arbon, T. (2003). Leadership succession in New South Wales, Catholic schools: identifying potential principals. *Educational Studies, 29*, 2–3.

Eisner, E. (1991). *The enlightened eye*. New York: Macmillan.

Elmore, R. F. (2000). *Building a new structure for school leadership*. Washington, DC: The Albert Shanker Institute.

Elmore, R. (2005). *Agency, reciprocity, and accountability in democratic education*. Boston, MA: Consortium for Policy Research in Education.

Fullan, M. G. (1991). *The new meaning of educational change*. New York: Teachers College Press.

Galton, M., & MacBeath, J. (2002). *A life in teaching?* London: National Union of Teachers.

Garbar, & Seligman, M. (Eds.). *Human helplessness*. New York: Academic Press.

Gladwell, M. (2002). *The talent myth: Are smart people overrated?* New Yorker.

Goleman, D. (2002). *The new leaders: Transforming the art of leadership into the science of results*. London: Time Warner.

Graubard, A. (1971). *Free the children*. Vancouver, Washington, DC: Vintage Books.

Greenleaf, R. K. (1977). *Servant leadership*. New York: Paulist Press.

Gronn, P. (2003). *The new work of educational leaders: Changing leadership practice in an era of school reform*. London: Paul Chapman.

Hargreaves, A. (2004). *Sustainable leadership*. Keynote address delivered at the International Conference on School Effectiveness and Improvement, Rotterdam, January.

Hargreaves, A., & Fink, D. (2005). *Sustainable leadership*. San Francisco: Jossey Bass.

Hargreaves, D. (1967). *Social relations in a secondary school*. United Kingdom: Routledge & Kegan Paul.

Harris, J. R. (1998). *The nurture assumption*. London: Bloomsbury.

Heifetz, R. A. (1994). *Leadership without easy answers*. Cambridge, MA: Harvard University Press.

Hertling, E. (2002). Retaining Principals. ERIC Digest.

Hesse, H. (1957). *The journey to the east* (Hilda Rosner, Trans.). New York: Noonday Press.

Hesselbein, F., Goldsmith, M., Beckard, R., & Drucker, P. (1996). *The leader of the future*. San Francisco: Jossey-Bass.

House of Commons. (1998). 9th Parliamentary Report on Education & Employment.

Illich, I. (1971). *Deschooling society*. New York: Harper and Row.

Ingersoll, R. M. (2003). Is there really a teacher shortage? Center of the Study of Teaching and Policy, University of Washington.

James, C., & Whiting, D. (1998). The career perspectives of deputy headteachers. *Educational Management and Administration, 26*(4), 26–34.

Johnson, S. M. (2005). *Dimensions of leadership: Principles, practice and paradoxes*. Retrieved from http://www.nationalpriorities.org.uk/Resources/Miscellaneous/NCSL/Voxpop.html

Jones, N. (1999). The real world management preoccupations of primary school heads. *School Leadership and Management, 19*(4), 483–495.

Katzenmeyer, A., & Moller, G. (2001). *Awakening the sleeping giant: Helping teachers develop as leaders* (2nd ed.). Thousand Oaks, CA: Corwin Press.

Lieberman, A. (2005). *Dimensions of leadership: Principles, practice and paradoxes*. Retrieved from http://www.nationalpriorities.org.uk/Resources/Miscellaneous/NCSL/Voxpop.html

Livingston, I. (1999). *The workload of primary teaching principals*. A New Zealand Survey Wellington, Chartwell Consultants.

Louden, W., & Wildy, H. (1999). Short shrift to the long lists: An alternative approach to the development of performance standards for school principals. *Journal of Educational Administration, 37*(2), 99–121.

Lovely, S. (2004). Staffing the Principalship: Finding, Coaching, and Mentoring School Leaders, Association for Supervision & Curriculum Development.

MacBeath, J., & Galton, M. (2004). *A life in secondary teaching?* London: National Union of Teachers.

MacBeath, J., Oduro, G., & Waterhouse, J. (2004). *Distributed leadership in schools*. Nottingham: National College of School Leadership.

Martin, P. R. (1997). *The sickening mind*. London: Flamingo.

Martin, R. L. (2002). *The responsibility virus*. London: Prentice-Hall.

Michaels, E., Hartford-Jones, H., & Axelrod, B. (2001). *The war for talent how to battle for great people*. Harvard Business School Press.

Milgram, S. (1964). Group pressure and action against a person. *Journal of Abnormal and Social Psychology, 69*, 137–143.

Mulford, B. (2003). *School leaders: Changing roles and impact on teacher and school effectiveness*. Paris: OECD.

OECD. (2001). *Teacher exodus – The meltdown scenario*. Paris: Education Policy Analysis.

Senge, P. (1990). *The fifth discipline: The art and practices of the learning organization*. New York: Doubleday.

Senge, P. (2000). *Schools that learn*. New York: Doubleday.

Sergiovanni, T. (2001). *Leadership: What's in it for schools?* London: RoutledgeFalmer.

Sobel, D. (1997). *Longitude*. London, Fourth Estate, pp. 12–13.

SooHoo, S. (1993). Students as partners in research and restructuring schools. *The Educational Forum, 57*, 386–392.

Southworth, G. (2002). Leadership in English schools: Portraits, puzzles and identity. In A. Walker & C. Dimmock (Eds.), *School leadership and administration: Adopting a cultural perspective*. London: Routledge.

Spencer, L. (1974). *Soft skill competencies*. New York: Wiley.

Spillane, J. P., Halverson, R., & Diamond, J. B. (2001). Investigating school leadership practice: A distributed perspective. *Educational Researcher, 30*(3), 23–28.

Spillane, J. (2005). *Dimensions of leadership: Principles, practice and paradoxes*. Retrieved from http://www.nationalpriorities.org.uk/Resources/Miscellaneous/NCSL/Voxpop.html

Spillane, J. P. (2006). *Distributed leadership*. Jossey-Bass.

Szreter, S. (2001). Social Capital Roundtable, Glasgow, November.

Thomson, P., Blackmore, J., Sachs, J., & Tregenza, K. (2003). High stakes principalship – sleepless nights, heart attacks and sudden death accountabilities: Reading media representations of the United States principal shortage. *Australian Journal of Education, 47*(2), 118–132.

Thrupp, M. (1999). *Schools making a difference: Let's be realistic*. Buckingham: Open University Press.

Tucker, M., & Codding, J. (Eds.). (2003). *The principal challenge: Leading and managing schools in an era of accountability*. The Jossey-Bass Education Series.

3. WHAT IS SCHOOL CULTURE?

INTRODUCTION

School Culture portrays more than the personality of an institution. It is the heart and soul of a system, representative of a collective.

The word 'culture' does not have a precise meaning. It appears to have its roots in the Latin word 'cultura', meaning 'cultivating' or 'tending'. This meaning links the word to agriculture. Another two different connotations of 'culture' can be distinguished: the older meaning - 'high culture' of a society, classical literature, music or art, and the sociological and anthropological use of the word for 'a style of life'. The meanings are interrelated in that all indicate a specific way of living or doing things. School culture is clearly related to the latter but it is also open to a wide range of interpretations. To understand the concept of school culture, it is necessary to place the concept within the context of the generic meaning of 'culture'.

According to Merriam Webster Dictionary, culture is –

> The integrated pattern of human knowledge, belief, and behaviour that depends upon man's capacity for learning and transmitting knowledge to succeeding generations.

School culture, being specific to the context of a particular institutional environment, portrays in miniature the culture that exists in a society. But it does more than this: school culture is selective in the aspects which it conveys, and each school makes its own contribution to its culture.

The culture of a society includes: the kind of value system people practise, the norms they follow, their code of conduct, their beliefs, their stories of the past, the heritage and tradition that mark them as different from others, the nature of the communication amongst people in the community and so on. As Fleming and Amesbury (2001) put it,

> Culture in its broadest sense can be defined as the 'way of life' of an entire society. (p. 30)

According to the sociologists, culture refers to 'values, customs and acceptable modes of behaviour' that typically define a society or groups

T. Townsend and I. Bogotch (eds.), The Elusive What and the Problematic How: The Essential Leadership Questions for School Leaders and Educational Researchers, 33–55.

within a society (Giddens, 1997). All three components are equally valid for the concept of school culture. Let us consider a quotation from Marsh and Keating (2006):

> This general notion of culture is directly related to social behaviour through the moral goals of a society (its values), the status positions of its members (social roles) and the specific rules of conduct related to society's values and roles, which are known as norms. (p. 20)

If we add the word 'school' before 'culture' in the first line and replace the word 'society' with 'school', the statement becomes equally applicable to school culture. The quotation also highlights that 'values' and 'roles' are at the centre of the concept of any culture.

HOW ARE VALUES AND ROLES RELATED TO SCHOOL CULTURE?

In the form of a decision making process, human values are the core guiding factors of all our actions. The following section discusses the relevance of values, specifically in school culture, with an emphasis on how the school community goes through a complex process of psychological adjustment while shaping a desirable learning environment. Although inevitably the process involves a much wider periphery (including society and the nation) than the physical boundary of the school, the discussion below focuses on the school as an educational institution.

Pupils come to school from a variety of economic, social and cultural backgrounds. If every family in every community within a society is considered as a unit, then every unit has its own rules of behaviour and code of conduct. Pupils' attitudes towards learning begin to be shaped by the core value system in the society through their individual backgrounds. Eventually, school culture also plays a significant role and influences the process of learning. According to Shinn (1972),

> The cultural interplay between the community and the school is an on-going event with no conspicuous demarcation where the involvement of both begin and end in the educational process of the child. (p. 364)

This refers to a complex construction of the school culture within other cultures. Although in the school different traits from different cultures are integrated in the form of another evolving culture, it is important for teachers to be aware of the variety of children's backgrounds and share a common set of values towards learning in order to express a collective institutional goal. This is a crucial job for the people involved in the process of teaching and learning. It is also a difficult task when we consider the fact that teachers themselves are individuals exposed to different cultures both inside and outside schools. To quote Robertson and Toal (2001):

> This means that several cultures or subcultures may exist within a school – among different groups of young people, among different sets of staff and among parents. (p. 105)

Teaching approaches are very personal and it is likely that teachers may unconsciously influence pupils with their personal value systems. How can we minimise the inconsistency in practices based on conflicts between personal and institutional values and create a shared understanding of a 'professional identity'? The point is discussed in the following paragraphs.

In effective schools, code of conduct should be related to the purpose and vision, in other words the goal, of the institution (Mortimore *et al*,1988). This harmony reflects a characteristic quality of an 'effective' school culture. Handy and Aitken (1994) argue,

> If discontinuities in the treatment, learning or development of children are to be avoided, then a corporate purpose is needed. (p. 244)

In an ideal scenario, what is behind this purpose and vision is a shared understanding of a common set of institutional values amongst the people in the learning community. At the micro level of the individual, these values can mean different things according to different subjective interpretations. However, the choice of the ways of working together as a team can and does make a difference in the outcome of a common pursuit (Das, 2006).

The moral goals of a school that are based on its core values are directly linked with (or ideally, should be) and reflected through its decided course of actions. Often aims or goals are documented in school brochures and policy booklets. In most cases, the problem arises when these 'decided courses of actions' are being 'implemented'. As Ballantine (1983) argues:

> It is in the schools that stated goals must be translated into action; in this process conflicts over purpose and interpretation may arise. (p. 122)

The implementation process involves areas that are potentially prone to creating complexity, simply because often it involves more than one method of doing things and more than one person implementing it. Moreover, many schools prefer to have a shared 'knowledge-making' process (Joyce, Calhoun and Hopkins, 1999). The complexity of this process involving various *role-conflicts* (King, 1983), sometimes results in effective innovations. At other times, it may result in chaotic conditions, leading to less effective learning outcomes.

The 'decided courses of actions' in the form of specific goals, such as raising pupils' attainment to a certain level within a specific period of time, can be implemented in various ways. The style of management adopted reflects the preferred guiding values, which in turn contribute to a specific learning culture in the school. For example, the school authority can decide to provide extra resources and moral support and arrange for in-service training programmes for the teachers to enable them to work more effectively towards the goal. Alternatively, the school authority can decide to create 'pressure' on the teachers by imposing added paperwork for monitoring purposes and ignore (or pay less attention to) the fact that this type of extra work can take planning time away from the teachers. Monitoring a process is important to ensure effectiveness but over-emphasis on 'control' can produce the opposite result. Sometimes what happens in the latter case (as in the above example) is that the teachers may still reach the targets in time, but at the cost of effective planning time. This is likely to produce less 'effective' learning outcomes for the pupils. Through this process, the school's short-term goals of attainment targets may be achieved, but the long-term goal of 'helping pupils to become effective life-long learners' is compromised. Thus some of the 'institutional values' have preference over others (here, efficiency over long-term effectiveness) while implementing the decided courses of actions in schools.

Of course, it can be argued that 'efficiency' is an important value to foster when it comes to professionalism and especially if it mirrors the nation's culture and value preferences. But then we need to consider who constitute the nation, who constitute our society and who decide on the guiding values for practice. The answer is that we all play a part through our roles in the individual contexts. So, in a way, we do have a choice to decide how we want to shape our reality. It is important to be aware of the fact that an over-emphasis on efficiency can be counter-productive in shaping an 'effective' learning culture in school.

This situation illustrated in the example may be described in another way. It is possible that sometimes when the decisions are made in schools, if there is no deliberate effort to emphasise preferred institutional values, incoherence in overall learning outcome may come as a surprise to the school community (Donnelly, 2004). Individual teachers' personal values that are 'implicit' in the process may take over, and as a result some may prefer 'efficiency', others, 'effectiveness'. The school community, in the example, may not collectively value 'efficiency' over 'long-term effectiveness' (or vice versa) but if the decision-making process and the decided courses of actions do not focus on the preferred institutional values, confusion can be created. Either way, the teachers' roles become important in shaping a teaching and learning culture for the pupils. Inevitably, teachers'

> ...values and beliefs influence the type of structure they create in the classroom and their responlses to pupils. (Ames, 1992, cited in Stoll, Fink and Earl, 2003, p. 38)

To avoid the misunderstanding described in the above example, resulting in undesired consequences, what needs to be done in these situations is to make the intention/s behind a goal explicit. Transparency and clear communication are essential for shaping an effective school culture. Following an agreed code of norms helps to maintain 'stability' in such a complex process of guiding a chosen teaching and learning environment in school (Evans, 1998). According to Fidler (2002), organisational culture has a powerful 'conditioning effect' on schools. He maintains:

> Unless cultural influences are made explicit, they may lead to strategic possibilities being prejudiced with the rejection of those that are not consistent with the prevailing culture. (p. 16)

Fidler (2002) describes such a situation as 'disastrous'. While discussing the process of 'change' in culture, he also emphasises that failing to question existing cultural assumptions can produce the same unwanted result for a school community. In addition, we need to be aware of the 'politics' of stating the usual long-term goals in the school brochures and mission statements, using vague phrases such as 'achieving full potential' or 'helping pupils to become life-long learners'. These phrases are perhaps kept vague and open to different interpretations intentionally, in order to accommodate the various interplay of role and values-conflicts discussed here. It is important to remember that we as individuals are in a position to choose what *role* we want to play in the process of shaping a desirable learning environment.

As argued earlier, the choice of a 'desirable' teaching and learning environment may vary between schools. This appears to be the case either because of a deliberate choice of certain values to guide specific school cultures. Alternatively, it varies according to differing understandings or interpretations of certain values by individual school communities. For example, the notion of a 'positive' ethos or culture carries different meanings for different school communities because of differences in national and local community cultures and sub-cultures. Fleming (2000) describes positive ethos as a concept where a culture of 'cooperation and achievement' exists. Elaborating the argument he asserts:

> It is likely to be the result of a vision shared by all staff, good selection and training procedures and effective policies which give staff and students a clear sense of direction, together with considerable autonomy and responsibility. It is likely that in these schools staff have high expectations of students and each other and that there is a strong belief in involving students in decisions about their learning. (p. 31)

The description provides a picture of an effective learning environment. Although many schools may claim to foster positive ethos in their brochures, the concept is not interpreted in the same manner in every context.

In a recent study (Das, 2006), the concept of school culture was explored in four primary schools in the city of Aberdeen in Scotland. All four schools had different socio-economic and cultural backgrounds. School D is situated in a deprived area of the city. One of the core values, as part of the 'positive' ethos practised in this school, focused on 'learning together' as a community. This is an effective approach to learning, but in School D's case it also reflected a response to the threat of closure, a characteristic quality of need for survival. (The 'survival model' of systems theory is relevant here.) The school had been facing frequent proposals for closure over the past few years due to competition from other local schools in the area. The school community believed in working 'together' so strongly that the members at one point unconsciously started compromising the quality of their 'learning'. Instead of using reflective practices to boost positive ethos, their focus was on 'getting on'. Harmonious relationships amongst staff were fostered at the cost of critical awareness.

A second example illustrates a different scenario. With a predominantly middle class pupil background, School A also practised a 'positive' ethos by using the code of 'learning together' as a community. The difference was that School A encouraged diversity in opinions to enhance the effectiveness of learning during collaborative activities in the classrooms as well as at the staff level. (The 'effectiveness model' of systems theory is relevant here.) To a certain extent, both schools managed to establish a 'positive' ethos reflecting pro-academic learning environments through their individual approaches but the quality of the learning outcome was different. Pupils in School A not only produced better academic results, but also they were found to be confident and generally happy children who enjoyed being engaged in creative and innovative projects. These examples emphasise that much depends on conscious approaches to shape a desired learning environment or culture in schools. Applying conscious approaches requires prior knowledge about school culture and understanding about its shaping process.

'ABSTRACT, ELUSIVE AND COMPOSITE'

Words commonly used to describe the concept of school culture or ethos include 'abstract', 'elusive' and 'composite'. It is abstract because its structure is based on a range of factors in various combinations: patterns of behaviour, attitudes and perceptions, which some authors have defined as the 'personality' of the institution (Hoy and Sabo, 1998), as well as the history, tradition, fostered values, norms and emergent interactions (Deal and Kennedy, 1982). The former set of factors is described as *school climate* by organisational psychologists (Halpin and Croft, 1963) and the latter as *school culture* or *ethos* by anthropologists and sociologists (Lortie, 1975; Munn, 2002).

School culture is elusive because some of these factors are not visible in concrete form. Sometimes they are documented in mission statements as aims or goals but often the real account vary according to our understanding of the phrases such as 'achieving full potential'. This particular characteristic 'elusiveness', is reminiscent of the term 'hidden curriculum', which by definition is the reverse of 'written or overt curriculum'. Jackson (1968) uses the term 'hidden curriculum' in arguing that education is a socialisation process and therefore schools not only facilitate learning to pass on knowledge to pupils but also are responsible for 'transmission of norms and values'. The socially constructed learning process in schools helps pupils to learn the formal curriculum as well as the informal rules, beliefs and attitudes. How are these informal rules, beliefs and attitudes transmitted?

The school community, including the members of staff and the pupils contribute consciously, subconsciously or unconsciously to shaping a particular learning environment in the school through everyday practices. This may be taken to imply that teachers as individuals create unique classroom cultures for different groups of pupils in the same school. However, Meighan (1981) argues that, if general social values influence the overall structure of the educational process, then it is likely that similar practices will be adopted across all classrooms in one school or indeed across all schools. The structure of a society often accommodates different groups of people fostering different value systems. Moreover, the same values can be practised differently according to different levels of understanding and subjective interpretations amongst individuals. Meighan's assumption does highlight a strong point that the schools are likely to mirror some of the core values in our society. Thus the complexity in understanding the concept of school culture refers to the composite structure of its making. Perhaps school culture should be acknowledged as a more powerful and complex phenomenon than any other area in educational research, as it embraces all interlinked elements of everyday school life and thereby potentially shapes a desirable environment for teaching and learning.

WHAT IS SCHOOL CULTURE?

There is little agreement on the definition or meaning of the terms, school culture or school climate or ethos or atmosphere or organizational climate. The terms are generated by different groups of people, carrying different focuses of interests. Hoyle (cited in Harris and Bennett, 2001) argues,

> ...values are central to the concept of culture and... climate focuses upon the quality of relationships between members of an organization. (p. 126)

> School climate is a term which we tend to intuitively understand, but one for which there is no single accepted definition. (p. 24)

Similarly, Torrington and Weightman (1993) believe that school culture is often felt rather than expressed. The 'slippery' concept thus remains vague and incomprehensible in some researchers' eyes. Despite attempting to understand how we shape school cultures, Deal and Peterson (1999) added culture is 'something extremely powerful but difficult to describe' (p. 2). However, Prosser (1999) strongly disagrees:

> To rest on the assumption that climate (or culture) is something 'felt', as many did, is a wilful lack of precision that limits our understanding and neglects its full constituency. (p. 5)

There are some ways of life in schools that we cannot see but feel everyday as we grow accustomed to the practices. These apparently invisible factors are visible only in the form of human attributes. In an effort to articulate the meaning of the concept, Hargreaves and Hopkins (1991) state:

> School culture is difficult to define, but is best thought of as the procedures, values and expectations that guide people's behaviour within an organization. (p. 17)

Thus, identification of specific traits of various school cultures requires closer examination of these everyday attributes in schools.

Dale argues (1972) that 'school culture' is constructed by the way we attempt to organise activities within a context, through a structure that involves human beings as 'actors'. When these actors try to pursue a common **goal,** by sharing a **set of values and code of conduct,** they interact. They interact as individuals, who bring in their own **attitudes and attributes** to their workplace. The actors require a common understanding of 'working together' in an organisation. Aspects of school culture such as codes of conduct (written or unwritten) help to formulate this common understanding.

From a different angle, Handy and Aitken (1986) argue similarly when they refer to school as a 'society in miniature'. A school has its own **system of communication, a structure to divide work as well as to define relationships between people** who are involved in the process of schooling. According to these organisational psychologists, school is an organisation with certain **rules and code of conduct**. The classrooms are mini-organisations,

> ...in which all the laws of group behaviour, motivation, leadership, communication and relationships apply. (p. 13)

Durkheim (cited in Ballantine, 1983) also described classrooms as 'small societies'. It is important for the members of staff in the school community to have a shared **set of values and expectations,** particularly as they are involved in the process of transmitting values to young children who are growing up to be independent learners. A collective **purpose** for the organisation is essential if the members are to feel motivated and encouraged by the fact that they are valued professionals and partners in educating children in school.

Dale (1972) considers **'time'** as an important part of school culture. He believes that there are certain factors which we take for granted, as we become used to a particular pattern of school life. He refers, for example, to the way time in school is divided into periods and intervals: we do not stop to think about how the structure has a subtle way of organising our work for the day or even our patterns of thoughts over periods of time; it has just become a part of the culture. Following the analogy, it may be difficult to conceive of such an abstract illustration of time as a part of a school's culture. But when there is a practice of doing certain things in certain ways at certain times over a certain period, these practices become **traditions** and thus eventually part of the **history** of the organisation. This is how 'time' becomes a part of school culture.

A government publication with the authority of the National Inspectorate in Scotland (*Scottish Education Department, Management of Educational*

Resources: 2 Effective Primary Schools, 1989, p. 9) suggests a number of factors concerning school ethos that are associated with a supportive teaching and learning atmosphere, promoting an effective academic outcome and 'good' social attitudes and behaviour among pupils.

These are:

- high but attainable **expectations** of pupils' standards of work and behaviour;
- **teacher commitment and** good **morale**;
- positive **attitudes** towards pupils and a concern for their well-being, coupled with a recognition of the motivating effect of praise;
- strong and purposeful **leadership** by the headteacher, including a high level of support and encouragement of the class teachers;
- **a sense of identity and pride** in the school;
- recognition of the importance attached to appearances and to creating a **welcoming environment**;
- a concern to establish good **relations** with parents and the wider community;
- effective **communication** with parents and pupils; and
- a willingness on the part of the pupils and staff to be involved in **extra-curricular activities**.

Although this list identifies a number of important key factors responsible for positive ethos, often descriptive words such as 'good' **(morale)** or 'strong and purposeful' **(leadership)** are used loosely without defining the characteristic qualities. The list also does not acknowledge history and tradition as contributing factors in a direct manner. The reference is vaguely implied within the fifth factor, **a sense of identity and pride** in the school. Any culture of a school is bound to have evolved through the events and the guiding beliefs and attitudes of the past. According to Stoll (1999) the **history, context and the people** of an organisation are important factors in the shaping process of culture. The **age** of the institution influences its cultural context. Stoll describes culture as 'a screen or lens' through which we observe our reality. This metaphor is particularly appropriate because when something is viewed through a lens, the image is slightly distorted through the process of refraction. When we observe a particular culture to gather knowledge about a context or a group of people, what we perceive is subconsciously filtered by our own value system. Thus, we interpret the gathered knowledge about the culture of a community through our individual subjective understanding. This can be applied to the members of the school community, who are involved in the constant culture-shaping process. Schein (1985) argues that, although cultural traits are visible through observed **behavioural patterns, practised norms,**

values, rituals and language, 'the deeper level of *basic assumptions* and *beliefs*', in other words the **implicit values,** are the guiding factors of an organisation's culture. Unlike an outsider viewing the culture of a school through a lens, the members of the school community require a common understanding about both the explicit or practised values and the implicit values, in order to fulfill the institutional goals in a coherent manner. On the other hand, often the value-conflicts arising from a lack of shared understanding in such situations create the unique characteristic traits of individual school cultures. Thus, each school exhibits 'situationally unique' patterns of practices (Beare, Calwell and Millikan, 1989; Stoll, 1999).

Nias *et al.* (1989) consider school as an organisation and therefore attempt to define school culture as 'organisational culture'. In their view, individuals in schools interact in groups and develop certain **codes of conduct** in the process. These researchers suggest a number of elements that comprise school culture – **beliefs and values, history, understandings, attitudes, meanings and norms, symbols, rituals and ceremonies**. They also consider **group dynamics** as one of the significant aspects of school culture. According to Nias *et al.* (1989):

> Though rooted in beliefs and values, culture develops through interaction, especially talk, between group members. (p. 12)

The statement echoes the idea of culture, as observed by Stenhouse (1975) and Thacker (1998), that it is a product of **social interaction.** School culture develops through formal and informal interactions between the members of the school community, including the pupils, teachers and the non-teaching members of staff. When these people interact, they pass on, negotiate and re-negotiate their values, beliefs, attitudes and understandings about various school-related matters to each other.

Geertz (1973) describes culture from an anthropological view. According to him, culture represents a 'historically transmitted pattern of meaning'. To define the term 'school culture', Stolp and Smith (cited in Stolp, 1994) extend the idea as

> ...the historically transmitted patterns of meaning that include the norms, values, beliefs, ceremonies, rituals, traditions, and myths understood, maybe in varying degrees, by members of the school community. (p. 1)

Peterson's (2002) arguments are similar: he defines school culture as the set of **norms, values and beliefs, rituals and ceremonies, symbols and stories** that make up the 'persona' of the school.

...In positive cultures, these features reinforce learning, commitment and motivation, and they are consistent with the school's vision. (p. 1)

Thus the authors have suggested a number of factors that constitute school culture. To extend the understanding further, these factors can be grouped into categories.

THE COMPRISING FACTORS

Previous research and the in-depth case studies conducted in four primary schools in Scotland (details in Chapter 9) indicate that the following factors are responsible for shaping school ethos or culture.

Historical Factors:	
history	symbols
tradition	rituals
beliefs	stories
ceremonies	myths
Behavioral factors:	
goals/purpose	norms and values
code of conduct	expectations
sense of identity	attitude
Organizational factors:	
group dynamics	
structure to divide work and define relationship	
system of communication	

Figure 1: Key Factors

The *historical factors* of a school, its tradition, beliefs, rituals define the character of the organisation. The *behavioural factors* set the scene and the third category, the *organisational factors*, indicates activities and inter-relationships between people in the school community. Based on these factors, prior to conducting the case studies, a working definition of an 'effective' school culture was adopted. The definition was used as a hypothesis. Following the Grounded Theory method, the hypothesis was revisited throughout, and as a result the adopted definition was developed further in the process of exploring the concept of school culture.

The absence of a sense of belonging to an organisation with a unique history, where people do not follow a code of practice consistently or do not share a particular set of values coherently or do not respect a specific way of communication in pursuing a common goal towards children's learning, identifies a situation where an effective school culture does not prevail. Therefore, the culture is liable to foster a lesser degree of security amongst the members of the school community. Here, the level of 'awareness' of the school's culture amongst the members is often non-existent. This description illustrates a 'less effective' school culture.

An effective school culture can be defined as one where there is a sense of belonging to an organisation with a unique history,
people follow a certain code of practice,
share a particular set of values, and
respect a specific way of communication in pursuing a common goal towards children's learning.

The presence of an effective school culture creates a strong sense of security amongst the members of the school community. 'Awareness' about the school's culture in the culture-shaping process is considered as important as the practices and guiding values.

Figure 2: An Effective School Culture

The definitions mark the opposite ends of the effective school culture continuum. Collective purpose, coherence in practices and shared values guiding everyday school activities are necessary to achieve an effective school culture. Awareness of the culture-shaping process is crucial to ensure effectiveness of learning outcomes. On the contrary, inconsistencies in practices and lack of shared values and goals mark a less effective culture, where also (not surprisingly) awareness of school culture amongst the members of the school community is often non-existent. Depending on the level of awareness, theoretically all schools could be located on this effective school culture continuum (from effective to less effective). Fostering a less effective culture sometimes gives birth to 'counter-culture' or, as Deal and Peterson (1999) called it, 'toxic culture'.

What is 'toxic culture'? If there is no agreement among the members of the school community about the purpose of the institution, and direction or guiding values are not made explicit, often sub-cultures become more powerful than an overall school culture. And if these sub-cultural practices demonstrate values that are contrary to the academic or social goals of the school, the overall school culture aimed for eventually becomes submerged in the process and a powerful counter-culture takes over. For example, the teenage pupil sub-culture in secondary schools generally exhibits significant traits. This sub-culture is influenced by the wider community's culture, displayed through behaviour patterns and certain codes of conducts. Some schools decide to work with this sub-culture and incorporate some of

45

its traits and values within the school's existing overall culture. Others often fail to notice the discrepancies in practices or codes and neglect the growing problems resulting from culture-conflict. Toxic cultures reinforce negative values; they are counterproductive; they foster an environment which works against the stated academic and social goals (Deal and Peterson, 1999). In the worst-case scenario, the resulting culture clashes can eventually lead to school closures.

The characteristics of an effective culture, a less effective culture and a toxic culture are determined by the degree of alignment between the stated goals of a school and the demonstrated cultural practices that aid the process of achieving such goals. In other words, whichever goal a school targets to fulfil, how the members of the school community work towards it determines the nature of their culture and effectiveness of their learning outcomes. This is why understanding school culture and its effect on learning is crucial in the process of schooling.

TYPOLOGIES OF SCHOOL CULTURE

As an alternative to general definitions of the term, some authors have chosen to identify different styles or typologies of school culture. The various categories identified are based on different criteria. Some of these typologies have been developed on the basis of the locus of control and the nature of dynamics through interactions between people in the school community. For example, Handy and Aitken (1986) described four types of organisational cultures – club culture, role culture, task culture and person culture. They studied schools as organisations and through this typology attempted to discuss how schools work in different ways depending on where the power lies in the structure of management and how its dynamics involves human agents to accomplish certain goals. The descriptions of these cultures used symbols to illustrate the above characteristics.

Club Culture

This type of culture (also called 'power culture') was described symbolically by Handiy and Aitken (1986) as a spider's web. Schools practising such a culture are likely to have a strong leader with vision in the centre of the power structure. The culture portrays a concept of a club with like-minded people, in which the relationships between people are based on trust and commitment. The strength of this culture lies in the clear and quick communication channels through the short and interconnected lines of the web. Weakness of this style or organisation is that if the 'spider' in the middle is weak or corrupt, the organisation is likely to project similar characteristics.

Role Culture

People fostering role culture are known to work with a strong focus on logic and rationality. The symbol used for this culture is a Greek Temple, for the pillars in the temple symbolise different roles of the staff and their departments. They are controlled by a narrow band of senior management at the top of the temple. Organisations with this culture are dominated by rules and procedures. This is a culture where roles are often more important than the individuals who shape it. Traits of this culture are more likely to be found in secondary schools than primary. Role culture-oriented organisations offer security and predictability to individuals but they are slow to perceive the need for change or bringing in change once the need is felt.

Task Culture

Task culture is based on individual expertise. It is suitable for small jobs or projects. Individual talents are valued in organisations practising such culture, through raised status and responsibility. Thus, jobs in these schools are done efficiently by fostering a satisfactory feeling of accomplishment. In these schools, leaders always look out for the right people for the right task. The organisation groups and re-groups the individuals according to the need of the different projects. The culture is symbolised by a net, where cords can be pulled when necessary, as it requires placing certain experts on different jobs at different times. Task culture is very adaptable. People usually have easy working relationships with colleagues, which are based on mutual respect and their capacity for work rather than status or age. The culture is also very much end-product-oriented.

Person Culture

In the other three cultures, irrespective of various roles, individuals' primary goal is to help the organisation achieve its purpose. The symbol used for person culture places the individuals at the centre. The organisation exists to help each of these individuals to achieve his/her purpose. People with their own specialities gather together to construct a loose circle. The experts in this circle are not mutually interdependent but they share an organisation for the benefit of their individual career development. Self-identity and freedom is very much preserved in person culture. As every individual has the right to veto any decision to be made in organisations fostering this type of culture, the decision-making process becomes a process of negotiation. Schools are not very likely to foster person culture, as a sense of centred self-interest is almost the main focus of this type of culture, instead of a collective goal.

The typology captures the intricate relationships and dynamics at work in organisations that affect the outcome in various ways. The descriptions discuss the strengths and weaknesses of each culture. However, when applied to schools, very few project only one type of these four organisational cultures. Often a mixture of elements from all four is found. According to Handy and Aitken (1986), the way in which the schools develop a unique culture and become different from each other depends on the mix of cultures that they choose.

Another typology of culture, devised by A. Hargreaves (1994) specifically for the context of the school, identified five different teacher cultures: *Individualism, Collaboration, Contrived Collegiality, Balkanisation* and *Moving Mosaic*. This assumes that teacher relationships are an important element in school culture. The typology essentially portrays the patterns of interactions amongst the teaching staff.

Individualism – The culture is described using metaphors of classrooms as egg-crates or castles, where individual teacher's autonomy is preserved through isolation and insulation. Consequently, in this culture blame and support are avoided.

Collaboration – In this culture, teachers work together spontaneously and voluntarily without an external control agenda. Here, sharing ideas and resources and learning though reflective enquiries are common features.

Contrived Collegiality – The term suggests that, in this culture, collegial working relationships are imposed. Such practices are compulsory and usually limited to fixed times and places set for collaboration.

Balkanisation – Teachers here do not work as a whole school. They are not isolated either. People work together in smaller collaborative groups, solving problems on similar issues.

Moving Mosaic – In this type of culture, teachers' professional relationships with their colleagues are flexible and they are creatively engaged in different problem-solving tasks. The task orientation signifies a focus on continuous learning and improvement. People here work collaboratively with adaptable partnerships and alliances. They group and re-group according to the need of the circumstances and contexts.

The self-explanatory categories are based on patterns of work dynamics between colleagues and on professional orientation towards institutional goals. Practised professional autonomy is also a hidden criterion used for this typology to portray how the use of power creates various patterns of work relationships resulting in different outcomes. It implies that increased professional autonomy (as portrayed in the description of *Balkanised* culture) does not necessarily produce better learning outcomes. Unless the autonomy is combined with a sense of direction and collective orientation towards a specific way of learning (as portrayed in the description of *Moving Mosaic* culture), there is still room for improvement to increase the effectiveness of a learning culture. The dynamics of *Moving Mosaic* is similar to that of the *Task Culture*, mentioned in the previous typology. Both indicate a primary focus on task and learning. MacGilchrist *et al.* (1995) in their analysis of learning environments in schools, suggest that school culture is manifested through three dimensions – professional relationships, organisational arrangements and opportunities for learning. A. Hargreaves's typology of teacher culture reflects all three of these dimensions. Although A. Hargreaves's (1994) typology and Handy and Aitken's (1986) categories of organisational cultures reflect the world of the adults' work culture in school, they do not take into account how the pupils' sub-culture fits into the concept of school culture. In fact, hardly any evidence was found in the studies of whole school culture where pupils' views were considered as an important contributing factor in shaping specific school cultures.

D. Hargreaves (1999) offers an alternative. He describes four types of school cultures on the basis of two aspects - social relationships and orientation towards learning with regard to social control, which include both the pupils and the members of staff.

Formal – The characteristic of this type of culture projects pressure on students to achieve learning goals but with weak social cohesion between staff and students. Approaches to practices are traditional in nature.

Welfarist – In this culture, the relationship between the staff and the students are relaxed and friendly but there is little academic pressure on students. A caring and cosy atmosphere prevails.

Hothouse – Here staff and students are pressurized to participate in all aspects of school life, both academic and social. Social control is high on the agenda.

Survivalist – Poor social cohesion and low academic achievement is perceived in this type of culture. Low morale and insecurity are common features amongst staff and pupils.

This typology also suggests that the 'ideal' or 'effective' culture would carry a balance between social cohesion and social control. The concept of social control implies the role of leadership as a significant element in a school's culture.

The typologies discussed above imply that school leaders are in an unique position to shape a school's culture in a specific direction, through their chosen approaches to implement the process of schooling. However, depending on the level of awareness of school culture and its influence on everyday school life, the members of the school community enjoy different forms and levels of professional autonomy. Figure 3 illustrates a new conceptual model of classification of school culture (Das, 2006) on the basis of three dimensions – *knowledge, process* and *power*. (All three dimensions and their components in Figure 3, both horizontally and vertically, should be treated as continuums.) On the *knowledge* dimension, school culture can be described as either conscious or sub-conscious or unconscious.

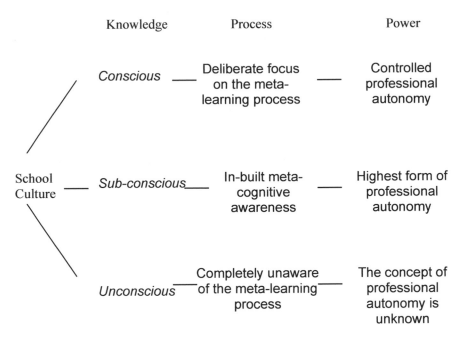

Figure 3: School Culture Classification

Conscious - On the *process* dimension, when the culture-shaping process is a 'conscious' act, often leaders are found to be quite strong and forceful in imposing their values and visions on the members of the school community. In this culture, a deliberate focus on the meta-learning process of culture-shaping is observed. It is an articulated process: frequently rules, codes and norms are discussed explicitly amongst the members of the school community, along with the expected outcomes, in a rigid fashion. Values in this type of culture are mainly acquired through a process which is best described by the 'inculcation' model (Crittenden, 1978; Musgrove and Taylor, 1969). The model advocates the transmission of values through deliberate promotion. When the outcome is predictable in the conscious culture of schooling, in most cases members of the school community enjoy only a limited form of professional autonomy. The exercise of power is controlled by the leaders who are managing the *process*. On the *power* dimension, this indicates less freedom of choice.

Sub-conscious - When the culture-shaping process is at a 'sub-conscious' level, the relationship between the members of the school community and the leadership exhibits a strong element of trust. Although the codes and norms are not frequently articulated, people in this culture intuitively act with a sense of collective consciousness. Their actions are guided by their previous experiences of working together. Both the 'inculcation' and 'socialisation' model (Cole, 1991; Jordan, 1991) of value acquisition are relevant for this type of culture. Predominant values are emphasised through the process of direct reinforcement in everyday practices as well as implicitly through subtle methods of socialisation. In a sub-conscious culture, implicit values fostered by the members of the school community are usually aligned with the explicit or stated ones. Leaders here, however, need to be skilled enough to know when to step in and take necessary action in case something goes against the school's goals. On the *power* dimension, in this culture, individuals enjoy the highest form of professional autonomy.

Unconscious – This is a culture where the school community is completely unaware of the culture-shaping process and the members look up to the leaders for directions and instructions. The *process* becomes mechanistic. Here, the element of reflective practice is absent in everyday activities, including the decision-making process. Relationships between the members of staff are generally cordial and harmonious. Predominant values are mainly practised through the 'socialisation' process. The concept of 'professional autonomy' is almost non-existent and unknown to the members of the school community. Most of the time the locus of control lies in the hands of the school leaders, as it is in the conscious school culture but the difference is that in the unconscious school culture, the leaders are not even aware of the fact that 'power' is concentrated in their hands. Potentially this type of culture portrays a great danger of misuse of *power* out of ignorance.

Theoretically, most schools with effective cultures would be found in the 'sub-conscious' category. This type of culture is capable of nourishing an effective learning community, where the locus of control shifts from place to place, depending on the need to accomplish a common goal at different points of time. Leaders in this culture usually opt for a democratic approach to management and have a strong sense of working together with school staff and pupils as a community. Coherence of opinion is generated with less effort as relationships between the members are based on trust and honesty. In contrast, sometimes in schools with 'conscious' school culture, the leaders opt for an autocratic approach to management against the majority's will and thus generate conflict. However, 'conscious' school cultures are often very useful when a strong 'change agent' is required for a particular context to steer towards a new direction. Which direction the school's culture should pursue might be debatable with the outcome depending on the approach (of the leadership) to management, but where the need for a culture change is required a 'conscious' school culture often produces the desired and predictable outcome.

CONCLUSION

We live in a constantly and rapidly changing world. The field of education amongst many signifies continuous development through the process of evaluation and adaptation. To evolve consciously within this intricate process, we require the knowledge and understanding of the interrelated elements that shape our world. For school leaders, it is not enough only to know 'what' produces effective learning anymore; the need to understand 'how' a desirable school culture can be fostered in order to achieve such outcomes has become equally crucial.

School culture is a powerful force, which operates from behind the scene with its subtle dynamics, influencing the everyday life in school. The concept is complex. It is also abstract, which adds to the complexity. In addition, to grasp the concept of culture as a coherent whole, it is important to take into account how people (individuals as well as groups) in the school community perceive their culture and contribute to shaping it in different ways.

When a concept is abstract, we tend to use metaphors as explanatory terminology; thus, those who write about school culture use words such as 'atmosphere' or 'climate' or 'environment'. One of the major difficulties in understanding the concept of school culture results from capturing a mixture of some 'tangible' and some 'not so tangible' factors within one boundary. This paragraph refers to the three categories of factors mentioned in Figure 1. Various combinations of these factors create the abstract notion of school culture. History, tradition and beliefs (*historical* factors) are elements that we cannot see or touch. We can only feel their influence or presence through different 'ways of doing things'. As Handy (1985, cited in Nias, *et al,* 1989) argues, a culture cannot be precisely defined, for it is something perceived, something felt. (p. 11)

On the other hand, the *behavioural* factors give us evidence of structured norms in an organization. It is the blend of these two types of factors that makes the concept complex. The third category of *organisational* factors indicating human interactions, adds yet another dimension to the concept. The interesting point is that often the *behavioural* and *organisational* factors become a part of the school culture as tradition (*historical* factors) over time. In this way the 'tangible' factors become 'intangible' as a part of organisational history through the process. 'Culture is evolving', says Morgan (cited in Preedy, 1993). Whether we are aware of it or not, culture changes in a subtle way over a period of time. Whether we want to be aware of the process in order to have a choice in shaping our school culture, is another question.

REFERENCES

Ames, C. (2003). In L. Stoll, D. Fink, & L. Earl (Eds.), *It's about learning*. London: Routledge.

Ashkanasy, N. M., Wilderom, C. P. M., & Peterson, M. F. (2000). *Organizational culture and climate*. London: Sage Publications, Inc.

Ballantine, J. H. (1983). *The sociology of education: A systematic analysis*. London: Prentice-Hall.

Beare, H., Calwell, B. J., & Millikan, R. H. (1989). *Creating an excellent school: Some new management techniques*. London: Routledge.

Bolam, R., McMahon, A., Pocklington, K., & Weindling, D. (1993). *Effective management in schools*. London: HMSO.

Bulach, C. R., Malone, B., & Castleman, C. (1995). An investigation of variables related to student achievement. *Mid-Western Educational Researcher, 8*(2), 23–29.

Cole, M. (1991). Class values, political values and education for equality: A reply to Dr. B. R. Singh. *Cambridge Journal of Education, 21*, 81–83.

Crittenden, B. (1978). Bearings in moral education: A critical review of recent work. *Australian Educational Review, 12*. Victoria: Australian Council for Educational Research.

Das, S. (2006). School culture: The evolving design of a study. *The International Learning Journal, 12*, 193–202.

Das, S. (2006). *School culture: Exploring a concept*. University of Aberdeen.

Das, S. (2007). Should power dynamics embedded in school culture be treated as a threat or an opportunity to create collective knowledge? *International Learning Journal, 14*(7), 1–8.

Dale, R. (1972). *The culture of the school*. Bucks: Open University Press.

Deal, T. E., & Kennedy, A. A. (1982). *Corporate culture: The rites and rituals of corporate life*. Harmondsworth: Penguin Books.

Deal, T. E., & Peterson, K. D. (1999). *Shaping school culture*. San Francisco: Jossey-Bass.

Donnelly, C. (2004). Defining the integrated ethos: perspectives from two integrated primary schools in Northern Ireland. *Education in the North, 11*, 27–35.

Durkheim, E. (1983). In J. H. Ballantine (Ed.), *The sociology of education: A systematic analysis*. London: Prentice-Hall.

Etzioni, A. (1960). Two approaches to organisational analysis: A critique and a suggestion. *Admin. Sci. Q., 5*, 257–278.

Evans, L. (1998). *Teacher morale, job satisfaction and motivation*. London: Paul Chapman Publishing Ltd.

Fidler, B. (2002). *Strategic management for school development*. London: Paul Chapman Publishing.

Fleming, P. (2000). *The art of middle management in secondary schools*. London: David Fulton Publishers.

Fleming, P., & Amesbury, M. (2001). *The art of middle management in primary schools*. London: David Fulton Publishers.

Freiberg, H. J. (Ed.). (1999). *School climate*. London: Falmer Press.

Geertz, C. (1973). *The interpretation of cultures*. New York: Fontana Press.

Giddens, A. (Ed.). (1997). *Sociology: Introductory readings*. Cambridge: Polity Press.

Glaser, B. G., & Strauss, A. L. (1980). *The discovery of grounded theory: Strategies for qualitative research*. Chicago: Aldine Publications.

Gleeson, D., & Husbands, C. (Eds.). (2001). *The performing school: Managing teaching & learning in a performance culture*. London: Routledge and Falmer.

Goldstein. (1980). The statistical procedures. In B. Tizard, T. Burgess, H. Francis, H. Goldstein, M. Young, J. Hewison, et al. (Eds.), *Fifteen thousand hours: A discussion* (pp. 21–25). London: University of London.

Greenbank, P. (2003). The role of values in educational research: The case for reflexivity. *British Educational Research Journal, 29*, 791–801.

Halpin, A. W., & Croft, D. B. (1963). *The organisational climate of schools*. Chicago: University of Chicago.

Handy, C., & Aitken, R. (1986). *Understanding schools as organizations*. Middlesex: Penguin Books.

Handy, C., & Aitken, R. (1994). The organisation of the primary school. In A. Pollard & J. Bourne (Eds.), *Teaching and learning in the primary school*. London: Routledge Falmer.

Handy, C. (1985). *Gods of management*. London: Pan Books.

Handy, C. (1989). In J. Nias, G. Southworth, & R. Yeomans (Eds.), *Staff relationships in the primary school*. London: Cassell.

Hargreaves, A. (1994). *Changing teachers, changing times: Teachers' work and culture in the postmodern age*. London: Cassell.

Hargreaves, D. (1999). Helping practitioners explore their school's culture. In J. Prosser (Ed.), *School culture* (pp. 48–65). London: Paul Chapman.

Hargreaves, D. H., & Hopkins, D. (1991). *The empowered school: The management and practice of development planning*. London: Cassell.

Harris, A., & Bennett, N. (Eds.). (2001). *School effectiveness and school improvement: Alternative perspectives*. London: Continuum.

Hoy, W. K., & Sabo, D. J. (1998). *Quality middle schools: Open and healthy*. CA: Sage.

Hoyle in Harris, A., & Bennett, N. (Eds.). (2001). *School effectiveness and school improvement: Alternative perspectives*. London: Continuum.

Jackson, P. (1968). *Life in classrooms*. New York: Holt, Rinehart & Winston.

Jordan, B. (1991). Competencies and values. *Social Work Education, 10*, 5–11.

Joyce, B., Calhoun, E., & Hopkins, D. (1999). *The new structure of school improvement*. Philadelphia: Open University Press.

King, R. (1983). *The sociology of school organization*. London: Methuen.

Lortie, D. (1975). *School teacher: A sociological study*. London: University of Chicago press.

MacBeath, J., & Mortimore, P. (Eds.). (2001). *Improving school effectiveness*. Buckingham: Open University Press.

MacGilchrist, B., Mortimore, P., Savage, J., & Beresford, C. (1995). *Planning matters: The impact of development planning in primary schools*. London: Paul Chapman.

Marsh, I., & Keating, M. (Eds.). (2006). *Sociology: Making sense of society*. London: Pearson Education Limited.

Meighan, R. (1981). *A sociology of educating*. London: Holt, Rinehart & Winston.

Morgan. (1993). Strengths and limitations of the culture metaphor. In M. Preedy (Ed.), *Managing the effective school* (pp. 30–43). London: Paul Chapman.

Mortimore, P., Sammons, P., Stoll, L., Lewis, D., & Ecob, R. (1988). *School matters: The junior years*. Somerset: Open Books.

Munn, P. (2002). In J. Murray (Ed.), *Building on success*. Edinburgh: Scottish Schools Ethos Network.

Musgrove, F., & Taylor, P. H. (1969). *Society and the teachers' role*. London: Routledge & Kegan Paul.

Nias, J., Southworth, G., & Yeomans, R. (1989). *Staff relationships in the primary school*. London: Cassell.

Peterson, K. D. (2002). Positive or negative? *Journal of Staff Development, 23*(3).

Pollard, A., & Bourne, J. (1994). *Teaching and learning in the primary school*. London: Routledge Falmer.

Preedy, M. (Ed.). (1993). *Managing the effective school*. London: Paul Chapman Publishing.

Prosser, J. (Ed.). (1999). *School culture*. London: Paul Chapman Publishing Ltd.

Reynolds, D. (Ed.). (1985). *Studying school effectiveness*. London: The Falmer Press.

Riddell, S. & Brown, S. (Eds.) (1991). *School Effectiveness Research: its messages for School Improvement,* London: The Scottish Office.

Robertson, P. & Toal, D. (2001). Extending the quality framework: Lessons from case study schools. In J. MacBeath & P. Mortimore (Eds.), *Improving School Effectiveness* (pp. 102–121), Buckingham: Open University Press.

Rutter, M., Maughan, B., Mortimore, P. & Ouston, J. (1979). *Fifteen Thousand Hours,* London: Open Books Publishing.

Schein, E. H. (1985). *Organizational Culture and Leadership.* San Francisco: Jossey-Bass.

Scottish Education Department (1989). *Management of Educational Resources: 2 Effective primary schools,* London: HMSO.

Shinn, R. (1972). *Culture and School,* London: Intext Educational Publishers.

Snyder, K. J., Acker-Hocevar M., & Snyder, K. M. (2000). *Living on the Age of Chaos: leading schools into the global age,* Milwaukee: ASQ Quality Press.

Stenhouse, L. (1975). *An Introduction to Curriculum Research and Development,* London: Heinemann.

Stoll, L. (1999). School culture: black hole or fertile garden for school improvement? In J. Prosser (ed.), *School Culture* (pp. 30–47), London: Paul Chapman.

Stolp, & Smith in Stolp, S. (1994). Leadership for school culture. *ERIC Digest 91,* Eugene: University of Oregon.

Stronge & Jones in Bulach C. R., Malone, B., & Castleman, C. (1995). An investigation of variables related to student achievement. *Mid-Western Educational Researcher, 8,* 23–29.

Thacker, V. J. (1998). *Using Cooperative Enquiry to Raise Awareness of the Leadership and Organizational Culture in an English Primary School,* Lewiston: The Edwin Mellen Press.

Torrington, D., & Weightman, J. (1993). The culture and ethos of the school. In M. Preedy (ed.), *Managing the Effective School* (pp. 44–55), London: Paul Chapman.

LEJF MOOS, JOHN KREJSLER AND KLAUS KASPER KOFOD

4. WHAT IS SUCCESSFUL LEADERSHIP?

INTRODUCTION

Success – contested term

When talking about successful leadership and successful principals, one realizes that success can be a rather arbitrary term. First, success is not a precise term until one has unveiled the criteria one employs for measuring success. Second, successful is something everyone wants to be. Therefore, success will always be a contested term. Third, there are currently strong tendencies that link success and quality, as well as other empty signifiers, to a global knowledge economy discourse, which gives the push for international comparisons of educational systems a particular direction. These tendencies are inspired by trans-national organizations like the OECD (PISA, TIMMS) (Moos (Eds.) 2006) and the like, which are then taken up by national governments to secure high competitiveness.

Commonalities and differences

Public debate about schools, education and school leadership is increasingly influenced by international comparisons, the large-scale OECD initiated PISA (Program for International Student Assessment) comparisons being probably the most influential – albeit contested.

However, when we compare schools, school leadership and school systems across nations, we must be careful not to overlook particularities of regional, national and local contexts in our search for commonalities. This is why we find it very timely to present in this chapter the issue of successful leadership through a three-level strategy: First, we shall present a survey of commonalities and differences from countries across the world. Second, we shall present the case of Denmark, represented by two local schools in the Copenhagen area. We thus want to highlight how commonalities seem more visible at the more general comparative level of international surveys, whereas differences become more important the closer you come to the local context. This is also our reason for wanting to introduce the concept of 'isomorphs', which serves to illustrate the problem

T. Townsend and I. Bogotch (eds.), The Elusive What and the Problematic How: The Essential Leadership Questions for School Leaders and Educational Researchers, 57–71.

of discussing schools and educational leadership across cultures: "By isomorphs is meant social conditions or values postures which appear to share the same shape or meaning from country to country but actually are structured of quite different elements." (Begley 2000)

It is important to be as clear as possible, because both researchers and policy makers indulge in policy borrowing from other cultures and countries and many educational and leadership discourses tend to use the same terminology to describe activities in different countries. One example could be the PISA comparisons. This may create an illusion of understanding because of the familiar terminology that is used in contexts, which, on more precise analysis, have significant differences.

In our research, we found that many concepts on successful schools and school leadership are isomorphs, which makes comparisons very challenging. A core question in discussing successful principals is whether or not we judge the success of schools according to the same set of criteria. Is the core purpose and function of schools seen to be the same?

THE INTERNATIONAL SUCCESSFUL SCHOOL PRINCIPALSHIP PROJECT

The International Successful School Principalship Project (ISSP)[1] aims to identify what counts as successful leadership practices in schools of varying sizes, geographic locations, and socio-economic conditions. The participating countries are US, UK, Australia, China, Canada, Sweden, Norway and Denmark. Multi-site case study methods are utilized as a research methodology in all participating countries. This approach is based on the assumption that the concept of 'success' when applied to school leadership is a contextualized and relational construct, as well as an attribution on the part of those who experience such leadership (Day et al. 2000, Leithwood et al. 1999). As such, it had to be investigated initially in reference to multiple perspectives within schools, and the research design incorporated multiple methods.

In all countries in our project national or state authorities have devolved authority to the local level and to the school level and therefore the project considers issues of site based management. In this way there are similarities between schools, however there are also differences. The relations between national/state level and schools differ – as an example – from rather strict regulation through detailed standards to more loose connections through target and framework management.

The concepts of success are constructed on the basis of the national and local regulations and discourses in the interactions in each individual school. We therefore look closer at those circumstances also. In most of the schools in the international project there is talk about distribution of leadership.

In most schools in the project there is discussion about how principals set the direction for the school. That seems to be very similar, but in some schools the direction is found and formulated by the principal him- or herself, while in other schools the direction is a product of dialogue, negotiations and shared knowledge production and sense making (Weick 2001c).

A parallel phenomenon can be seen when looking at principals creating strong communities. There seems to be different reasons and rationales for the creation of communities and also different ways of practising membership of communities, communal norms and relations within communities (Starrat 2001, Wenger 1999).

Different contexts, yet similar developments

The situation for schools has been markedly changing since the early 1980s in some countries like UK, US, Australia and Canada, and since the early 1990s in other countries like Norway, Sweden and Denmark. Beginning at that point in time government launched neo-liberally inspired New Public Management reforms (NPM) with decentralization of finances and administration from states to local authorities or to institutions as a powerful tool to make the educational systems more responsive to the demands of the market and to make public sectors more efficient and cost-effective. However, China seems to relate to that situation somewhat differently (Jacobson et al. 2005a).

This decentralization has been coupled with interest in more centrally developed curricula and standards for student achievements that generally has served two purposes. One is a back-to-basics inspired return to subject-oriented curricula with a particular emphasis on literacy, numeracy and science areas. Another purpose is the usefulness of such curricula to develop standards up against which students and local schools can be compared to each other nationally, and – when it comes to literacy and numeracy - internationally as well. This situation has meant a strong public management from the state level in UK, US, Canada and Australia in the first wave and in the other countries in the second wave. In federal unions like the US and Australia education is by tradition and by constitution a state issue, but the federal authorities have started to show a greater interest in education and in formulating goals for education. The initiatives are often accompanied by a system for allocating resources that makes it difficult for state authorities not to participate in the new programs. This development has been strongly supported by trans-national organizations.

In many societies and educational systems there used to be the understanding that schools were the major cultural institution that societies established and maintained because they wanted to make sure that the next generation of citizens were brought up and educated to take over, maintain and develop the society. Thus educational purposes were often described in broader terms: Schools should educate students to become enlightened, participating, active and collaborating citizens. Schools were therefore also about social justice, equity, empowerment and community. These notions still live in schools in most places, but are not always furthered from the level of politicians and administrators.

It is a clear tendency that policy makers and practitioners in countries like US, UK and Canada, that joined the NPM-trends early on (in the 80's) are more accustomed to the managerial and market-place thinking and values than practitioners in countries like Norway, Sweden and Denmark, where the trend hit at a later stage. But the implementation of accountability, performativity and marketisation depends very much on the means and technologies that governments deploy.

This short account demonstrates an astonishing trend towards uniformity and harmonization, that probably is an effect of Glocalization forces, the efforts of trans- and supra-national agencies' policies.

But the account also implies that national or local traditions, values and cultures are pivotal when trying to understand not only the official and explicit intentions but also the actual practice of education and leadership. We shall discuss that later on.

Successful leadership across nations

Within the frameworks of the different – yet similar – contexts described above, we see (Jacobson et al. 2005b) that principals interpret the signals given from legislators, the local community and administrators in ways that respond to the particularities of the national, state and local contexts. These responses are articulated in different visions and criteria for success in schools and they are identified and promoted in the interactions and relations between principals, (and) teachers and students in schools as the pursuit of successful leadership.

In Australia, principals are seen in all case schools as single heroic leaders that have strong values and beliefs and they use their influence to get things done, but they also distribute tasks and responsibilities to teachers. Principals underline the inclusive values that 'all children can learn' and 'all children matter'. In Tasmania the principals strive for a culture of collegiality and collaboration in which principals set directions. Principals in Victoria, on the other hand, tend to be strong leaders, who lead through decisions and support and act as role models to staff.

With the implementation of New Public Management (NPM) measures principals in the Canadian case use the provincial and district initiatives as a point of departure for setting goals for their schools. They communicate clear goals and high expectations for student achievement to staff. They give individualized support, intellectual stimulation and they act as role models. They act as members of various work teams and give teachers as well as parents significant decision making roles. They exercise strong management skills and use systematically collected evidence. In order to maximize learning, principals protect learning time from external, excessive and distracting demands. They give teachers room to manoeuvre to choose the means of instruction, but monitor student outcomes and teachers practice closely.

In China (Shanghai) a hierarchy of superintendents shows the direction of development, and at the case schools, there are strong top-down communities. The principal's task is handling the bureaucratic management carrying out decisions made by the federal senior management. Principals establish 3-year plans for their schools on the basis of policy decisions. Whenever a plan has been decided on, it is the middle managers that are kept responsible for the implementation. These plans often comprise both academic goals and extracurricular goals in sports or arts. Chinese schools have traditional, national Chinese goals of education. Order, control and collectivism are essential elements of schooling, and good behavior and group responsibility are main goals.

In Denmark leadership is distributed in various degrees from the school's leadership to staff teachers, and in some cases to the students in specific areas (e.g. the project work method). There is usually a leadership team and teacher teams. The distributed structure seems to resonate simultaneously with the traditional educational rhetoric of education for 'democratic citizenship' and with the NPM trend of decentralization. The purpose of schools used to be described in rather broad terms that were left to schools and to individual teachers to interpret. In recent years Government has formulated more detailed goals and demanded more rigorous forms of accountability from schools. Therefore, principals are now beginning to describe directions for the school and to discuss them with teachers in order to develop a shared set of goals. Most schools strive to accomplish high outcomes over a broad range of academic, social and personal competencies, which all contribute to building the participatory democratic citizenship competences.

In Norway students' learning is the focal point for the schools' philosophy. That is expressed in the need for a productive, collective learning culture and interactions between teachers and students. The demands in the national curriculum have lately been made more visible because a new national accountability system has been put in place. The distribution of leadership has been decided in such a way that the principal still retains the final powers of decision, but at a general level teachers are involved in school development issues and are expected to take significant responsibilities and decisions in their everyday work. Students are encouraged to participate in planning and evaluating teaching and learning. The criteria for selecting 'beacon schools' are very important to the case schools too.

In Sweden, although principals are loyal to the Government's policy on high performance on academic and social competences, and to the testing system, there is a feeling that that is not good enough. "The students must perceive that they actually have learned something," says one principal. Therefore principals and teachers emphasize in accordance with Government policies the need for an open and participatory school structure and culture based on fundamental democratic values. It is very important to them to enable teachers to take on responsibility and decisions and to demonstrate trust in teachers' competences and values. Therefore many schools form teacher teams and distribute both responsibility and decision making to them.

In the UK principals are seen to be responsible for ensuring that Government's targets for improving pupils' achievements are met through rational forms of management planning and monitoring. However many principals think that the vision of what is needed to achieve better examination results fails to address the need to provide an education which matters both for the individual and for society, including holistic development, equity and social justice. Thus the principals find themselves in a context full of contradictions, tensions and dilemmas. Principals clearly set directions for their school and education, but also delegate task and responsibilities for implementing those visions to teacher teams. Principals also spend much time in developing relations with parents and local community in order to include them in the efforts of their schools.

In the USA (New York State), schools in challenging circumstances are confronted with the New York State performance standards in literacy and numeracy. Principals use standards and testing as a way to focus teachers, parents and students in raising expectations for improved student achievement. Some teachers oppose this move, but even so the testing data are used to determine school goals and improvement plans; to stimulate collaborative dialogue, shared learning and to monitor progress. Sometimes goals are determined collaboratively, sometimes unilaterally. Leadership is in some instances distributed to teachers, giving them opportunities for teachers to take on instructional leadership, and also leadership in teacher teams. Some principals found time for shared planning in teacher teams.

Common trends

The general trend towards a more uniform, low-trust model (Ball 2003) for relations between state/local authorities and schools, building on detailed standards for students' achievements in some basic subjects and a tight testing and examination system, has been shown to have fundamental impact on the ways schools are managed and led. However, successful principals seem to challenge these instrumental changes by asserting that they are not enough to meet the needs of their vision for educating the whole child, for inclusiveness and 'education for all'.

Principals in schools in the more 'mature' accountability and perform- ativity countries (UK, US, Canada, China and Australia) are more inclined to accept the standards and testing as a fact of life. However most of them find that the national standards are not good enough indicators for a good or a successful school. They agree with principals in the younger accountability countries (Denmark, Norway and Sweden) that the school's core purpose is broader than basic skills.

There is a broad understanding that the core purpose of schooling is to give a holistic education that is focusing on education for citizenship and education for democratic citizenship. The reasons why this is the main purpose include that the school is an important cultural institution in every society with a special purpose to contribute to the education of the next generation to become active, knowledgeable and caring citizens of their societies. Therefore the purpose of schools is to provide a comprehensive education with a responsibility to community – education for democratic citizenship – and learning, also called 'Bildung' a German concept (Moos 2003b), so the students can grow or develop into being independent and enlightened adults who are action-competent, concerned with equity and social justice. That means that the individual is able and willing to be a qualified participant in society.

These descriptions are nonetheless at a very general level. For instance, distribution of leadership seems to be a common denominator of successful leadership in this cross-national material. However, it is often very difficult to see whether distribution just means the powerful principal's delegation of power, or whether distribution is implemented through democratic procedures or though rational argumentation (Spillane 2006). In order to determine that, one will have to come closer to the actual contexts of particular schools, which is exactly what we shall do in the following section.

DENMARK AS AN EXAMPLE, A CASE STORY

In order to show how differences become more visible the closer you get to the local context we shall now move to illustrate this by means of approaching what successful leadership is seen as through the lens of the empirical data from Danish schools. First, however, we shall briefly introduce the Danish context and an education system in transition.

The Danish context

The 20th century Danish comprehensive school evolved out of the development of the Danish welfare state (a largely Social-Democratic project) and a consensus-building dialogue across political parties. The school was looked upon as a vehicle for promoting equal opportunities and as a place for acquiring knowledge, skills, and values that prepare the student for life in a broader sense. That was done with reference to the concept of 'Bildung', traditional egalitarian and nation-building school ideas and inclusive welfare thinking. The Act on The Folkschool thus states: "The school prepares the pupils for participation, co-responsibility, rights and obligations in a society with freedom and democracy. Hence, education and everyday life of the school must be based on freedom of spirit, equality and democracy". (Act on Folkeskole 1995).

Since the beginning of the 90s, however, the Danish comprehensive educational system has been undergoing a process of thorough transformation under the influence of strong international currents: neo-liberal currents have linked educational thinking very closely to the economy and to neo-conservative trends of back-to-basics, more subject-oriented teaching, re-introduction of testing at all levels of primary school, pressure to harmonize within the European Union, inspiration from and fear of PISA (Program for International Student Assessment), individualization and so forth. The understanding of leadership, professionals, and learning are thus under profound change (Krejsler 2005, Moos 2003c).

For example the responsibility for finances and administration of the 'Folkeskole' (primary and lower secondary school, students aged 6-16) was devolved to municipalities and from there to schools. The school leader now manages very large parts of the budget in collaboration with School Boards, which have a parental majority membership. The Acts, and therefore the responsibility for objectives of the schools, remain in the hands of Parliament/the Ministry of Education but the interpretations and administration of the curriculum – which is fairly broad in its demands – is given to municipalities (which very often leave it unattended) and to schools themselves. At present the general notion of New Public Management (NPM) tendencies that focus less on processes and more on outcomes and on accountability, is gaining momentum. In Denmark the schools must post the results of school leaving tests on the Ministry's website. The government issues binding national 'goals' (usually every two years) that are much tighter and more prescriptive than the curriculum used to be and has also introduced plans for more testing of students in grades 2, 4 and 6 in addition to the end of school test in grade 9. There is also a focus on economic incentives like merit pay for teachers. In addition there is a focus on top-down management and decentralization across the system and on decentralization and top-down management within institutions.

School leaders, it seems, (Moos et al. 2000) are caught in the cross-fire between first, the national objectives for schools, which focus on liberal education (the 'Bildung/Dannelse' of children to become citizens in a democratic society); second, the local authorities' demands for financial accountability; and third, the school culture – teachers who are used to being very autonomous and are not eager to be managed or led by the 'new, strong, visible' school leaders described by Government and local authorities .

Danish schools

In our empirical studies successful principals were usually inspired by approaches like the learning organization and distributed leadership, when responding to the new emerging context for Danish schools. There were, however, considerable variations among the schools and principals. One principal is to a large extent the driving force at the school. However, she works hard to keep up to date with the wishes, problems and under-standings of almost each individual at the school in order to make her decisions on the background of that knowledge. She is open to recurring reformulations of the vision and suggestions to implementations. At another city school the principal is much keener to ensure that a certain vision of the learning organization is employed. At still another city school a much larger portion of relationship management is distributed to the teams, and the principal more looks upon himself as the one making the bullets, and expects his employees to fire them themselves with a large degree of autonomy.

The first of the above-mentioned principals could serve as an example as to how the interplay between principal and staff may typically work at a relational level. At her Copenhagen suburban middle-class school she found it important to set the direction by demanding commitment from all stakeholders in order to accomplish the purpose of the school. Her vision was explicitly moulded upon the theoretical framework of the learning organization (Senge 1990). Her vision of developing people was built on a firm conviction that the exercise of one's professional role cannot in a modern society be disconnected from sincere personal commitment (Krejsler 2002, 2005).

Two Copenhagen schools

The Danish case material consists of eight schools: six "folk-schools" (primary and lower secondary schools for 6- to 16-year-olds), one upper secondary school and one vocational school. We chose to focus on one primary and one lower secondary school in this chapter.

The North School is located in an affluent suburb of Copenhagen whereas the Inner City School is located in a challenging social area of the city. Those two schools are probably among those schools in Denmark that have been working most intensively towards team structuring and self-organization of teachers.

In the North School we interviewed the principal, department leaders, teachers, students, parents and superintendents. At the Inner City School we held a round of interviews with the principal, heads of departments, teachers, students and parents. In both schools we also observed the principal, the deputy, a teacher and a student for a whole day and then interviewed them on the basis of the observations.

First Case: The North School

The North School has a policy of qualifying pupils to take part in education at the highest possible level: "All kids should learn more," is the way the superintendent put it. The school vision is very much in line with the visions of the other schools in our study: "Respect, tolerance, and responsibility; curiosity and active participation; experience, happiness and self esteem; professionalism and competence". The chairman of the school board says that education at the school does not only prepare pupils for upper secondary school, which 80% of the children ended up attending, but also for life.

A picture of the local community

The school's catchment area is characterized by upper-middle-class parents. The school is, like many Danish schools, a three form entry school with three departments: one for the introductory level, one for the middle level and one for senior level. There are currently approximately 630 pupils at the school, and there are about 55 teachers. In the last few years quite a few new young teachers have come to the school. In order to adapt the school's buildings to the new educational principles a major rebuilding of the school was begun, aimed at separating the three teaching levels physically so that they each had their own "home area". At each level, teaching is organized by self-governing teams of teachers. Every single teacher did his/her entire teaching within the team. Once the teachers have chosen their teams, the choice was binding for a number of years.

Stakeholders' perception of success: The school is considered successful by most of the stakeholders. The principal emphasizes that they have succeeded in achieving a paradigm shift towards a new concept of learning with a focus on student competencies. A common language about learning complying with the municipality's learning philosophy has been developed. Finally, the organization of teachers into teams is considered a sign of success because it has given greater flexibility in the creation and composition of groups of pupils. The pupils thrive at school in part because the school's new structure makes it possible to give more care and attention to each individual child. They are listened to, students and teachers say, and they are often given room for manoeuvre.

Evidence of success: The superintendent considers it a sign of success that the school has the second highest marks on average at the national level in 2002 and that first grade's reading tests only show 4% insecure readers, a figure well below the national average. It is even said that families have moved to the municipality because of this school.

A picture of the principal: The male principal has been principal in this school for nine years. He is well liked and respected and has a great deal of authority. He is described as industrious, and he generally follows matters through. He has excellent cooperation with the deputy head teacher.

The principal's successful reorganization of the school gains everybody's respect. He has extraordinarily good relationships with central administration and politicians. He is respected by the teachers because he fights for the things he feels are right. Sometimes he might seem harsh because there is a feeling that there is no room for teachers who do not comply, one teacher said.

Some teachers describe the school's leadership team as decisive in creating the positive climate at the school through their leadership example, initiatives and democratic disposition. The leadership team is skilled at encouraging teachers without steamrolling them, teachers say. Teachers' opinions about initiatives are heard. The principal has turned the school around by his fierce involvement in the school development project right from the start. And he has succeeded in obtaining widespread support among staff for the project. Many mention that he only interferes if things go wrong. But the principal is also described as humble towards his job, good at delegating tasks, and someone who makes himself visible through precise visions and plans. No one has any doubt about the pedagogical direction in which the school is moving, but the principal's influence remains of a more indirect kind.

Second case: The Inner City School

The school is a three-form entry school. Currently, approximately 800 students attend the school. The buildings are open-plan with six houses, each containing a center room with classrooms around it. A head of department is connected to each block. Each department carries out its own planning with regard to teaching. However, "shadow-planning" is also made by the school management in case anything goes wrong with the block's planning. Most of the budget is decentralized to the single blocks.

Roughly 30% of the school's students come from an immigrant background, and this percentage is rising.

The teachers emphasize that there is a strong sense of cohesiveness between them. This is supported by the block structure, which makes it easy to get close to each other.

The Senior Management Team (SMT) has given the teachers great freedom and trust. At the same time, however, it expects that the teams keep discipline among themselves. The teachers have accepted the responsibilities and the room for creativity that has been distributed to them and there is a marked feeling that the school is a democratic working place. People respect and treat each other as equals: the teachers among themselves, and in relation to parents, students, and management.

Stakeholders' perspectives on success: The school is described by the teachers as successful because, seen through their eyes; there is great liberty of action in their daily work and both students and teachers say that they are listened to and very often included in negotiations about the development of aspects of school practice. Furthermore, the school is sought by twice as many students as the present architectural frame can contain.

The principal emphasizes the success of the delegation of decision-making competence from the SMT to the teachers in the self-governing teams. He also draws attention to the fact that almost all the children either continue in the education system or get a job.

The students stress that it is a good school because they are actively engaged in many activities.

DISCUSSION

In this chapter we wish to compare schools, school leadership and school systems across nations with the purpose of stressing the points that on the one hand international comparisons can be very fruitful and give plenty of insight; whereas on the other hand we must be careful not to overlook particularities of regional, national and local contexts in our search for commonalities. This is why we have found it very useful to present the issue of successful leadership through the three-level strategy of presenting first a description of commonalities and differences from countries across the world. Secondly, we presented the case of Denmark, represented by two local schools in the Copenhagen area. We hereby highlighted how commonalities seem more visible at the more general comparative level of international surveys, whereas differences become more important the closer you come to the local context.

The description of similarities and differences between the eight educational systems showed a general trend towards a more uniform, low-trust model for relations between state/local authorities and schools building on detailed standards for students' achievements in some basic subjects and a tight testing and examination system. However, successful principals in most countries seem to challenge these instrumental changes by asserting that they cannot meet the needs of their vision for educating the whole child, for inclusiveness and 'education for all'.

Some educational systems are more 'mature' in accountability and performativity (UK, US, Canada, China and Australia). Even if principals here are more inclined to accept the standards and testing as normal aspects of school life, most of them agree that national standards very often are too narrow as indicators for a successful school. They agree with the principals in the other countries in the project that school's core purpose is more than just basic skills.

Principals on a broad front find that the core purpose of schooling is to give a holistic education that is focusing on education for citizenship and education for democratic citizenship.

In the Danish case we see that principals are clear when it comes to prioritizing the main purpose of the school: Because schools are important societal and cultural institutions they must strive to promote the comprehensive project of democratic 'Bildung.' Basic skills like literacy and numeracy are seen to be important ingredients in the enlightenment of students, but not the end goal of education. On the same note, Danish principals are eager to find ways of leading schools, teachers and students that give students room for participation, deliberation and civil rights.

As this discussion clearly shows, it is hard to be very specific when comparing across a wide range of different nations, whereas focusing on a few schools in one country makes it possible to go very much into detail. Consequently, the former will abound with what looks like similarities. However, as a closer scrutiny of any one country will show – the case of Denmark in this chapter – those similarities may not be very similar at all when particular contexts and their richness are consulted. This basically goes to confirm that point that Begley made when he coined the concept of 'isomorphs' as quoted in the beginning of this chapter.

The comparison showed a number of similarities between the understanding of success on the political level in the two groups of countries, the 'accountability and performativity mature' countries (UK, US, Australia and Canada) and the younger accountability countries (Norway, Sweden and Denmark). So between the two groups one can talk about concepts of success being isomorphs. However there are even bigger differences to the accountability way of success when one looks closer at the actual practice of school leadership, as the Danish case shows and as cases from other countries will show too.

NOTES

[1] The International Successful School Principalship Project (ISSPP) has participation from the US, UK, Australia, China, Canada, Sweden, Norway and Denmark. Part of the data presented here are included in Moos, L., Krejsler, J. & Kofod, K. (2006): Communicative Strategies among Successful Danish School Principals, in: Leithwood, K. and Day, C. (Eds.) (2006): Successful School Principals: International Perspectives. Dordrecht, Springer

REFERENCES

Act on Folkeskole (1995). Consolidation Act No. 55 of 17 January.

Ball, S. J. (2003). Professionalism, managerialism and performativity. In L. Moos & J. Krejsler (Eds.), *Professional Development*. DPU Press.

Begley, P. (2000). Cultural Isomorphs of Educational Administration in *The Asia Pacific Journal of Education*.

Day, C., Alma, H., Mark, H., Harry, T., & John, B. (2000). *Leading Schools in Time of Change*. Open University Press.

Day, C. (2005). Sustaining success in challenging contexts: Leadership in English schools. *Journal of Educational Administration, 43*(6), 573–583.

Gronn, P. (2002). Distributed Leadership. In K. Leithwood & P. Hallinger (Eds.), *Second International Handbook of Educational Leadership and Administration* (pp. 653–696). Kluver Academic Publishers.

Jacobson, S. L., Christopher, D., & Kenneth, L. (2005a). The international successful school principal project in *Journal of Educational Administration, 43*(6), 532–629.

Krejsler, J. (2005). Professions and their Identities - How to explore professional development among (semi)professions in *Scandinavian Journal of Educational Research, 49*(5).

Krejsler, J. (2002). Teacher Professionalism and Terminology of Self-Determination in *Nordic Educational Research, 22*(1), 25–37.

Leithwood, K., Doris, J., & Roseanne, S. (1999). *Changing Leadership for Changing Times*. Open University Press.

Moos, L. (2003a). Leadership for/as 'Dannelse'? In L. Moos (Ed.), *Educational Leadership*. Danish University of Education Press.

Moos, L. (2003b). Pædagogisk ledelse - om ledelsesopgaven og relationerne i uddannelsesinstitutioner [Educational Leadership - On the leadership assignment and the relations in educational institutions]. Børsen.

Moos, L., Stephen, C., Olaf, J., & Jill, M. (2000). *Skoleledelse i Norden*. Nordisk Ministerråd.

Moos, L. (Eds.). (2006). What kinds of democracy in education are facilitated by supra- and transnational agencies? *European Educational Research Journal Special Issue* (forthcoming).

Senge, P. (1990). *The Fifth Discipline*. Century Business.

Spillane, J. P. (2006). *Distributed Leadership*. Jossey-Bass.

Spillane, J. P., Richard, H., & John, B. D. (2004). Towards a theory of leadership practice; a distributed perspective. *Journal of Curriculum Studies, 36*(1), 3–34.

Starrat, R. J. (2001). Democratic leadership theory in late modernity: an oxymoron or ironic possibility? *International Journal of Leadership in Education, 4*(4), 333–354.

Weick, K. E. (2001). *Making Sense of the Organization*. Blackwell.

Wenger, E. (1999). Communities of Practice. Learning, Meaning and Identity. Cambridge University Press.

Woods, P. A. (2004). Democratic leadership: drawing distinctions with distributed leadership. *International Journal of Leadership in Education, 7*(1), 3–26.

ALMA HARRIS AND PAT THOMSON

5. LEADING SCHOOLS IN POOR COMMUNITIES: WHAT DO WE KNOW?

INTRODUCTION

The challenge of improving schools in the most disadvantaged contexts is currently high on the political agenda in many countries. It remains the case that many schools in disadvantaged contexts face acute levels of socio-economic deprivation compounded by sets of external factors that adversely affect their ability to perform. Incidences of crime, drug abuse and violence tend to be significantly higher within areas of deprivation and social disadvantage. As a consequence, the socio-economic challenges facing schools in poorest communities are acute and the task of school improvement is a particularly difficult one for those principals and teachers committed to working within these contexts.

The educational reform agenda in many countries reflects a renewed interest in improving schools in the most difficult or disadvantaged circumstances. The issue of 'underachievement' has a high political profile and considerable attention plus resource has been directed towards addressing the problem (West and Pennell, 2003). However, it remains the case that certain groups of pupils consistently fail to reach their potential while other groups of pupils consistently succeed. Research has shown that children from low income families do not on average overcome the hurdle of lower initial attainment (Piontek et al, 1998). It also highlights that class differences affect children long before they start school and have a growing influence as they get older. The odds, it would seem, are 'still stacked against schools in poorer areas' and the social class differential remains a powerful indicator of subsequent educational achievement (Gray, 2001:1).

Schools located in poor communities often face a myriad of social problems, such as high levels of unemployment, physical and mental health issues, migration of the best qualified young people and, not least, low educational achievement. These powerful, interlocking variables render the teaching and learning processes, accepted and expected in schools in more challenging circumstances, particularly difficult. As Power et al. (2003) conclude in their study: [educational] outcomes in deprived areas are worse

T. Townsend and I. Bogotch (eds.), The Elusive What and the Problematic How: The Essential Leadership Questions for School Leaders and Educational Researchers, 73–83.
© *2008 Sense Publishers. All rights reserved.*

than those in non-deprived areas, whether they are measured in terms of qualification, attendance, exclusions or 'staying on' rates. Inner-city areas, in particular, feature as having low achievement outcomes and lower attainment levels. (p. 26). The study also points to the need to reduce the 'compositional effects that appear to result from high concentrations of disadvantaged students' (p. 65). The 'social mix' of students has been shown to be an important contributor to a school's performance therefore making it more difficult for schools in challenging circumstances to improve.

In addition, schools in poor communities are often a recipient of higher than average numbers of pupils with diverse ethnic backgrounds and low literacy levels on entry. In many cases, these schools also take a high proportion of refugee children or pupils that have been excluded from other schools. Not only does this make the student population inherently transient and diverse but it also presents teachers with the daily task of teaching pupils who they have not taught before. Inevitably this places great demands on teachers and often leaves the school in a position of having difficulty with teacher recruitment and retention. Inevitably, with disadvantage comes diversity and the more severe the disadvantage the greater the diversity within the student population (Harris and Chapman, 2004).

In summary, schools in poor communities not only have students who vary in terms of their religious, ethnic and cultural backgrounds but also vary from their teachers in terms of aspiration, experience and other attributes directly linked to success at school. In schools in poor communities the social stratification or class of students may be relatively homogeneous while differences in race, ethnicity, religion and language can vary enormously. These variations expand disproportionately the lower down the socio-economic scale schools go. Consequently, there are two inherent and persistent problems facing these schools. The first is the influence of social mix of the school population, i.e. a high proportion of young people from low SES backgrounds (Thrupp, 1999). The second is the sheer challenge of the teaching task presented by a less affluent student population and a community disengaged from education. Students from disadvantaged backgrounds can challenge teachers' conceptions of what to teach, what to expect of students and even how to communicate with them (Knapp, 2002). This is not to suggest a deficit model of teaching in schools in disadvantaged circumstances but simply to acknowledge the extent of the task in securing levels of performance that schools in more affluent areas achieve with relative ease.

Research has shown that in order to achieve and sustain improvement in such schools teachers must exceed what might be termed as 'normal efforts' (Maden, 2001). They have to work much harder and be more committed than their peers in more favorable socio-economic circumstances. In addition, they have to maintain that effort in order to sustain improvement as success can be short-lived and fragile in difficult or challenging circumstances (Whitty, 2001:109). It cannot be denied therefore that there is a strong negative correlation between most measures of social disadvantage and school achievement. However this should not translate into a position of believing that there is little that can be done with schools in difficult or challenging contexts. While it is important to recognize the socio-cultural factors that sustain inequalities in educational achievement, cultural deficit models underestimate the potential of schools, teachers and students to 'buck the trend'. There is increasing evidence that schools facing difficult and challenging circumstances are able to add significant value to levels of student achievement and learning (Maden and Hillman, 1999:2002). There is also evidence to show that schools in poor communities can sustain improved levels of student performance and achievement (Gray, 2001; Harris et al, 2003).

It is interesting to note that the school improvement literature has not been overly concerned with schools facing difficult or challenging circumstances. Only relatively recently have researchers focused their expertise and attention upon schools in poor communities (e.g Stoll and Myers, 1998; Gray, 2001; Harris and Chapman, 2001; Harris et al, 2006). As Gray (2001:33) concedes 'we don't really know how much more difficult it is for schools serving disadvantaged communities to improve because much of the improvement research has ignored this dimension- that it is more difficult, however, seems unquestionable'. So while social disadvantage may not be an excuse for poor achievement in academic terms it certainly remains a powerful factor and source of explanation.

The contemporary research evidence shows that schools in challenging circumstances can improve levels of student performance and achievement (Borman et al, 2000; Harris et al, 2003) and highlights that the quality of leadership is a major contributory factor of this success (Reynolds et al, 2001 and Hopkins 2001). It shows that leadership of schools in poor communities is one of the major levers for subsequent success and achievement (Harris et al, 2006). The existing empirical base highlights the importance of leadership in securing long term change and development in schools but also highlights the limitations of the charismatic, autocratic single leader in securing any form of sustainable improvement (Hill, 2006). The idea of turning around 'failing' schools through the leadership efforts of one person has been shown to be misguided and has proved to be generally less than successful. While the leadership of the principal is undoubtedly important, any individual's efforts however great is unlikely to generate the momentum needed to improve performance unless there is deep engagement and involvement from staff, students and parents in the community. The evidence suggests that the most successful leaders of schools in poor contexts are those who distribute leadership widely and recognize the importance of connecting the school to its wider constituency and community (Harris et al, 2006).

LEADING IN POOR COMMUNITIES

The importance of leadership as a lever to secure improvement in schools in difficult contexts should not be surprising. The research base is pretty unequivocal about the importance of leadership in securing successful school change, development and improvement (Fullan, 2001). It points towards the fact that successful school leaders exercise an indirect but powerful influence on the effectiveness of the school and on the achievement of students, explaining up to a quarter of the school level variance in pupil achievement (Hallinger & Heck (1998). It is also well known that school leadership plays an unprecedented role in determining a school's success and there is a very strong belief in the ability of leaders to promote and generate school improvement. This is reinforced in the research literature which consistently emphasizes the powerful relationship between leadership and school development.

The dominant message is unequivocal – effective leaders exercise an indirect but powerful influence on the effectiveness of the school and on the achievement of students (Leithwood and Jantzi, 2000). The research evidence consistently demonstrates that the quality of leadership determines the motivation of teachers and the quality of teaching in the classroom. Based on a series of comprehensive and systematic reviews of the literature across all types of schools, Hallinger and Heck (1996) concluded that the effects of school leadership on pupil outcomes were educationally significant. In summary, leadership makes a difference to school effectiveness and school improvement.

Contemporary evidence about schools in challenging circumstances (Harris and Chapman, 2002; Harris et al, 2006) has identified some common features or characteristics of successful leadership practice. While it is clear that more research is needed in order to gain an in-depth and comprehensive understanding of effective leadership in such contexts, these studies offer a contemporary snapshot of leadership in schools in disadvantaged contexts. The breadth of data collected in both empirical studies provides an important source of evidence about the leadership styles and qualities in such schools.

The data revealed some common themes about the leadership of the principals in these school settings. It showed that of central importance to the leaders of schools in poor communities was the co-operation and alignment of others to their set of values and vision. The principals communicated their personal vision and belief systems by direction, words and deeds. All of the principals reinforced the fact that they had deliberately chosen to work in school in a poor community. It was clear that their vision and values emanated from a core belief in the ability of all children to learn and in the school's potential to offset the effects of disadvantage on student performance.

Second, the data showed that the principals' vision was shared both within and outside the school. Through a variety of symbolic gestures and action, the principals were successful at aligning staff, parents and students to their particular view of what the school stood for and how it should operate. They had a great optimism around learning and all subscribed to the view that within their school there was huge potential for student growth and development. They respected staff and students and treated each person as an individual. They trusted others and required trust from others. They recognized the need to be actively supportive, caring and encouraging as well as challenging and confrontational when necessary.

Third, vision was an inherent part of their leadership relationships which helped them communicate a sense of direction for the school. The vision and practices of the principals in schools in poor communities were organized around a number of core personal values concerning the modeling and promotion of respect (for individuals), fairness and equality, caring for the well being and whole development of students and staff, integrity and honesty. It was clear from everything said by the principals that their leadership values and visions were primarily moral (ie, dedicated to the welfare of staff and students, with the latter at the center) rather than primarily instrumental (for economic reasons) or non-educative (for custodial reasons). Their values and visions both constructed their relationships with staff and students and were constructed within them.

In summary, both studies illustrated that the principals of schools in poor communities displayed 'people-centered leadership' as their core leadership behavior. This was premised upon respect, trust and a core belief in developing the potential of both staff and students. Their ability to invite others to share and develop their vision was frequently commented upon by staff and students alike. Alongside these qualities however, were examples of the principals being firm (in relation to values, expectations and standards), and, on occasion taking very tough decisions, for example, tackling teachers who were consistently under-performing. The principals did not gently cajole staff and students towards success but provided both pressure and support while concurrently building positive relationships. The way they interacted with others was the common denominator of their success. The human qualities they possessed enabled them to lead others effectively and to establish confidence in others that their vision was worth sharing. The data also revealed a number of common leadership themes.

VISION AND VALUES

Of central importance to leaders in all schools, but particularly in schools in poor communities is the co-operation and alignment of others to a shared set of values and vision. Establishing a clear vision and communicating a sense of direction for the school is a critical task for leaders in schools in difficult circumstances. A lack of direction or common purpose can be a contributory factor to a downward spiral of performance amongst staff in schools in challenging circumstances. Re-establishing direction and regaining staff confidence is essential if subsequent changes are to be successfully implemented. The emphasis upon core values such as respect, fairness, equality, integrity and honesty is a way of defining or re-defining the moral code of the school and setting in place minimum standards of conduct. With a well defined vision and established values in place, the possibility of raising staff and pupil expectations of performance is enhanced in all schools but particularly those in challenging circumstances.

Leading Learning

For the all the principals, effective leadership was centrally concerned with building the capacity for improved teaching and learning. They were quick to dispel the 'cultural deficit' notion prevalent in many schools in poor communities and were committed to the belief that every child can learn and succeed. They made decisions that motivated both staff and students and placed an emphasis upon student achievement and learning. The principals talked about creating the conditions that would lead to higher student performance and they were deeply concerned about the welfare and the educational experiences of minority children. They set high expectations for students, emphasized consistency in teaching practices and provided clear rules about behavior and stressed discipline.

Their developmental focus was on improving the quality of teaching and learning. In this sense, they were instructional leaders as the emphasis was upon student attainment and achievement. The principals created learning opportunities for both students and teachers. They focused their strategic attention upon the classroom and engaged staff in dialogue about teaching and learning issues rather than issues of behavior or classroom management. They were able to make clear links between their core values and their vision for improved student achievement and learning.

Investing in Professional Development

A main concern for the principals in challenging school contexts is often one of maintaining staff morale and motivation. In a number of the schools in both studies staff morale had been low and individual self-esteem had been eroded by ongoing criticism of the school. In response the principals consistently and vigorously promoted staff development whether through in-service training, visits to other schools, or peer support schemes. It was noticeable also, that such development did not only focus upon needs which were of direct benefit to the school but also those which were of direct benefit to the individual. The development needs of non-teaching staff were also included. The emphasis principals placed on the continuing development of their staff was an endorsement that teachers were their most important asset and that, particularly in difficult times, it was important to support and value them. Consequently, the principals were highly skilled at using a combination of pressure and support to promote the efforts of teachers, particularly when working with the most difficult students. They encouraged teachers to take risks and rewarded innovative thinking.

The principals set high standards for teaching and teacher performance. The focus and emphasis upon improving teaching and learning was common across all schools. In most cases, time was provided to allow teachers to meet to discuss teaching approaches and they were able to observe each other teaching. In addition, teaching performance was monitored and individual assessments made. Poor teaching was not ignored or tolerated within the schools. Where it did exist, it was challenged and strategies were agreed for improvement. Where this did not occur, the necessary steps were taken by the head teacher to deal with the problem. In the majority of cases, a combination of support, monitoring and an individual development program addressed the problem of poor quality teaching. For all the principals, effective leadership was about capacity building in others and investing in the social capital of the school.

Distributing Leadership

Evidence suggests that highly creative approaches to tackling complex problems are required in schools in poor communities and that the leadership task is one that cannot be undertaken by an individual. This implies distributed or shared forms of leadership where tasks are not the sole responsibility of one person or indeed, the leadership team. All the principals in both studies invested in the leadership of others. In such schools often the decision to work with and through teams as well as individuals is a common and effective response to the management of change. Successful principals in such contexts tend to distribute certain strategic leadership responsibilities or core developmental work to teams or individuals within the school.

While principals in schools in poor communities clearly recognize the need to take responsibility for all decisions made, they also acknowledge the importance of empowering teachers who are not necessarily in positions of responsibility or authority to lead important initiatives or developments on behalf of the school. The overarching message is one of the principal building the community of the school in its widest sense i.e. through developing and involving others in leadership and innovation.

Community Building

Recent research has reinforced the importance of school leaders connecting with the community and of hearing and taking account of parent (and student) voices (Chrispeels, Castillo, & Brown, 2000).The principals in both studies were acutely aware of the need to engage with their community. They visited homes, attended community events, communicated regularly with the parents about successes and engendered trust by showing genuine care for young people. They understood the forces within the community that impeded learning, they were aware of the negative forces of the sub-cultures and they listened to parents' views and opinions regularly. The principals tried to create integral relationships with the families in the communities they served. They recognized that 'family, school and community relationships directly affected student outcomes' hence the need to connect with the community was of paramount importance to the success of the school.

The principals were also highly responsive to the demands and challenges placed upon their school by other external forces. Schools in poor communities are often in receipt of much more attention and intervention from the district and central government level than schools in more affluent circumstances. The schools in both studies were under constant scrutiny and pressure to implement numerous innovations and interventions aimed at improving performance. The principals saw their role as protecting teachers from unnecessary intrusion or burdens by acting as gatekeepers to external pressures. While there were innovations and new initiatives at each school, these had been carefully selected to ensure that they matched the developmental needs of the school and would not simply compete for teachers' classroom time and energy.

The principals were good at developing and maintaining relationships. They were considered to be fair and were seen as having a genuine joy and vibrancy when talking to students. They generated a high level of commitment in others through their openness, honest and the quality of their inter-personal relationships. The principals engaged in self-criticism and were able to admit to others when they felt they had made a mistake. They placed a particular emphasis upon generating positive relationships with parents and fostering a view of the school as being part of, rather than apart from, the community. Stoll and Fink (1996) describe 'invitational leadership' as a form of leadership where leaders place a high premium upon personal values and inter-relationships with others. The principals in both studies did reflect many of the dimensions of invitational leadership. They placed an emphasis upon people rather than systems and invited others to lead. It was clear that while they possessed a range of leadership strategies to address the diverse sets of issues and problems they faced, at the core of their leadership practice was a belief in empowering others.

COMMENTARY

The evidence suggests that leadership within schools in poor communities takes two forms. The first is concerned with the implementation of policies and initiatives aimed at addressing structural concerns within the school. The second is concerned with cultural change and development where leadership has a transformational intention and quality. The principals displayed both kinds of leadership and had instigated many changes and deployed many strategies aimed at improvement. They had deliberately and carefully selected key areas for development and change.

The principals acknowledged that there had been times when the quality of the relationships between staff and also between staff, students and parents had not been at an optimum. In some cases relationships had deteriorated over time resulting in a negative culture within the school characterized by low expectations and a high degree of mistrust. Therefore they had invested a great deal of time in creating opportunities for more positive relationships to be developed. For staff, opportunities were provided to work together, to work across teams and within teams, social events were organized and staff development activities included the expertise and involvement of those within the school. For students, staff-student committees were organized, student councils were established, lunch time and after hour clubs were set up and trips were organized. For parents, there were evening classes and 'drop in' sessions, all parents' evenings included a social component and there were more opportunities created to give parents positive feedback and to invite them into the school. An emphasis was placed upon breaking down social barriers and creating a climate within school where staff, students and parents had more opportunities to talk.

Leadership is a complex undertaking in any school, but for schools within disadvantaged contexts, it presents extra challenges. The core message about successful leadership in schools facing difficult or challenging circumstances is one of building capacity through empowering, involving and developing others and by providing systems of learning support, guidance and assistance. Capacity building should be the central aim of all schools but for those in challenging circumstances it is imperative to ensure that school improvement is long term rather than short lived. While there are no 'quick fixes' for schools facing challenging circumstances (Stoll and Myers, 1998), there is an emerging evidence base to suggest that distributed forms of leadership and more contextually specific approaches to development are more likely to contribute to raising attainment in schools in difficulty (Harris and Chapman, 2006).

Increasing external scrutiny, intervention and pressure upon schools facing challenging circumstances are strategies that are least likely to bring about improvement in schools in the poorest communities in the long term. An alternative approach is one where improvement approaches are carefully matched to individual schools and to the individual school context. This requires leaders to accurately diagnose and prioritize problems and to put in place strategies for improvement that fit the developmental stage and needs of their school. It also implies moving away from highly prescriptive forms of leadership practice to more evolutionary approaches that are responsive to individual school context and circumstances.

No one close to schools in challenging circumstances would ever think that providing them with leadership is an easy task. The work of these leaders is hectic, fast paced and demanding. Successful leaders in poor communities are constantly managing tensions and problems directly related to the particular circumstances and context of the school. The main leadership task facing them is one of coping with unpredictability, conflict and dissent on a daily basis without discarding their moral purpose and core values. Successful leaders of schools in poor communities tend to be, above all, people-centered combining a willingness to be collaborative with a constant striving for improved teaching and learning. The evidence suggests that while the demands upon such leaders are considerable, the personal and professional benefits far outweigh them ensuring that there is leadership continuity, capability and continuity in our most challenging school contexts.

REFERENCES

Borman, G. D., Rachuba, L., Datnow, A., Alberg, M., Maciver, M., & Stringfield, S. (2000). *Four Models of School Improvement. Successes and Challenges in Reforming Low-Performing, High Poverty Title 1 Schools*. Baltimore: Johns Hopkins University, Center for Research into the Education of Students Placed At Risk.

Chapman, C, & Harris, A. (forthcoming)' Improving schools in difficult contexts: towards a model of differentiated intervention' *Educational Research*

Chrispeels, J. H., Castillo, S., & Brown, J. (2000). School leadership teams: A process model of team development. *School Effectiveness and School Improvement, 11*(1), 20–56.

Fullan, M. (2001). *Leading in a Culture of Change*, San Francisco: Jossey Bass

Gray, J. (2000). Causing Concern but Improving: A Review of Schools' Experience. London, DfEE.

Hallinger, P., & Heck, R. (1996). Reassessing the principal's role in school effectiveness: a critical review of empirical research 1980-1995. *Educational Administration Quarterly, 32*(1), 5–4.

Harris, A., & Chapman, C (2002). Effective Leadership in Schools Facing Challenging Circumstances, Final Report, NCSL, Nottingham www.ncsl.org.uk

Harris, A., Muijs, D., Chapman, C., Stoll, L., & Russ, J. (2003). Improving Schools in Disadvantaged Areas – A Review of the Research Evidence, DFES Moorfoot.

Harris, A., Clarke, P., James, S., Harris, B., & Gunraj, J. (2006). *Improving Schools in Difficulty*, London: Continuum Press.

Hill, R. (2006). *Leadership that Lasts*, Association of School and College Leaders (ASCL)

Hopkins, D. (2001). Meeting the Challenge. An Improvement Guide for Schools Facing Challenging Circumstances. London: Department for Education and Skills.

Knapp, M. S. (2002). Policy, Poverty and Capable Teaching in Biddle, B. (2001) *Social Class, Poverty and Education,* Routledge Falmer, New York.

Maden, M. (Ed.). (2001). *Success Against the Odds: Five Years On*. London: Routledge.

Maden, M., & Hillman, J. (Eds.). (1993). Success Against the Odds: Effective Schools in Disadvantaged Areas. London: Routledge.

Power, S., Warren, S., Gillbourn, D., Clark, A., Thomas, S., & Kelly, C. (2003). *Education in deprived areas. Outcomes, inputs and processes*. London: Institute of Education, University of London.

Stoll, L., & Myers, K. (1998) *No Quick Fixes: Improving Schools in Difficulty*, London: Falmer Press.

Whitty, G. (2001). Education, social class and social exclusion. *Education & Social Justice, 1*(1), 2–8.

.

6. REBUILDING NEW ORLEANS PUBLIC SCHOOLS: THE CASE OF ALGIERS CHARTER SCHOOL ASSOCIATION

June 4ᵗʰ, 2006
Algiers Teachers,

This letter is written to thank you for all you have done this year. Truly, sincerely, and from my heart, thank you. What we have created and done this year is extraordinary ...and it has been done through your efforts. The exertion teachers, counselors, security guards, secretaries, our school leaders and more that all have exhibited – have all played a part in our story. I know each of you has sacrificed. Some travel a far distance, some live in houses under repair, some teach in unfamiliar surroundings and unfamiliar subjects, some live with relatives or friends, but all have given their all – their best. If you just stop and think where we were just six months ago think and realize that we graduated over 80% of our seniors in attendance. Extraordinary!

Each grade and subject has a story, and each has a struggle, but please take the time to look past that to the success and you can see you are part of something VERY SPECIAL...and I thank you....from our community, from our students, from me....

Sincerely,
Brian Riedlinger, Ed.D.
CEO
Algiers Charter School Association

INTRODUCTION

The purpose of this chapter is to analyze the case of rebuilding public schools in the city of New Orleans, post-Katrina. We do so through the lenses of critique and voice. The focus here is on the "what" of school improvement as we raise questions regarding the ideological influences created by accountability measures and the marketization of public schools as charters. Given the urgency of rebuilding a city and its schools, versus the more

T. Townsend and I. Bogotch (eds.), The Elusive What and the Problematic How: The Essential Leadership Questions for School Leaders and Educational Researchers, 85–98.

common practices of school improvement, we ask whether rebuilding can accommodate context and cultural uniqueness – of New Orleans – given the dominance of educational accountability measures and the market forces unleashed in this city. This chapter traces the trajectory of School Effectiveness/School Improvement (SESI) research findings from the 1980s to the present in order to assess the opportunities that New Orleans can successfully rebuild schools rather than reproduce pre-Katrina educational patterns.

Why School Effectiveness/School Improvement reforms as a lens? SESI tenets have gained a privileged status within policymaking circles regarding school improvement. For this reason, it is logical to expect to see ideological influences of SESI within the New Orleans rebuilding efforts, especially when focusing on one segment of school reform, that is, the Algiers Charter School Association. Within this unprecedented context, we have observed how the push and pull of school reform was progressed during Years 1 and 2 of the rebuilding. In other words, there is not only the reality of having to rebuild schools; there is also the reality of the ghosts of past practices and negative perceptions regarding New Orleans public schools. The tensions between these two realities are embedded in how reform efforts have and continue to address best practices, good teachers and teaching, good schools, accountability, and world class curricula.

CRITIQUING IDEOLOGICAL DOMINANCE

Arguably, School Effectiveness/School Improvement research has been one of the most debated research reform movements in education over the past quarter century. Its axioms, variables, and measures have dominated the school reform landscape primarily because of the appeal that "school matters." This is a professional judgment that educators themselves favor; but it also has had great appeal to governmental and philanthropic organizations. While the names James Coleman (1966) and Ronald Edmonds (1979) framed the initial debate, a small number of seminal studies in the 1980s and 90s has become an abiding framework for school reform in many countries including the U.S. At the same time, SESI research and researchers have offered self-critiques and have adopted significantly new directions and methods associated with SESI research in the last decade. Nevertheless, global and standardized measures of accountability as well as market forces linked to early SESI research findings, have ignored emerging SESI frameworks for school improvement based on contexts, cultures, and voices. Is there a lesson in this for the educators in New Orleans?

In the beginning, school effectiveness research (SER) was an attempt to counter James Coleman's 1966 finding that schools did not alter outcomes for low SES black students in the US. Rather than blaming the school, however, Ron Edmonds (1979) argued that schools mattered because of what people were doing inside of them. With the right structures, processes, and behaviors, low SES students were found to be learning.

Rather quickly, however, school effectiveness researchers settled upon a set of managerialist routines with direct, univariate measures used in input-output research designs. Thus, everyday instructional practices of effective schooling were measured and correlated to outcomes, typically standardized test scores. Within-school measures were constructed without close attention of who the students were, where they came from, and what their interests were. The same protocols were used in measuring teacher and administrator effectiveness. Consequently, SER research and resulting practices ignored the underlying values residing in history, communities, and relationships among teachers, administrators, and students. School effectiveness was associated with a rational delivery model that was behavioral, prescriptive, and formulaic. By not questioning the deeper meanings of within-school relationships and processes, and by never explicitly asking the question 'effective for what?' the general public was not educated to see the educative meanings and values behind the measures. They have learned to watch schools the way they watch the stock markets. Were test scores moving up or down? That was all they needed to know. That was all anyone needed to know if school effectiveness questions and measures were the whole of the school reform discussion. Unfortunately, and in spite later SESI researchers' own efforts to broaden its initial research agenda, this ideological mindset has continued to dominate many of the state and national accountability models, including *No Child Left Behind* in the U.S.A.

As a result of its own self-critiques as well as critiques from outside SESI (Slee and Weiner, 2001; Thrupp, 2001), school effectiveness/school improvement researchers slowly began to understand that while studying within-school variables, it could not ignore what happened out of the school (Townsend, 2001). So, by the new millennium, the school improvement side of the school effectiveness equation was emerging more vigorously than it had in the previous two decades.

Some of the later SESI findings were significant in terms of challenging past effectiveness measures, methods, and ideologies. That said, these new debates seem to be limited to researchers themselves rather than revising policymakers' original positions regarding school effectiveness. While in the past, SESI research had not taken sufficient notice of the importance of studying educators, including pupils' perceptions of their own experiences of school. Recent work has moved to correct these methodological limitations. One example is the work of Karatzias, Power, and Swanson (2001) who developed a scale for measuring students' experience of the quality of school life. In addition, Weiner (2002) conducted a qualitative study of failing schools to listen critically to the voices from participants such as teachers and school administrators. Van Landeghem, Van Damme, Opdenakker, De Frairie, & Onghena (2002) studied the effects of schools and classes on non-cognitive outcomes. Murillo and Rincon (2002) pointed out the ethnocentric nature of SE and SI and demonstrated that assumptions about education systems held by SESI researchers in first world contexts were shown to be inappropriate when applied to programs in the third world. Consequently, Murillo and Rincon (2002) initiated an organization to carry out research with a Latin American focus. Sheldon and Van Voorhis (2004) studied the development of a program which had family involvement as a desired outcome. Finally, John MacBeath and his colleagues at the Learning School, have documented the significance of student voices (2006). Collectively, these new directions corrected many of the limitations of earlier SER studies.

The question we have, however, is that despite these new directions and advances, why have governments and policymakers themselves not made the transition away from first generation school effectiveness research and measures? Why have policies governing classroom and school-wide practices and their effects on student learning been treated as procedural rationalities in contrast to the complex pedagogical and organizational problems found in schools and in relational contexts outside of schools? Why have the multiple purposes of education and, therefore, the political difficulties of different constituencies not been listened to by policymakers (Walford, 2002)? Why has the influence of standardized measures remained persistently evident in national systems even as they dedicate themselves to establishing "world class" reputations?

Clearly, policymakers and the general public have embraced simple measures regarding school improvement at the classroom, school or system levels. While central governments reduced their responsibility for running public institutions, they have maintained ideological influence and direct control through 'audits' (Biesta 2004). By focusing on accountability, the central authorities trample teachers' understandings of their work and professional identity. In other words, the 1970's New Right agenda (Walford, 2002) built upon school effectiveness findings continues to set subsequent educational agendas into the 21st Century throughout the world, particularly within the U.S. Through the publications of national and school league tables, the idea that the purpose of schooling is based on test scores has intensified the critiques on participants within schools.

As we see how educational research has served national and global publics, we can also see how harmful were the effects on students, teachers, administrators, and the educational research community. Noteworthy efforts to better understand the "what" of school reform has led to a greater focus on disadvantaged schools and children who attend them and increased attempts to expand research into non-Western cultures. Nevertheless, the criticisms we make are more fundamental in terms of epistemology, methodology and politics. We must take up these challenges by questioning such knowledge and conduct as school leaders and researchers. So long as we work inside of reductionist policies established and controlled by central authorities, positivistic theories of teaching, learning and leading will be measured by results that have little to do with the higher purposes of education. By avoiding engagement with the politics and sociology of education, school improvement [as research and practice] inadequately addresses the problems of social class contexts and the professional and moral judgments of educators. School curriculum and school effects continue to be accepted as 'given.' Consequently, centralized authorities, notably governments, have used educational research findings in political ways that have had harmful effects on pupils, teachers, and administrators. How can New Orleans escape and rebuild?

THE CASE OF NEW ORLEANS

Our focus on these dynamics of research and policymaking now shifts to the case of New Orleans. The city of New Orleans was depopulated through mandatory and voluntary evacuations, by nature – Hurricane Katrina – and by edict. While the following case study addresses returnees to the city, it is important to keep in mind that other publics who have scattered across the United States and may not be returning to the city are relevant, too. That is, the decisions to stay, to leave, or to return are all significant past, present, and future aspects of this case study.

Context

The case of New Orleans post-Katrina brings into focus a unique context that covers the full gamut of human emotions. It is a story that cannot be told without looking at the people of New Orleans, those who stayed, those who are still returning, and those who remain as evacuees. Homes [200,000] and families [half the population] were destroyed as were most of the city's public schools. Practically everything beyond the downtown

French Quarter has had to be rebuilt. New Orleans had and still has one of the oldest school systems in the nation-public, parochial, and private. Its public school system is the focus here, and that particular school system was deeply in trouble long before the hurricane blew onto shore.

The destruction brought about by Katrina has made it a necessity to be creative as part of everyday living. Traffic patterns have changed; shopping is different. There are too few hourly workers in the city to provide efficient services in the local economy. Creativity and learning new routines are part of the rebuilding processes, economically, emotionally, socially, politically, and educationally.

At the same time, we have argued above, using SESI as an example, that the past holds ideological power over the present and future directions of educational research. This ideological and cultural context is evident in the story of the New Orleans school rebuilding in terms of policies, politics and in everyday school practices. The empirical question is whether school rebuilding, unlike the dominance of school effectiveness and school improvement research, can meet the challenges of this ravaged city. Specifically, we wondered whether the realities of rebuilding would be dominated by the ideologies of accountability, marketization, and prescriptive managerial and behavioral routines being promoted by local, state, and national authorities inside of post-Katrina New Orleans.

Conversely, we wondered whether we would see the emergence of underlying educational values and personal educational meanings as part of the rebuilding schools' reform. If so, we imagined that there would be a renewed emphasis on individual school contexts and cultures over system-wide measures of student achievement and accountability. Likewise, we might expect to see an emphasis on educational leadership processes that are associated with schools relating to communities, rather than to structures that buttress the standardization of administrative processes and rules. Rhetorically, would we hear discussions of the multiple realities inside and around the rebuilding of public schools coupled with a discourse of system-wide change? Our hopeful assumptions were that the impact of Katrina had been so devastating that people needed to come to terms with a new reality and think of radically new ways for rebuilding schools, not just reproduce school effectiveness and school improvement.

It is within this historically unique context of New Orleans and its public schools that case study methods seemed, at first, to be most appropriate. The information gathered had to be both practical and significant in terms of what school rebuilding on the ground looked like. It is precisely in such extreme conditions that the need to discover the purposes and values of education emerges, and the limitations of traditional school reform and educational research become most visible.

Specific Case of the Algiers Charter School Association

Under Dr. Brian Riedlinger's leadership, The Algiers Charter School Association opened five schools on December 14, 2005 and hired administrators and teachers. Among the newly hired administrators is a Distinguished State Educator, from St. Charles Parish Schools, a system recognized as a lighthouse district in Louisiana. Only one of the newly hired administrators would be returning to assume his "old" role as the new principal of one of the two high schools. All of the educators hired by the Algiers Charter School District competed for their positions, winning out over many experienced and talented Louisiana educators.

Eschewing the unions' rules of hiring teachers based on seniority, teacher applicants had to demonstrate knowledge, skill, and dispositional competencies across the board. In terms of math and language arts knowledge, kindergarten teachers had to pass the same exams as their high school peer teachers. Each candidate had to demonstrate a "can do" attitude as opposed to a "wait and see" attitude. What's more, those who failed the written tests were not put back into the pipeline for later consideration. Over 500 teachers applied; only 100 were selected for the original schools. Dr. Riedlinger, described the selection and placement processes as akin to the "major league draft." As Behrman Elementary School principal, Ms. Lewis-Carter said, "For the first time, we are building a staff instead of staffing a building." The schools have kept the same names; but their faculties and mission are far different. This personnel process, in itself, signalled to the public a radical change in how public education in the city was going to proceed. There would be as a stated goal of instruction quality in every classroom supported by policies and practices.

On-the-ground and in the Political Backrooms

Prior to the hurricane, the New Orleans School District hired the consulting firm Alvarez and Marsal to avoid going into receivership. Act 35, passed by the Louisiana state legislature changed the definition of "academically unacceptable" specifically for schools in a district in "academic crisis." This allowed the state to take over control of any school with a School Performance Score less than the state average, including some schools that had earned exemplary academic achievement rewards for exceeding their growth targets. The State took over the majority of local New Orleans' public schools, and labeled them the Recovery District. A number of city-wide access schools (CWAS) schools, scattered throughout the city, were locally chartered by the school district and their constituencies of teachers, administrators and families, i.e., parents and children, followed them to new locations after the storm. The school board itself was left to operate four schools which had received passing grades.

On the West Bank of New Orleans, across the Mississippi River from the French Quarter, an area of the city was not as severely damaged as other sections, a publicly chartered district called the The Algiers Charter School Association was created. While the new landscape of the city as a whole and its many publicly chartered schools are still in stages of development, our focus here is on the West Bank schools only. There is much need for city-wide research studies as well as in-depth case analyses of different schools and school systems in New Orleans.

Here is our close up look at the various publics, students, teachers, administrators, and parents, whose hopes and concerns were expressed at professional development sessions (Bogotch, 2006) and during on-site school visits.

Local New Orleans' Publics

At professional development sessions, teachers and administrators expressed their hopes and concerns regarding the school year, the first school year post-Katrina. From the beginning, we heard administrators call for positive interactions between teachers and students. "All children would experience success everyday." The schools will demonstrate on a daily basis how much they care about the children and appreciate them. As Brian Gibson, the new AP at Walker high school told us, "The schools are going to have a lot of loving."

The New Orleans' administrators outlined their expectations for educating the students. Students would:
- Be engaged in learning from the first moment of instruction;
- Feel special at school;
- Experience a qualitative change from their prior every day life at their previous schools in New Orleans;
- See the transparent processes of their school;
- Learn what they desired and needed.

The principals and their assistants said that they hoped they would hear students say the following on the last day of school: "I can't wait to return to school next year." Having administrators and teachers say out loud what their goals and objectives were was not a straightforward process however. Most of these administrators in New Orleans had learned to work "under the radar," outside of any close scrutiny. Now, post-Katrina, they were all living and working in a fishbowl with the sun shining on them. We could see how this dramatic difference was interpreted. For some principals and their assistants, just saying the right things was a positive first step in believing that things would be different from the past. No one was naïve enough to ignore the historical patterns and powers that would be present pulling them back away from their new visions. It was up to them and their staffs and communities to resist reverting to past practices. But words themselves were not sufficient. In professional development sessions, time for reflections and sharing new ideas [and on-going concerns] were prioritized.

At the beginning of one session, Dr. Riedlinger, the system's CEO, asked the school administrators to write down on a sheet of paper the three biggest problems they faced the previous day. He then collected the "problems" and told the administrators they could pick them up at the end of the day's session. Thus, materially and symbolically, the message that professional development and reflection [reflective practice] were as important, if not more so, than everyday problems was communicated to these educational leaders.

While the curriculum still mandated Louisiana Content Standards and grade level expectations, neither the standards nor the tests of accountability would be the end goal of every teacher or student. Rather, it was stated that the content standards would serve as benchmarks and minimum requirements to be taught inside of a curricular philosophy based on giving every child the capacity for mastering deep understandings of important ideas along disciplinary lines. Even in the hurry up atmosphere of diagnosing children on Day One, student assessments would not be the center of instructional importance inside the schools. How will these educators bring the larger world beyond the West Bank and Algiers to students? In a walk through, the following account was recorded (Porter, personal communication):

> I noticed students working in small groups, at centers and at their desks, and students sitting on the carpet in a circle with teachers either on the floor, too, or in a small chair. A lot of discussion was going on, the doors to the classrooms were open and the rooms were inviting. I heard teachers encouraging students, gently giving correction, sometimes in private and one on one. [Teachers were teaching] ... All students were on task. As I passed through the older students' halls, I saw similar interactions]. Teachers were outside of their doors at the change of class, greeting the students pleasantly. There was the beginning of an altercation between two boys and a teacher stepped in and hugged them both while encouraging them to move on without letting it get out of hand. The students complied with the teacher's

request. It just seemed warm and friendly, a place I would not mind sending my kids.

At a similar walk through at Karr High school

He (The Principal) introduced me to students by name, real impressive. These were all seniors so he probably has seen them at school for 4 to 6 years, if they went there for middle school when that was still there. He has a very good rapport with the students. They run up to him to shake his hand or even hug him. He treated the teachers respectfully when he spoke to them.

The in-school notations above seem more about relationships than academics, yet the focus in the professional development was on teaching and learning.

PAST MEETS PRESENT: TENSIONS

The teaching and learning challenge for the principals and teachers was: "Can we hold onto the vision of world class schools?"- a phrase used to describe practices outside the experiences of the local educators - and "not get pulled back." The fear was that the school leaders and the teachers would fall back into their comfort zone, and given the huge challenges in simply gearing up to open schools post-Katrina, would not be able to sustain the momentum necessary to achieve lasting transformation. The unspoken fear was that these school leaders would revert to patterns pre-Katrina, the national consensus of which ranked New Orleans near the bottom of urban big city school systems.

These tensions of past, present, and futures were palpable. Those teachers who were returning to the same schools they had left before the storm felt a need to either rebuild or discard the past culture depending upon the school's historic reputation in the city. Those teachers who came from other schools brought with them fixed ideas on what a 'good' school is. They intentionally wanted to remake their new schools into their old schools by bringing programs and fully developed models they had known previously. Many of their past experiences, of course, were positive. Yet at one school, a group of teachers who had come from a Montessori school were convinced that their 'new' school should also become a Montessori school. The teacher-leaders needed to understand that it was the concepts and practices, not the name Montessori, that would be [or not] important for rebuilding a new school culture. All this was new to the participants who began to see new leadership roles for themselves in terms of professional development and teacher leadership outside of the hierarchy of administrative roles as they had experienced them before Katrina.

However, it must be remembered that this rebuilding was unique. Everyone felt pressures to solve problems overnight. Nobody had time to plan or contemplate change. Everything in their world and that of their students had already been changed for them and for others. The old New Orleans no longer existed. There was a pressing need to create something new, not bring back something old and possibly out of place. Thus they asked: what do those who have stayed in New Orleans want for their children? Yet in answering the question, there were pressures to act that did not always allow for maximum community, school and parental input. Yet, the city needed to rebuild community centered schools. How would both necessities be accommodated? Parents needed input and voice; but, in so many residential areas, people were displaced and not given a voice in local neighborhood decisions. To its credit, the Algiers Charter Association held public forums, but could not assure everyone that all voices had been heard.

New relationships and communications had to be initiated; new and better school cultures had to be created. That was certainly true for one of the two high schools located in Algiers. In the past, this particular high school was known for violence and warehousing of African-American students. Now, in these professional development sessions, the administrators and teachers of the school were talking about it being a privilege to work there. They called it an honor to serve. There was new transformational leadership which foretold of rituals grounded in the teaching of youngsters and inexperienced teachers by their elders.

Even the central authority structures of the Algiers Association were different than in the past. From its inception, Algiers had only three central office administrators in total! Thus, building administrators had direct access to their supervisors for support. The autonomous nature of the charter schools in Algiers, moreover, meant that the principals would be able to hire all new staff who, while they would be subject to district salary scales and benefits, also enjoyed greater professional flexibility. Last, not unlike any world class system, Algiers' parents would be asked to complete customer surveys on satisfaction and safety.

One residue of the past was the perpetuated inequities within the city itself. Rather than re-naming the West Bank schools, a decision was made to keep the old/original names. This decision would mean that New Orleaneans would have to disassociate pre-Katrina meanings to rebuilt schools with the same names. Old reputations, past experiences, and perceptions have to be addressed publicly. There is, however, an irony. That is, New Orleans has been home to many world class educational institutions including Tulane and Xavier Universities, and, Jesuit (parochial), Newman (private), and Franklin (public) high schools. Dozens of other schools, at every level and in every neighborhood, had been offering children and the community quality programs. The children of two of the authors of this case study were educated inside of the public school system. Unfortunately, New Orleans was known mostly as having a dysfunctional urban public school system that warehoused, rather than educated, the mostly poor African American children. Since the retirements of Superintendent Drs. Everett Williams and Morris Holmes in the 1990s, the city has had a succession of forgettable School Superintendents. But the ineptitude and corruption was not only at the top of the system. There were management and financial problems that affected classroom instruction. This was the reality that educators such as Dr. Scott Cowan, President of Tulane University, and Dr. Brian Riedlinger, CEO of the Greater New Orleans School Leadership Center were determined to change in post-Katrina New Orleans.

The system now being created is a hybrid of the old and new. Some of the schools want to return to the old ways; other schools need to re-culture quickly. It is always about perceptions and status, tradition and history. There are tensions. How will New Orleans emerge? Not everyone hopes that New Orleans' schools will be different.

In reframing the dynamics of The Algiers Charter School "experiment," we return to the dynamics of SER/SESI reforms and research. It has been the outcome measures, the objective evidence, that have driven the "successes" of SESI. State and federal government support for Algiers will also depend on such measures if support by policymakers is to be continued. Evidence and measures are important. But so, too, are the peoples' stories. So far, the stories among the educators themselves are hopeful. "New" schools are scheduled to open, indicating perhaps that families are sending their children across the river to attend "good" schools. Nevertheless, the normative classifications of good and bad are directly linked to the ideological and social class divisions that dominated past New Orleans' thinking.

Our on-site observations suggest that the school improvement strategies that have been put in place in Algiers do NOT strictly follow old formulae. In our conclusions, we describe a number of processes to support some new directions. They reflect the dynamics of professional development, reflective practice, relationship building, and moral judgments.

THE FUTURE: ON-GOING PROFESSIONAL DEVELOPMENT, REFLECTIVE PRACTICE, NEW RELATIONSHIP BUILDING, AND MORAL JUDGMENTS

In reframing the New Orleans case study as School Effectiveness/School Improvement, it is apparent to us that professional development, reflective practice, building new relationships and moral judgments, as opposed to models, mandates, and test scores are the predominant modes of school improvement. Teachers and administrators are participating in on-going professional development. Some of the knowledge transmitted has to do with doing current practices better, but there is a shift in the discourse and knowledge to new ideas, new practices. Some of the professional development will come from within (Barth, 1990). Some will come from outside consultants. Leadership teams were shown a PBS video documenting that math is taught differently in other countries than how it is taught in the US, even by our best teachers. The phrase, "a mile wide and an inch deep" referring to curriculum and instruction has been rhetorically challenged in terms of looking at state standards and indicators. Teachers are being asked to prioritize indicators and to trust that by teaching conceptualizations, not all specific facts, formulae and procedures need to be drilled.

Making time for professional development and reflective practice means putting aside daily problems. It requires a different mindset that is not focused exclusively on problem-solving. Nevertheless, the central administration must address inequities and problems as they arise. For example, a concern shared by all the elementary schools was that the children were not being fed properly by the outside food vendor. When this was voiced, it became clear that high schools were receiving one to two hot meals a day. It was a striking contrast that was at the time inexplicable. The problem was brought to the central administration because the principals on site had not been successful in solving the lunch problem.

At this time, it is fair to say that not all of the local participants have been able to make this transition to reflective practice and relationship building. The problems are overwhelming: where to live, where to shop, how to get health care. Teachers and administrators as first responders were also victims of the storm. These issues will continue for years to come. As one debriefing session ended, a participant said he had to go furniture shopping. For most Americans, furniture shopping has a particular meaning. That is, it is to add a functional piece to an existing household. In this case, in New Orleans, it may mean refurnishing temporary living quarters. It may mean that a bed to sleep on that night is needed.

While it may be unfair to challenge educational research findings on the basis of how national, state, and local authorities have used the reforms and research for their own political purposes, published research has served to both maintain and improve systems as they are currently given. Fortunately or unfortunately, that is not an option in New Orleans. The moral imperative is to educate children who, in turn, will try to convince their parents to stay in the city despite the difficult living and working conditions. That will be the true test of public school accountability. Clearly, without "good schools," redefined by New Orleaneans, non-New Orleaneans will not even consider moving here. That is a certainty. So, the future lies with New Orleaneans themselves, and with those who have left the city as evacuees. How many of them will return? That is still being debated today, more than three years after Katrina. Will the people who have remained learn to trust the educators and will the educators learn to trust the people? If not, then which new public school system will emerge? Will the old rigid dichotomous variables reemerge as effective schools and non-effective schools? Or, will the new public schools in Algiers and elsewhere throughout the city redefine public education as a valued institution, vital to the rebirth and rebuilding of the city?

REFERENCES

Barth, R. (1990). *Improving Schools from Within*. San Francisco: Jossey Bass.
Biesta, G. J. J. (2004). Education, accountability and the ethical demand. Can the democratic potential of accountability be regained? *Educational Theory, 54*(3), 233–250.
Bogotch, I. (January, 9, 2006). Rebuilt schools can be a U.S model. *South Florida Sun – Sentinel* (p. 23.A).
Coleman, J. et al. (1966). *Equality of educational opportunity*. Washington, D.C. U.S Department of Health, Educational and Welfare, Office of Education: The Superintendent of Documents, U.S Government Printing Office.
Edmonds, R. (1979, October). Effective Schools for the Urban Poor. *Educational Leadership, 37*, 15–24.
Karatzias, A., Power, K. G., & Swanson, V. (2001). Quality of school life: Development and preliminary standardization of an instrument based on performance indicators in Scottish secondary schools. *School Effectiveness and School Improvement, 12*, 265–284.
MacBeath, J. (2006). Finding a voice, finding self. *Educational Review, 58*(2), 195–207.
Murrillo, J., & Rincon, L. (2002). The Ibero American Network for Research on School Effectiveness and School Improvement: A Way to Increase Educational Quality and Equity, *School Effectiveness and School Improvement, 13*(1), 123–132(10).
Sheldon, S., & Van Voorhis, F. (2004). Partnership Programs in U.S schools: Their Development and Relationship to Family Involvement Outcomes, *School Effectiveness and School Improvement, 15*(2), 125–148.
Slee, R., & Weiner, G. (2001). Education Reform and Reconstruction as a Challenge to Research Genres: Reconsidering School Effectiveness Research and Inclusive Schooling. *School Effectiveness and School Improvement, 12*(1), 83–98.
Thrupp, M. (2001). Sociological and political concerns about school effectiveness research: Time for a new research agenda. School Effective. *School Effectiveness and School Improvement, 12*(1), 7–40.
Townsend, T. (2001). Satan or savior? An analysis of two decades of school effectiveness research. *School Effectiveness and School Improvement, 12*(1), 115–130.
Van Landeghem, G., Van Damme, J., Opdenakker, M-C., De Frairie, D. F., & Onghena, P. (2002). The Effect of Schools and Classes on Noncognitive Outcomes, *School Effectiveness and School Improvement, 13*(4), 429–451.
Walford, G. (2002). Redefining school effectiveness. *Westminster Studies in Education, 25*(1), 47–58.
Weiner, G. (2002). Auditing failure: Moral competence and school effectiveness. *British Educational Research Journal, 28*(6), 789–804.

7. WHAT IS CULTURAL COMPETENCE?

The principal, Dr. Stevenson, at Flamingo Elementary school, has always been concerned with the climate and culture of her school. This is evidenced by the way she talks about it with the faculty, students, and parents. Her interactions with others are frequent, respectful, and solution-based. Dr. Stevenson embraces the challenge of her job, but at the same time is brutally aware of the pressure to ensure that all students make adequate academic progress in math, reading, and science. Her school is located in the southern section of the district. This section of the school district is almost always the subject of conversation when other educators and parents mention, "those schools." Dr. Stevenson often thinks about these conversations, and much to her chagrin, she has even been part of those same conversations. Before inquiring about her position in the district or work location, other educators or administrators frequently plunge into negative comments about the schools that are responsible for the overall low academic rating of the district and, "if something could just be done about those children in those schools, then maybe the entire district would be better off." Dr. Stevenson knows all too well that, "those schools," and "those children," are actually code phrases for schools in neighborhoods populated by people of color and their children. Children from diverse ethnic and racial backgrounds, as well as children who do not speak English as their first language, have traditionally not received effective instruction, but Dr. Stevenson is sensitive to the debates surrounding the impact of cultural differences on learning and the responsibilities teachers have to respond to such differences. She has heard the comments from teachers "Are you trying to tell me that good teaching doesn't count anymore," or "Culture and race are issues for the Social Studies and Language Arts teachers, not me, I'm a science teacher." Each of these comments offers insight into the plethora of issues concerning students from diverse backgrounds. Dr. Stevenson's situation is by no means isolated. Administrators, educators, and parents alike are all faced with questions surrounding the vast number of children from diverse backgrounds in schools and how these cultural differences impact learning. How does one's cultural background impact one's capacity to learn? What do educators need to know about culture? In short, what is cultural

*T. Townsend and I. Bogotch (eds.), The Elusive What and the Problematic How: The Essential
Leadership Questions for School Leaders and Educational Researchers, 99–116.*
© *2008 Sense Publishers. All rights reserved.*

competence and does this competence have any bearing on the basic conventions of teaching and learning? The relentless pressure to ensure that all students make academic progress weighs heavy on educators and administrators. The continued reports of large-scale student failure, necessitates a different orientation to student learning. A new orientation to education must include explicit attention to the nature of cultural competence, methods to help teachers develop cultural competence, and ultimately use this competence to facilitate student achievement.

The changing demographics of schools have overwhelming implications for parents, educators, and administrators. Concerns abound over a progressively interconnected world in which a comprehensive education must focus on academic content as well as the skills necessary to live in a multicultural society. Virtually every educator can intuitively understand and appreciate the uniqueness of students and readily engage in efforts intended to respect the nature of their learning needs. The sheer increase in the numbers of students from diverse backgrounds attending schools has challenged the traditional notion that in spite of unique student characteristics, it is customary to use effective instructional methodologies that address groups of students, rendering considerations of students' cultural background unnecessary. Cultural competence has become a critical aspect of the instructional repertoire. Not only is it important to develop cultural competence for the purpose of instruction, but it may even be necessary for teachers to incorporate the spirit of cultural competence in their daily work lives (Brown & Kysilka, 2002). Schools reflect the best and worst of our society and interactions between teachers and students can serve as a catalyst for change in the larger society, where there may be limited or non-existent opportunities to directly teach students about human relations.

In this chapter, the authors will provide an overview and meaning of cultural competence and its relationship to the larger topic of multicultural education. Cultural competence is not simply a pleasant notion shared by many intended to serve as the curriculum for sensitivity training designed for educators and administrators. Rather, cultural competence should be viewed as a starting point for how educators and administrators, intended and to a great degree, should impact instructional practices. Cultural competence serves as the basis for the development, implementation, and maintenance of a comprehensive educational system necessary in many urban schools (Obiakor, Grant, & Dooley, 2002). Then, the authors will present the rationale underlining the need for educators and administrators to develop cultural competence and why professional development cannot be passive. For some, any discussion about the uniqueness of individuals creates grounds for divisiveness and does not bode well for the overall well-being of schools (Ravitch, 1990). Clearly, divisiveness is not an intended or unintended goal of any effort to facilitate the development of a culturally competent educator. Making educators aware of cultural competence is yet another step on the road toward progressively creating a better understanding of students and the potential impact culture has on learning and the resulting trajectory of long-term academic achievement. Next, the authors will discuss the nature of adopting new professional practices, specifically relating to the issues of: (a) designing and delivering the necessary professional development activities intended to help educators learn the significance of cultural competence and (b) providing the support necessary for implementation of cultural competence. Cultural competence is not simply a substitute or stand-in for sensitivity training or a derivative there-of, but rather a clear directive for educators and administrators to seriously consider the impact that cultural and linguistic differences have on learning and achievement. Before turning to the main issues of this chapter, we will begin with a brief account of how the changing student demographic has affected general service delivery in schools.

HOW DID WE GET HERE?

The changing student demographic in schools is not a new phenomenon. In fact, the progressive increase in the number of students from diverse backgrounds is the result of many decades of immigration, emigration, and shifting employment patterns resulting in inadequately served urban populations largely made up of students who are ethnically, linguistically, and economically diverse (Shakespear, Beardsley, & Newton, 2003). Public education is overflowing with stories about students from economically deprived areas that "overcome the odds," and make more than adequate strides in academics to achieve, "the impossible." More often that not, this is not the case for a majority of students from diverse backgrounds living in economically depressed areas. Even a cursory review of services and facilities in many urban school districts will reveal that wide-scale success is a difficult task. In the past, explanations for academic achievement gaps between levels of particular groups were largely attributed to innate demographic features (see Herrnstein & Murray, 1994 and Fraser, 1995 for a response to such arguments). Family history and genetic features was the primary determinant for one's potential success in school, while cultural background and ineffective instruction never entered the conversation.

Currently, culture and effective instruction are critical issues in education and serve as primary candidates for contributing to the success or failure of all students. The marginalization of students was a common practice in the past and numerous examples exist in the history of American education (Byrne, 2005; Stroman, 2003). These exclusionary practices probably served as a "default response" to student differences. Educators were not required to make any concessions to accommodate student differences and these factors were not taken into account in regard to learning and overall achievement. Considerations for student difference are now a concern as mandated by the No Child Left Behind Act (NCLB) of 2001 and the reauthorization of the Individuals with Disabilities Education Improvement Act (IDEIA) in 2004. Both legislative documents contain statements that clearly call educators and administrators to action and strongly recommend that students make "marked change in academic progress" in the areas of math, reading, and science. The phrase all means all, has been a popular rallying cry for advocates of students with disabilities (see mission statement from TASH). The meaning behind this statement has now been interpreted to include students from culturally and linguistically diverse backgrounds. In short, all means, "children from economically poor or advantaged backgrounds, children from mainstream or marginalized cultural and ethnic backgrounds, and children with and without disabilities," (Edgar, Patton, & Day-Vines, 2002, p. 233). Thus, educators and administrators are charged with delivering educational services that include students with varying learning needs from varied backgrounds resulting in academic and social gains in school. This charge brings to the forefront many of the questions and concerns that were simply not considered in the past, namely the impact of culture on learning and how educators and administrators should effectively respond to differing student needs to ensure academic success. These concerns are nested in multicultural education and reflect some of the core issues that many advocates of multicultural education have argued for and continue to argue for today (Banks, 1991). Educators and administrators need access to a particular content, a set of principles that can be used to direct professional practice to respond to the current and ever expanding diverse student population. The development and effective use of cultural competence is a logical requirement for today's education professionals. Clearly, culture and language are issues that must be met head on, but what is really at issue? We now discuss the meaning and rationale behind the development of cultural competence in educators and administrators.

CULTURAL COMPETENCE

It is essential that educators and administrators have the ability and willingness to develop cultural competence for the benefit of their students (Ming & Dukes, 2006). The development and use of cultural competence must be framed in the larger context of efforts to help all students make adequate academic progress. A number of authors have conceptualized the meaning of cultural competence: (a) "cultural competence refers to the ability of educators and administrators to respond optimally to all children, understanding both the richness and the limitations reflected by their own sociocultural contexts, as well as the sociocultural contexts of students that they are teaching" (Barrera & Kramer, 1997 as cited in Craig, Hull, Haggart, and Perez-Selles, 2000), (b) "cultural competence is the ability to successfully teach students from cultures other than your own, it entails mastering complex awareness and sensitivities, various bodies of knowledge, and a set of skills that, taken together, underlie effective cross-cultural teaching" (Diller & Moule, 2005, p. 5), and (c) cultural competency in the classroom depends on an educator's capacity to perceive cultural diversity as a norm and, therefore, view it as fundamental to all aspects of schooling (Sheets, 2005). There are two common threads worthy of note contained in each of these definitions of cultural competence. First, awareness of one's own culture and the culture of others is absolutely essential. Acknowledging that culture is significant enough to recognize as a factor in the education of students is reason enough to require direct inquiry into culture and its implications for learning. Second, action is based on awareness of one's culture and the culture of others. Here, action is synonymous with several of the essential duties of educators: selection of curriculum standards, selection of materials, choosing and implementing effective instructional strategies, and evaluating student progress. There must be a clear connection made between one's awareness and subsequent action. Essentially, culturally component educators and administrators use their cultural competence as a guide for action when interacting with students, parents, and members of the community at large.

CULTURE AS A PHENOMENON OF STUDY

Almost any mention of the word culture, conjures a highly diverse set of opinions depending on the individual and context. The meaning attributed to the word culture is varied and thus, can lead to entirely different interpretations and implications. The study of culture has long been the purview of social scientist and has a history of causing methodological and interpretive problems for many (Goodwin, 2003). For a number of social scientists, empirical or conceptual inquiries into culture have resulted in difficulties. One of the most significant difficulties is the sheer political nature of inquiries into culture. Arguments about the validity of cultural practices can quickly lead some to make assumptions that one particular cultural practice is less than desirable and should be altered. Any discussion of culture that implies the supremacy of one culture over another, even if unintended, makes objective considerations of culture difficult at best. Another difficulty often encountered when studying culture is the development and use of methodology that allows for objective investigation. The conventions of science call for strict adherence to methods that lead researchers to, "rule out alternative explanations." This is an extremely difficult task when researching any aspect of culture. Humans are highly complex and engage in a vast range of different behaviors for a number of different reasons, making the determination of cause and effect relationships tenuous. Unlike social scientists, educators are not engaged in the same line of inquiry, but similar to social scientists, educators should be interested in attempting to understand cause-effect relationships to ensure that educational interventions are efficient and effective. Thus, studying culture and its impact on learning is a legitimate line of inquiry for educators. The challenge for educators is to understand culture and how knowledge of culture can translate into a set of skills that can be applied to instruction, resulting in academic progress.

Current inquiries into culture emphasize the intangible, symbolic, and ideational aspect of culture (Banks, 2002). They move away from considerations of material objects as the only representation of culture has influenced a closer examination of the "deeper" implications of culture and how intangible aspects of culture may impact the manner in which individuals develop and learn. It is through this understanding of students' that educators and administrators can begin to understand the impact of cultural background on acquisition and use of knowledge. Some may confuse efforts to understand students and their cultural backgrounds as a call for the individual to "study" each and every student and her unique cultural background. Contrary to this misconception, it is the revelation that understanding students' cultural background, in and of itself, can lead to a greater understanding of all students and how each learns. Thus, cultural competence is a call for educators and administrators to understand the impact of culture on learning and development. Further, this knowledge must be translated into skill that pervades the entire educational process. In review, knowing one's self is the first step and deliberate steps to become cultural competent should immediately follow. Cultural competence is a piece of the larger puzzle that is multicultural education. How does cultural competence connect to multicultural education? We now discuss the connection between the two.

CULTURAL COMPETENCE AS A PART OF MULTICULTURAL EDUCATION

The last four decades have seen an explosion in the number of ideas, concepts, and instructional recommendations related to multicultural education (see Sleeter, & Grant, 1988 for a historical overview). In spite of the vast size of the extant literature, confusion and misconceptions about multicultural education is still a reality for many individual educators and administrators. Part of this confusion stems from the, "narrow conception of multicultural education as merely content integration" (Banks, 2002, p. 13). Essentially, some educators have marginalized multicultural education and view its "addition," to the curriculum as the purview of certain educators and certainly not the responsibility of all educators across the entire curriculum. Thus, multicultural education is seen solely as a "curriculum" issue, but it is also viewed as largely the responsibility of only a few. This confusion is part of a larger issue relating to a misunderstanding about the nature and intent of multicultural education in general and cultural competence specifically.

Cultural competence and multicultural education are inextricably linked, with multicultural education serving as the knowledge base for the skill set contained within cultural competence. While awareness and respect for cultural differences is important, it is not the sole desired purpose of cultural competence or the greater mission espoused by advocates of multicultural education. Rather, the dimensions of multicultural education should lead directly to the development and use of fundamentally different practices from traditional educational interventions that clearly fall short of the comprehensive educational interventions necessary for the current demographic in many urban, suburban, and rural schools. It is necessary for educators to not only understand multicultural education, but also incorporate its dimensions as part of their instructional repertoire. The dimensions of multicultural education include: (a) content integration, (b) the knowledge construction process, (c) prejudice reduction, (d) an equity pedagogy, and (e) an empowering school culture and social structure (Banks, 2002, see Sheets, 2005; Brown, & Kysilka, 2002 for similar dimensions). Thus, the link between cultural competence and multicultural education is part of the, "dynamic process," that is multicultural education (Brown, & Kysilka, 2002). While it is all too easy to oversimplify multicultural education as something one "does," during the holiday season (e.g., eating certain foods or displaying certain posters), the dynamics of genuine multicultural practices call for all educators and administrators to take on a particular posture and adopt particular practices (Harry, Kalyanpur, & Day, 1999). We now turn to the learning process and the resulting impact culture exerts over this process.

THE IMPACT OF CULTURE ON LEARNING

Student achievement is currently at the forefront, in the light of federal legislation as well as general public concern for the vast numbers of students who do not make adequate academic gains. The dismal performance exhibited by large populations of students in many schools leaves many asking one basic question, "why"? While this may seem like a simple question, providing an answer to that question can be highly involved and complex. Why do so many students of color seem to under-perform in comparison to their peers, and how can educators and administrators help change this disturbing trend? For some, the issue is simple and explained by pointing to student demographic features (e.g., race) and claim that certain students do not have the mental capacity to perform as well as others. In short, many have innate deficits and will not be able to make comparable academic gains to students with superior innate abilities (see Parsons, 2003 for further explanation of the deficit model). Thus, the deficit exists "within" the child and external interventions, high-budget social programs, and the like ultimately will not make a difference for this population, and remedial efforts are futile. The prospect of such views paints an unsettling picture, not just for the students it posits to describe, but for parents, and even society in general. If the current state of schools is reality, then that implies that a great number of students of color who do not make academic gains will be followed by even more students who do not make academic gains and so on. Clearly, this is not the desire of a majority of educators, administrators, parents, or society in general.

There is an alternative vision for schools, one that does not claim to solve all ills, but brings to light a view that is nested in a solution-based notion about teaching and learning. Traditionally, many educators and administrators worked with homogeneous groups of students. Many of these students shared the same values and general notions about the purpose of schools. Most importantly, those students who did not or could not make adequate academic gains for almost any reason were simply excluded from the group of students who did have the capacity to learn. Systematic exclusion was the intervention of choice and therefore, created an unrealistic population of students that did not include students from diverse backgrounds with varying abilities. As the demographics of schools have changed, the progressive inclusion of students with disabilities, students from diverse backgrounds, and students who do not speak English as a first language, has moved forward at a breathtaking pace. The issue for educators and administrators has been that teaching and learning has not followed the same evolutionary pace. For a number of educators and administrators, traditional methods of instruction and supervision have predominated and these methods do not reflect a genuine consideration for effective instructional methods and the impact of culture on teaching and learning. This may be due in part to a clear misunderstanding about culture in general and multicultural education in particular. Many educators and administrators may "miss the point" about culture and view its inclusion in the conversation about teaching and learning as simply irrelevant to considerations about content, instruction, and assessment. This is not the case and one of the most significant implications of professionals developing cultural competence is the basic understanding that culture does impact learning and by adopting a significantly different posture, based on an understanding of the significance of culture, students from diverse backgrounds can make academic gains.

CULTURAL MISMATCH

Ignorance of different traditions, beliefs, values, and norms can result in unintentional clashes between individuals or groups who differ on these points (Ford, & Moore, 2004, p. 36). Many educators and administrators have a limited knowledge of culture and its impact on teaching and learning, thus prompting many to ponder the existence of a "cultural clash" (Necochea, 1997; Casteel, 1998; Cartledge, Kea, & Ida, 2000). Educators and administrators who lack the willingness and/or sufficient knowledge base to appreciate, celebrate, and utilize cultural competence may encounter difficulties when attempting to assist students to achieve academically. Culture is indeed a powerful concept, as evidenced by the way in which people organize their thoughts and shape their beliefs based in large part on culture (Sheets, 2005). In education, culture plays a unique role in the teaching and learning process. Thoughts are still organized and beliefs shaped, but in addition, culture can have an impact on the way in which educators and administrators develop and implement a wide range of educational practices.

Many scholars have highlighted the impact of culture on learning and subsequent educator reaction by conceptualizing a number of different issues: (a) movement styles or the way in which students of color use body language to communicate, often misunderstood by educators and administrators from the dominant culture (Neal, McCray, & Webb-Johnson, 2001), differentiated expectations or simply expecting that students from diverse backgrounds will not perform based solely on demographic features (e.g., race or ethnicity) (Warren, 2002), (c) field-dependent learners (learning by having problems placed in context) versus field-independent learners (learning by looking at the problem in a broad context) (Lee, 1998; Gay, 2004), and (d) assessment procedures that have external validity for students from diverse backgrounds

(Lee, 1998). Wading through the muddy waters of student achievement in today's schools is made even more difficult when culture is injected to the conversation. The preceding conceptualizations about culture highlight some of the various issues and concerns associated with the impact of culture on learning. The gap existing between where many students from diverse backgrounds currently perform and where their performance should be is vast. This divide is not solely based in cultural differences, but it is still necessary to take account of the profound influence of culture on learning (Turnbull, Rothstein-Fisch, & Greenfield, 2000). The full-scale impact of culture on learning is extremely difficult to bring into focus, as many educators and administrators view their work through "Westernized blinders" (Lamorey, 2002). Similar to many other areas of education, there is still a need to better understand the impact of culture on the teaching and learning process. While our understanding is limited there is still considerable information contributing to our understanding leading many to believe that there are distinct beliefs and practices that adequately take into account the impact of culture on learning, leading to improved outcomes (Foster, Lewis, & Onafowora, 2005). The question remains, how can educators and administrators reduce and/or eliminate the common barriers to developing and utilizing cultural competence? Thus, in addition to the challenge of learning the meaning and significance of cultural competence, educators and administrators must also face the challenge of actually adopting a new repertoire of professional practices.

PREPARING CULTURALLY COMPETENT PERSONNEL

Educators and administrators play a vital role in determining students' academic success or failure (Jacobson, 2000). When questioned about the prospect of making changes to their practices that may be beneficial to their students; many will answer in the affirmative. But, there is often a discrepancy between what educators and administrators report and what they actually do on a daily basis (Dukes & Ming, 2007). Some educators may even question the need for information about culture and view any specialized training in cultural issues as an accusation of racism or prejudice (Pang, 1994). The central question relating to the issue of cultural competence development is the manner in which competence can be achieved by a majority of educators and administrators. Traditionally in education, professionals have been prepared or "trained" in two different ways. Primarily, future educators attend a college or university and take relevant education course work in elementary or secondary methods. Secondarily, educators and administrators already working in schools attend workshops (i.e., training sessions) where information about one or perhaps several topics is presented. There is no consensus on the effectiveness of the latter method, as some view the use of "one-shot" (training sessions that meet one time only) as largely ineffective (Lenski, Crumpler, Stallworth, & Crawford, 2005; Voltz, Brazil, & Scott, 2003).

Teacher education programs

A majority of education professionals attend college or university teacher education programs for undergraduate and/or graduate course work. These programs are designed to impart the knowledge and skills necessary to prospective educators so that they can be successful in all schools with all students. A significant number of students attending teacher education programs are European American (White) females (Cockrell, Placier, Cockrell, & Middleton, 1999). While current research does not indicate an individual from one particular culture cannot effectively teach students from a different cultural background (Torrey, & Ashy, 1997), there is indication that "cultural clashes" can be a real phenomenon impacting student performance (Kea, & Campbell-Whately, 2005). When educators enter the profession without experiences with different groups of people with varied experiences, everyday classroom interactions (e.g., conversation between teacher and student) may be adversely affected. Educators, who have no prior knowledge of particular cultural norms, may mistakenly misinterpret a seemingly meaningless act as one of aggression. The term "clash" is often used, as inexperience and misinterpretations can result in referral to special education (Harris, Brown, Ford, & Richardson, 2004) and/or lowered expectations and negative stereotypes (Warren, 2002).

Cultural issues still have the potential to be marginalized and viewed as a matter of nothing more than one's attitude. If one is "open minded" and "doesn't see color," then is the adaptation of a multicultural perspective and practices really necessary? Further, is specialized training really necessary to learn cultural competence, or incorporate the principles of multicultural education into teaching (see Gallavan, 1998 for a related discussion)? The simple answer to the previous question is a resounding, yes! In order for educators and administrators to understand the significance of the impact of culture on learning and then appropriately examine this impact to improve students' achievement, requires preparation, specific implementation efforts, and active evaluation of those methods (Edgar et al., 2002; Ball, 2000). Garmon (2004) conducted an intensive interview of a single teacher candidate, to illuminate issues related to attitudes and predispositions toward culturally competent teaching practices. The interview sessions yielded a number of factors that contribute to the development of a culturally competent professional. Included among these factors are: self-awareness/self-reflections, commitment to social justice, intercultural experiences, educational experiences. Each of these factors point to specific activities embedded within teacher education or professional development programs as opposed to a passive reliance on individuals claiming themselves to be bias free.

In a related study, Cruz-Janzen and colleagues (2005), initiated a study across two universities, intended to gather information that could later be used to improve the university teacher education programs. A total of 38 students were interviewed in a series of focus groups. The students were asked questions about their overall experiences in the program and specifically about their field experiences with diverse populations. Results of the study indicated that many teacher candidates acknowledged the necessity to conduct self-reflection and actively engage in understanding the culture of others and how this knowledge can positively affect their professional practice. There were also those who viewed the multicultural content of the program as an affront to their beliefs and own cultural background. Some students expressed resentment to the entire process as a personal attack on their membership in the dominant culture. Each view is important to better understand the numerous perspectives possible when attempting to teach future educators about the impact of culture on teaching and learning. The university faculty involved in the study decided to make some changes to their respective teacher education programs based on the responses from students in the focus groups. Several of these changes involved more direct student involvement in experiences that could be used later as a source of reflection to help faculty members as well as students professionally grow from the experience. Again, this highlights the importance of the active involvement necessary to benefit from activities directed at building cultural competence. Depending on experiences gained in the university classroom alone in the absence of dialogue, reflection, and diverse field experiences can severely limit the lessons future educators learn while in school.

Teacher education programs consist of a number of different experiences. Each of these experiences will affect students in different ways and may or may not actually affect later professional practice. University and college faculty have a responsibility to create programs that not only convey the importance of cultural competence, but they also must help students gain an understanding of the "worth" of cultural competence. If cultural competence is relegated to a side note only relating to attitude and not directly linked to the principles of multicultural education and systematic effective instruction, then it is unlikely that all students will make academic and social gains. Allen and Hermann-Wilmarth (2004), argue for "cultural construction zones," where future educators and university faculty share the responsibility for bringing cultural considerations to the forefront of educational studies. Haberman and Post (1998) proposed 12 teacher attributes of a program reporting to teach multicultural education. Parts of these attributes include: self-analysis, relevant curriculum, and relationship skills. These attributes highlight the critical nature of teacher preparation and the necessity to ensure that these initial experiences bring "culture into focus," for teacher education students. The university or college should serve as the first and most significant basis for building cultural competence. Unfortunately, the reality is that for many, teacher education programs do not provide this necessary foundation and there is a need for additional in-service professional development.

Professional development

The potential for some to come into the field of education without having had formal training in a teacher education program is likely. An alternative route to certification has increasingly become a path toward certification (Ilmer, Nahan, Elliott, Colombo, & Synder, 2005). While the long-term outcomes of alternate entry into education have yet to be determined, there does seem to be one immediate result, in regard to direct experience with children. Many who enter the profession alternatively, have no or limited experiences with children, including children from diverse backgrounds. This reality, in urban, suburban, and rural schools, necessitates the extensive use of professional development directed at "filling in the gaps," for the numerous educators who do not have a complete knowledge base. Currently, many educators face two similar challenges in relation to the development of cultural competence. First, many educators are not keenly aware of the knowledge base associated with cultural competence and the principles of multicultural education. Second, the possession of the knowledge base must be further extended into skills. For a number of educators, translating cultural competence into the instructional practices is no easy task. The lack of knowledge and inability to utilize skills in the school context renders the entire intent of the multicultural education movement literally useless. Incorporating cultural competence into the actual instructional practices is one of the most critical issues facing educators and administrators. In the absence of educators actually using cultural competence to make instructional decisions and shape services, underserved children are still at a disadvantage.

In a study conducted by Saldana and Waxman (1997), a total of 76 teachers who were randomly selected from 12 elementary schools were observed during one of the following lessons: reading, mathematics, or social studies. Teachers were observed on two occasions, once at the beginning and once at the end of the school year, using the Multicultural Teaching Observation Instrument (MTOI). The instrument consists of 18 indicators grouped into three categories: teacher support, equity, and integration of culture. Results of the study indicated that teachers were highly supportive of their students, 94% respected students and 90% were willing to help each student most of the time. In contrast, the integration of culture scale did not indicate the same high level of implementation. Only 8% of teachers were observed using examples from other cultures and only 9% of teachers had books in the classroom representative of different ethnic groups in their classrooms. Conclusions drawn from the results yield several implications. First, teachers need frequent, easily accessed information about the principles of multicultural education and necessity of cultural competence. Second, classroom teachers need reliable and credible models for integrating this information into their teaching routines. Knowledge about multicultural education in the absence of direct application to teaching only provides teachers with "half the story" and may actually impede the use cultural competence, simply because teachers do not know how to use the information in the context of the classroom. Finally, administrators and curriculum supervisors must recognize the importance of professional development sessions followed by professional support of teachers in the classroom context. Teachers, who attend professional development sessions without related, long-term follow-up, may be more inclined to disregard the information (Ingvarson, Meiers, & Beavis, 2005).

In an ethnographic study conducted by Brown (2002), a veteran teacher of 25 years experience was interviewed and observed in her classroom, to gain insight into the "accommodation methods," used to integrate the principles of multicultural education into an elementary classroom. A literature review was conducted to identify effective classroom practices in line with the principles of multicultural education. The review yielded five main themes: (a) classroom management, (b) instruction, (c) assessment, (d) student/teacher interaction, and (e) parent/teacher communication. The investigator then used these themes as a basis for classroom observations and interviews. The single participant was observed on six different occasions in her classroom and informally interviewed either before or after each in-class observation. To effectively promote academic achievement and facilitate social engagement, Brown put forth the following, teachers must: (a) posses effective classroom management skills; (b) liberally include references to diverse cultures in the classroom environment (e.g., text books, instruction, and community resources); (c) be flexible and consistent when determining and using discipline practices to encourage students to assume responsibility for their action; (d) affirm student's home language; (e) develop and use assessment tools to identify student weaknesses and use this information to make instructional decisions; and (f) encourage partnerships with parents. Clearly, educators and administrators have a sizable challenge in developing and incorporating cultural competence into practice. The underlying theme of the multicultural education movement is change to professional practice. Changes in attitude are simply not enough, professional practice must be made an integral part of any discussion on multicultural education and cultural competence.

SUMMARY

Cultural competence is the accurate understanding of others' culture as opposed to acceptance of myths and stereotypes (Texeria & Christian, 2002). This all important disposition is supplemented by one's willingness to seek out accurate information about different cultural and ethnic groups and grapple with personal beliefs. Educators and administrators can and should cultural competence as the foundation for clearly understanding the principles of multicultural education and incorporating these principles into instructional and supervisory practices. Multicultural education is essentially a reform movement intended to bring about equity for all students, including those from diverse backgrounds and with disabilities (Banks, 1993). Reforming all schools and ensuring that all students can meet basic requirements in mathematics, reading, and science is the hallmark of federal legislation (e.g., *No Child Left Behind*), but also embodies one of the most basic tenants of teaching: children should learn and develop skills. Traditionally, demographic variables have been the main source of blame for the dismal underachievement for students from diverse backgrounds. Countless stories about little to no parent involvement, apathetic attitudes, and diminished cognitive capacity were passed off as definitive reasons for large-scale student failure. For years, advocates of multicultural education have argued that the movement is not just about revising curriculum materials, but about adopting specific principles that include: (a) content integration, (b) the knowledge construction process, (c) prejudice reduction, (d) an equity pedagogy, and an (e) empowering school culture and school structure (Banks, 2002). If educators and administrators are able to develop and use cultural competence and further learn and ultimately incorporate the principles of multicultural education in the teaching and learning process, many students who have traditionally been marginalized based on demographic reasons alone will have the opportunity make academic and social gains.

REFERENCES

Allen, J., & Hermann-Wilmarth, J. (2004). Cultural construction zones. *Journal of Teacher Education, 55*(3), 214–226.

Ball, A. F. (2000). Empowering pedagogies that enhance the learning of multicultural students. *Teachers College Record, 102*(6), 1006–1034.

Banks, J. A. (2002). *An introduction to multicultural education* (3rd ed.). Boston, MA: Allyn & Bacon.

Banks, J. A. (1993). The canon debate, knowledge construction, and multicultural education. *Educational Researcher, 22*(5), 4–14.

Brown, S. C., & Kysilka, M. L. (2002). Applying multicultural and global concepts in the classroom and beyond. Boston, MA: Allyn & Bacon.

Brown, E. L. (2002). Mrs. Boyd fifth-grade inclusive classroom: A study of multicultural teaching strategies. *Urban Education, 37*(1), 126–141.

Byrne, D. N. (Ed.). (2005). *Brown v. board of education: Its impact on public education, 1954-2004.* Brooklyn, NY: Word for Word Publication Co.

Cartledge, G., Kea, C. D., & Ida, D. (2000). Anticipating differences-celebrating strengths: Providing culturally competent services for students with serious emotional disturbance. *Teaching Exceptional Children, 32*(3), 30–37.

Casteel, C. A. (1998). Teacher-student interactions and race in integrated classrooms. *The Journal of Educational Research, 92*(2), 115–120.

Cockrell, K. S., Placier, P. L., Cockrell, D. H., & Middleton, J. N. (1999). Coming to terms with "diversity" and "multiculturalism" in teacher education: learning about our students, changing our practice. *Teaching and Teacher Education, 15*, 351–366.

Craig, S., Hull, K., Haggart, A. G., & Perez-Selles, M. (2000). Promoting cultural competence through teacher assistance teams. *Teaching Exceptional Children, 32*(3), 6–12.

Cruz-Janzen, M., Owens, J. K., Taylor, M. (2005). Impact of multicultural curriculum, content, and instructors: An assessment of a preservice program through teacher candidates' eyes. *Curriculum and Teaching, 20*(1), 79–97.

Diller, J. V., & Moule, J. (2005). *Cultural competence: A primer for educators.* Toronto, CA: Thomson Wadsworth.

Dukes, C., & Ming, K. (2007). The Administrator's Role in Fostering Cultural Competence in Schools. *ERS Spectrum, 25*(3), 19–28.

Edgar, E., Patton, J. M., & Day-Vines, N. (2002). Democratic dispositions and cultural competency: Ingredients for school renewal. *Remedial and Special Education, 23*(4), 231–241.

Ford, D. Y., & Moore, J. L. (2004). Creating culturally responsive gifted education classrooms: Understanding culture is the first step. *Gifted Child Today, 27*(4), 34–39.

Foster, M. Lewis, J., & Onafowora, L. (2005). Grooming great urban teachers. *Educational Leadership, 62*(6), 28–32.

Fraser, S. (Ed.). (1995). The bell curve wars: race, intelligence, and the future of America. New York: BasicBooks.

Garmon, M. A. (2004). Changing preservice teachers' attitudes/beliefs about diversity: What are the critical factors? *Journal of Teacher Education, 55*(3), 201–213.

Gallavan, N. P. (1998). Why aren't teachers using effective multicultural education practices? *Equity and Excellence in Education, 31*(2), 20–27.

Gay, G. (2004). The importance of multicultural education. *Educational Leadership, 61*(4), 30–35.

Goodwin, R. (2003). A brief guide to cross-cultural psychological research. In J. Haworth (Ed.), *Psychological research: Innovative methods and strategies* (pp. 78–90). London: Routledge.

Haberman, M., & Post, L. (1998). Teachers for multicultural schools: The power of selection. *Theory Into Practice, 37*(2), 96–104.

Harris, J. J., Brown, E. L., Ford, D. Y., & Richardson, J. W. (2004). African Americans and multicultural education: A proposed remedy for disproportionate special education placement and underinclusion in gifted education. *Education and Urban Society, 36*(3), 304–341.

Harry, B., Kalyanpur, M., & Day, M. (1999). *Building cultural reciprocity with families: case studies in special education*. Baltimore, MD: Paul H. Brookes Publishing Co.

Hernstein, R. J., & Murray, C. (1994). The bell curve: Intelligence and class structure in American life. New York: Free Press.

Ilmer, S., Nahan, N., Elliott, S., Colombo, M., Snyder, J. (2005). Analysis of urban teachers' 1st year experiences in an alternative certification program. *Action in Teacher Education, 27*(1), 3–14.

Ingvarson, L., Meiers, M., & Beavis, A. (2005, January 29). Factors affecting the impact of professional development programs on teachers' knowledge, practice, student outcome & efficacy. *Education Policy Analysis Archives, 13*(10). Retrieved July 3, 2006 from http://epaa.asu.edu/epaa/v13n10/.

Jacobson, L. O. (2000). Valuing diversity-students teacher relationships that enhance achievement. *Community College Review, 28*(1), 49–66.

Kea, C., & Campbell-Whatley, G. D. (2005). Quality instruction as a means of preventing problems: Emerging best practices of classroom instruction. In L. M. Bullock and R. A. Gable (Eds.), *Effective disciplinary practices: Strategies for maintaining safe schools and positive learning environments for students with challenging behaviors*. Reston, VA: The Council for Exceptional Children.

Lamorey, S. (2002). The effect of culture on special education services: Evil eyes, prayer meetings, and IEPs. *Teaching Exceptional Children, 34*(5), 67–71.

Lee, C. D. (1998). Culturally responsive pedagogy and performance-based assessment. *Journal of Negro Education, 67*(3), 268–279.

Lenski, S. D., Crumpler, T. P., Stallworth, C., & Crawford, K. M. (2005). Beyond awareness: preparing culturally responsive preservice teachers. *Teacher Education Quarterly, 32*(2), 85–100.

Ming, K., & Dukes, C. (2006). Fostering cultural competence through school-based routines. *Multicultural Education, 14*(1), 42–48.

Neal, L. I., McCray, A. D., & Webb-Johnson, G. (2001). Teachers' reactions to African American students' movement styles. *Intervention in School and Clinic, 36*(3), 168–174.

Necochea, J. (1997). When cultures clash. *Thrust for Educational Leadership, 27*, 20–23.

Obiakor, F. E., Grant, P. A., & Dooley, E. A. (2002). *Educating all students: Refocusing the comprehensive support model*. Springfield, IL: Charles C. Thomas.

Pang, V. O. (1994). Why do we need this class? *Phi Delta Kappan, 76*, 289–292.

Parsons, E. C. (2003). Culturalizing instruction: Creating a more inclusive context for learning for African American students. *The High School Journal, 86*(4), 23–31.

Ravitch, D. (1990). Multiculturalism yes, particularism no. *The Chronicle of Higher Education*, A44.

Saldana, D. C., & Waxman, H. C. (1997). An observational study of multicultural education in urban elementary schools. *Equity and Excellence in Education, 30*(1), 40–46.

Shakespear, E., Beardsley, L., & Newton, A. (2003, September). Preparing urban teachers: Uncovering communities. A community curriculum for interns and new teachers. Boston, MA: Author.

Sheets, R. H. (2005). Diversity Pedagogy: Examining the role of culture in the teaching-learning process. Boston, MA: Allyn & Bacon.

Sleeter, C., & Grant, C. (1988). Making choices for multicultural education: Five approaches to race, class, and gender. Columbus, OH: Merrill.

Stroman, D. F. (2003). The disability rights movement: From deinstitutionalization to self-determination. Lanham, MD: University Press of America.

Texeira, M. T., & Christian, P. M. (2002). And still they rise: Practical advice for increasing African American enrollments in higher education. *Educational Horizons, 80*(3), 117–124.

Torrey, C. C., & Ashy, M. (1997). Culturally responsive teaching in physical education. *Physical Educator, 54*(3), 120–127.

Trumbull, E., Rothstein-Fisch, C., & Greenfield, P. M. (2000). *Bridging Cultures in Our Schools: New Approaches That Work. Knowledge Brief*, ERIC Document number ED440954

Voltz, D. L., Brazil, N., & Scott, R. (2003). Professional development for culturally responsive instruction: A promising practice for addressing the disproportionate representation of students of color in special education. *Teacher Education and Special Education, 26*(1), 63–73.

Warren, S. R. (2002). Stories from the classrooms: How expectations and efficacy of diverse teachers affect the academic performance of children in poor urban schools. *Educational Horizons, 80*(3), 109–116.

Section Two: The How of School Leadership Research

8. LEADERSHIP MOMENTS: HOW TO LEAD

What leadership 'is' and the ways in which it manifests itself in the day to day work of schools and classrooms are so closely inter-related that the 'what' and 'how' of leadership are separable only in theoretical abstraction. However, we come closer to understanding what leadership is when we take a closer focus on the activity of schools and are able to spot the leadership moments which cut across status, position and hierarchy.

Investigating the 'how' of leadership was a central focus of a seven country international project Leadership for Learning (more commonly known as Carpe Vitam after its Swedish funding body). The project was titled Leadership for Learning because we started from the premise that learning is what schools are for and that for learning to occur and infuse an organization it requires leadership. As the 'how' is so closely dependent on a shared understanding of the 'what', we were to discover that we needed a great deal of conceptual ground clearing in order to identify a common language and common methodology which made sense to all the participants.

The project encompassed 24 schools in seven countries (Austria, Australia, Denmark, Greece, Norway, U.K. and U.S.), with three staff from each school coming together for the first time in Cambridge 2002 to establish some common ground and agreed methodology. Early discussion brought sharply to the surface the contested nature of 'learning' and 'leadership'. It takes an international project to show just how problematic both of these terms can be and exposes the difficulty in examining their inter-relationship when we approach the task with such different cultural and political baggage.

Our Danish and Norwegian partners pointed to the dangers of 'cultural isomorphs', 'concepts that look alike but are actually structured of quite different elements' (Moos and Moller, 2003, p. 360). The terminology of leadership may be shared but its underlying connotations are construed very differently in different places. Meaning is embedded in a historical, linguistic and cultural context and infused with implicit assumptions. These are most sharply realized across national borders but play out too within countries divided by a common language. Indeed, it may be argued that it is our very familiarity with language that makes it all the more difficult to

T. Townsend and I. Bogotch (eds.), The Elusive What and the Problematic How: The Essential Leadership Questions for School Leaders and Educational Researchers, 119–134.

perceive things in new ways, to know what we see rather than seeing what we already know.

Our 'habits of seeing' (Heschel, 1970) impact in very direct ways on the 'how' and it as we trace through what leaders and followers actually do that we gain new insights into the nature of learning and the processes of leadership. Through this focus on behavior and 'behavior settings' (Barker, 1986) the connections between leadership and learning become transparent and accessible to those who lead and follow in a complex interchange which flows across boundaries of status and institutional authority.

Challenging the assumptions that are brought to what is 'seen' and the way in which it is judged, Czarniawska (1997) coins the term 'outsidedness' to denote a form of knowing – by difference rather than by similarity. This is of particular relevance in an international context but is applicable in any context where stepping outside of classroom or school and stepping back in as a naïve stranger brings with it new ways of seeing.

It aims at understanding not by identification ('they are like us') but by the recognition of differences – 'we are different from them and they are different from us; by exploring these differences we will understand ourselves better.' (Czarniawska, 1997 p. 62)

By virtue of stepping out of the immediate demands of curriculum and testing and looking back in at the school, policies can be seen in a new light and with an anthropological perspective. As Richards (1992) comments, knowing yourself as an individual or an organization proceeds through three stages – first, separation from everyday practice and creating critical distance for systematic reflection; second, an encounter with new ways of doing things; third, the 'homecoming' in which new conceptions and the new experiences are brought 'home' (in both senses of that word). As Carpe Vitam participants consistently reported, viewing ourselves from the outside can be a salutary and formative experience. Reflecting on the challenge of other schools and her own journey through the Carpe Vitam project, a Norwegian teacher wrote:

> I have become more focused on learning in my own teaching, and I know that influences my work. I have also seen how important it is that we as teachers have time and space for discussing our teaching with colleagues, with a focus on learning. So much time is used on organization, administration and frustration. I think at my own school we focus too much on problems instead of opportunities and solutions.

Visiting a school in another country shakes the foundations of our 'thought world' – 'a set of basic assumptions that are taken as axiomatic; that is, it is assumed that they exist, that are shared by the majority in the field and their presence is evoked whenever a practice is challenged' (Czarniawska, 1997, p. 68).

Encouraging a discontinuity of perceptions proved to be one of the hallmarks of leadership. As prior conceptions have a tendency to 'overwrite', or sabotage, new knowledge, opportunities need to be created which require a revisiting and reframing, of what we know and what we are able to learn, as it were for the first time.

At the culmination of the project in 2005 a Brisbane principal attested to intellectual subversion among staff in these words 'a significant change in their mindset about being in the school and what's important'. In Seattle the research team reported that, two years into the project, intercultural travel, both geographical and intellectual, had helped to dislodge many of the preconceptions that principals and teachers brought with them. The dialogue had helped them to see past 'cursory practice' to deeper-lying principles

PRINCIPLES FOR LEADERSHIP AND LEARNING

One of the research strategies, both at the outset of the project and then two years later, was to shadow school principals over the course of a day, noting what they did, where they did it and with whom they engaged in the course of a working day. This was not a passive process as shadowing might imply but a process of constant dialogue, in which the researcher's naïve questions promoted reflection on, and explication of, the rationale for choices and decisions made.

Through a continuing dialogue over the three and a half years with principals and teachers in these 24 schools (21 still there by the end of the project) we arrived at five broad principles of practice. Primarily framed in terms of the 'how', these principles rested on a slowly emerging consensus as to the 'what' of leadership. These five principles of practice, discussed and refined many times, through a continuing cross country dialogue, we found to be applicable across the seven countries of our study but also with a wider resonance in other countries, other cultures. The five broad principles are:

Principle1
Leadership for learning practice involves a focus on learning in which it is assumed that:
– everyone (students, teachers, principals, schools, the system itself) is a learner
– learning relies on effective interplay of emotional, social and cognitive processes

- the efficacy of learning is highly sensitive to context and to the differing ways in which people learn
- the capacity for leadership arises out of powerful learning experiences
- opportunities to exercise leadership enhance learning

Principle 2

Leadership for learning creates and sustains conditions that favor learning, when there are:
- cultures which nurture the learning of all members of the school community
- opportunities for all to reflect on the nature, skills and processes of learning
- physical and social spaces that stimulate and celebrate learning
- safe and secure environments that enable pupils and teachers to take risks, cope with failure and respond positively to challenges
- tools and strategies which enhance thinking about learning and the practice of teaching

Principle 3

Leadership for learning practice involves an explicit dialogue which:
- makes LfL practice explicit, discussable and transferable
- promotes active collegial inquiry into the link between learning and leadership
- achieves coherence through the sharing of values, understandings and practices
- addresses factors which inhibit and promote learning and leadership
- makes the link between leadership and learning a shared concern for all members of the school community
- extends dialogue internationally through networking, both virtually and through face-to-face exchange

Principle 4

Leadership for learning practice involves the sharing of leadership by:
- creating structures which invite participation in developing the school as a learning community
- symbolizing shared leadership in the day-to-day flow of activities of the school
- encouraging all members of the school community to take the lead as appropriate to task and context
- drawing on the experience and expertise of staff, students and parents as resources

– promoting collaborative patterns of work and activity across boundaries of subject, role and status

Principle 5

Leadership for learning practice implies accountability by:
– taking account of political realities and exercising informed choice as to how the school tells its own story
– developing a shared approach to internal accountability as a precondition of accountability to external agencies
– maintaining a focus on evidence and its congruence with the core values of the school reframing policy and practice when they conflict with core values
– embedding a systematic approach to self evaluation at classroom, school and community levels
– maintaining a continuing focus on sustainability, succession and leaving a legacy

It is only when we explore the practical applications of these principles that we begin to appreciate how far reaching and subversive they really are.

MATTERS OF PRINCIPLE

That leadership requires a focus on learning was our first principle. All of the other four principles flow from this. There would be little disagreement among politicians, policy makers, parents and teachers that learning is what schools are for and that leadership is measured by how successful schools are in achieving their learning goals. Yet that very consensus is more likely to inhibit than to enhance the capacity of leadership to focus with integrity on what really matters in learning. The co-option of the language by policy makers and the equation of learning with performativity has brought with it an intensification of teaching, conspiring to crowd out a deep learning discourse. Without a quality of leadership that creates space for critical reflection, that supports principled dissent and nourishes an educationally subversive dialogue, schools and teachers risk being overwhelmed by the 'grand narrative'. 'There is no grand narrative that can speak for us all', writes Giroux (1992) arguing that:

> Teachers must take responsibility for the knowledge they organize, produce, mediate and translate into practice. If not there is a danger that they come to be seen as simply the technical intervening medium through which knowledge is transmitted to students, erasing themselves in an uncritical reproduction of received wisdom. (p. 120)

Inherent in this counsel are two main assumptions. One is that there are leaders able to foster a culture in which teachers' professional autonomy can be realized. The second assumption is that teachers have the strength, resilience and self-confidence to assume moral leadership in their own classrooms and beyond. The grand narrative of standards, targets, benchmarks and comparative performance is powerful and oppressive in its hegemony, hard to resist and virtually impossible for teachers to counter as individuals. If teachers are to take the responsibility and exercise the moral leadership that Giroux propounds, it requires a counterpoint and a counter culture which is premised on what we know and don't know about learning. It is through a culture of inquiry and self-evaluation deeply embedded in the daily routines of classroom life, that schools gain a strength of conviction to expose what constrains authentic learning and are able to illustrate how things can be different (our second principle).

In an educational context leadership, whether exercised by principals or by teachers, is inherently subversive. A continuous historical strand which links Socrates to the present day through Dewey and a long line of heretics, is the questioning of conventional wisdom which, in its original coinage, says Kenneth Galbraith (2004) referred to 'convenient truth'. It is the sacred mission of educational leadership to expose convenient truth and its detrimental impact on the lives of teachers and on the interests of the young people that teachers entered the profession to serve. It is this moral commitment to inconvenient truth that marks leadership in schools from corporate leadership which, however ethical in its conduct, simply cannot escape the bottom line of the profit motive.

A powerful illustration of the need for moral and intellectual subversion comes from a publication by an expert panel[1] in the U.S. of the ten most harmful books of the nineteenth and twentieth centuries. Included in the top ten alongside The Communist Manifesto and Mein Kampf is Dewey's Democracy and Education. While this may be dismissed as paranoia of an American right wing, there are parallels in the British context. Oxford's Richard Pring describes being approached by a splenetic Secretary of State (Kenneth Baker) who accused him, in collusion with John Dewey, of destroying education in English schools[2] Yet is it Dewey, perhaps more than anyone else, that has helped us to challenge inert ideas and to identify the intimate connections between learning and leadership. For Dewey it was the act of will, to appropriate learning for oneself, and take the initiative individually and socially that characterized the ability to lead rather than to simply passively follow.

As a footnote, one of the ten harmful books receiving 'honorable mention' is Adorno's study of the Authoritarian Personality. This is, in fact, a seminal study of how accession to authority made fascism possible, exposing the dangers of charismatic leadership and unthinking followership. Adorno's study continues to shock those who read the study or view the film footage because of the ease with which people can cede their own authority to someone in a leadership role. The connection between compliance and ceding of personal authority may, at first sight, not suggest obvious connections with a focus on learning. However, the more we worked with schools to tease out the connections the clearer these became.

David Perkins' (2006) playful metaphor of the Pod People, from the film Invasion of the Body Snatchers is a telling one. The film depicts alien invaders who develop out of pods and take over the bodies of hapless earthlings. While they have all the superficial characteristics of 'real' people they cannot take possession of the human qualities. The original author of the book on which the film was based (Finney, 1950) saw in his parable humans as losing the very qualities that made them human, masters of their own inventions, victims of a "rush to modernize, bureaucratize, streamline and cellophane-wrap". Siegel who directed the film admitted that the film was about the conflict between individuals and varied forms of mindless authority. He followed Finney's thesis that humans were losing much of their sensitivity in an authoritarian culture and 'to be a pod means that you have no passion, no anger, the spark has left you'. (www.gadflyonline. com/11-26-01/film-snatchers.html).

It is the emotion, the passion, and sometimes the anger, that connects learning as a subversive activity and leadership as a subversive activity. While the Pod People may learn behavior convincing enough to defy superficial inquiry, the vital lacking element is what Perkins terms 'proactive learning'. Proactive learning has two key components which are beyond the reach of the Pod People because these two components are affective in character – alertness, the predisposition to spot the learning moment, together with a desire for deeper engagement with the issue at hand. Schools, claims Perkins, present students with pre-defined problems which, by and large they are able to solve if pitched at the right level. However, what students are not good at, as his research team was to discover, is identifying problems when the field is open, as in real life problems. And even if students surmount that obstacle (through proactive alertness) the question is whether they care enough to engage deeply with the issue (affective engagement). It is not a hop from understanding to enactment, argues Perkins, but a giant leap – one that few students make in the course of their schooled learning.

The same principle may be applied at every level within a school. Mary Kennedy (1999) identified 'the problem of enactment' at the level of teachers, reporting that teachers experience great difficulty in translating good ideas and broad principles into effective practice. Like their students they need to perceive a need, to wish to move out of the comfort zone of the familiar and be exposed to practice which demonstrates how things might be different. The same would appear to hold true of principals and senior leaders too. We may be conversant with the 'what' of learning and leadership but the 'how' may continue to defy us.

MAKING LEARNING VISIBLE

A prior condition is making learning visible, explicit and discussable (our third principle). The problem to be confronted is that learning is generally invisible because 'we are used to it being that way'. (Perkins 2004:6) As educators, our first task, therefore, is to 'see the absence, to hear the silence, to notice what is not there'. Making learning visible requires having access to, or creating, a language, in which learning can be apprehended and discussed in new ways, with the blinkers of policy mandates removed. The blindness to learning is echoed in a blindness to leadership. In our research with teachers as to what leadership 'is' we found that while writ large in the body of the principal it was largely invisible elsewhere (MacBeath, Oduro and Waterhouse, 2004). Principals are seen to lead while teachers follow, just as teachers are seen to teach while children learn. In the words of a former Chief Inspector in England: 'Teachers teach and pupils learn. It is as simple as that' (Woodhead, 2002:15).

How learning becomes visible and discussable is illustrated in the following examples from Carpe Vitam schools in New Jersey and a school in Hertfordshire in England.

In a New Jersey school a principal described how student work is used to focus the learning conversation.

> Once a month at grade level meetings, teachers bring examples of student work and we discuss them. We developed a protocol that they use. Some of those meetings are done very well: teachers ask one another very good questions. It is wonderful to see a team of teachers who can look at student work and can ask good questions of other teachers, without 'attacking' the teacher, but in a helpful way
>
> ... asking them to think about the assignment that they'd given, for instance. Teachers have good conversations about student work, both within and across grade levels. (Principal interview)

Without a culture of trust and unconditional tolerance of difference, critical appraisal of student's work might have been seen as threatening to teachers, revealing to the scrutiny of their colleagues their professional judgments of quality and the inherent value of assignments administered. These issues go to the very core of pedagogy but in open and critically friendly sharing, they provide a forum for deep learning conversations when the professional culture is right. Learning conversations and collaboration growing informally and organically build cultures from the bottom up. However, as reported by Austrian schools, in the flow of everyday work it is like-minded teachers who seek out allies, exchanging experiences and materials but avoiding spending too much time with colleagues who have different opinions of teaching and learning and who adopt differing value positions. The dilemma for learning-focused leadership is either to foster the spirit of informal collegiality or to be bold enough to invite conflict, believing that schools grow as much through vigorous debate as through easy consensus.

In Barnwell School in England the strategic team constructed a mock-up of a brick wall on a notice board at the entrance to the staffroom, a site for spontaneous uninhibited and non-judgmental sharing of take-it-or-leave-it ideas.

> Whenever a teacher used a post-it to record an observation it would be posted on to the wall. Soon, posting observations took on a degree of competitiveness and it was clear which departments were contributing most because of the color of the post-its. As the wall grew, members of staff found that it was worthwhile to stop and read the post-its as they passed on their way into the staff room. These classroom obser-vations therefore became the catalyst for cross-cutting conversation about teaching and learning (Frost, 2005 p. 83)

How learning conversations extend from the teacher to the student discourse is described by a Barnwell teacher (Johnson, quoted in Frost, 2005).

> We now have a culture where it is not unusual for students to discuss their learning with both their teachers and their peers. One teacher reported that she often hears students talking about what they have done in lessons, how they prefer to learn, what they have found interesting and she finds this exciting as she has never worked with students who are so enthusiastic about their learning. (p. 83)

Such learning conversations do not occur spontaneously among students. They are the product of a strategic nurturing of a classroom dialogue. In Brisbane a welcome rise in student attendance and increased engagement in the classroom was described by the principal as a product of teacher student discussions at the end of the projects which not only gave permission for critical appraisal of learning and teaching but provided opportunities for leadership. As this principal put it:

> For a kid to stand up in class and say how about we do this, that's exercising leadership.

> Or [in] a little group you know where there's always someone who sort of seems to lead the group.

> I think that this whole process is actually producing leaders.

In this Brisbane school they instituted focus groups with students to explore the range of ways in which students were exercising leadership, and how they could extend their leadership capacity in other forums and alliances. These discussions contested the role of students as consumers, moving to one in which they were seen as resources for learning for their peers and for their teachers.

In a Seattle school a strategy for making learning visible lay in the creation of a school within a school. It was the initiative of one teacher who had been in the Carpe Vitam project since its inception and wanted to apply and test the principles in action. The idea was to build a smaller learning community in which young people could explore together with their teachers the nature and quality of deep learning and begin to undo the pattern of failure that was a feature of so many students' prior experiences.

These examples illustrate strategies for working within traditional disciplinary structures. A more radical approach is from Alan Luke in Australia and challenges the very edifice of subject kingdoms and 'warring tribes'.

> You've got warlords dividing up this curriculum. Then once it's divided up, children simply travel from kingdom to kingdom with little cross-curricular coordination. Now, 'rich tasks', enterprises, projects etcetera, were our attempts to force the warlords to the table to take each other seriously. Some schools in Queensland – one school in the north coast region – have begun to do this and have actually looked at re-organizing their curriculum like small universities or community colleges, so that there are three schools the kids study in – the School of Arts and Humanities, the School of Social Sciences and the School of Science and Technology – in which the kids in Year 10 are in the School of Arts and Humanities for two days a week and then they move across to Science and Technology. They've begun to look at radical ways of re-organizing the work of the school into communities of practice – into learning communities – that don't rely upon the kids

just going from cellblock to cellblock. There may be other ways of how you industrially organize your timetabling in your school; how you divide your staffroom up into warring intellectual tribes is reflected in the organization of knowledge and curriculum and then has direct impact on the kids' experience and uptake of knowledge.

(http://www.nationalpriorities.org.uk/resourcePages/resources.html)

LEADERSHIP CREATES TIME AND SPACE FOR WHAT MATTERS

As these examples illustrate, a focus on learning implies, as a leadership priority, to create time and space for what really matters. As one English headteacher concluded:

If you really want to try and effect change, you've got to get good people doing it, but you've also got to give them the time and space to make it happen.

This is what has been described as an 'expansive' learning environment, one that presents wide-ranging and diverse opportunities to learn, within a culture that values and supports learning. It increases what Billett (2001b) terms 'affordances' for learning whilst also increasing the chances that staff will want to make the most of those affordances. Fuller and Unwin (2003, 2004) term this boundary crossing—moving out of your own familiar patch to learn by engaging in a different environment.

The dilemma for leadership is that intensification and the pressure to reach prescribed targets mean that teachers are more inclined to welcome direction, structure and simple solutions. In a highly prescriptive environment off-the-shelf, ready-made packages lessen the need for teachers to invest time in planning and collaboration with colleagues, yet following this path diminishes opportunities for teacher leadership. It is the learning conversations, peer observation, and collaborative planning that are the lifeblood of professional development, creating a context and opportunity for shared leadership. As an English headteacher argues, this is only likely to happen when senior leaders stand back and create the space for others to lead (our fourth principle).

I think one of the biggest things is for people in the senior leadership position to have the confidence to allow others to lead and if your own need for affirmation and your own self-esteem requires you to be constantly lauded and feted as a great leader then it's very hard to allow anybody else to take up a leadership role. I think one of the biggest things within schools is being able to enjoy other people's success and as a headteacher that is absolutely crucial and one of the things that gives me most pleasure is when you see people taking, something that you know originally stems from you and running with it and it becomes theirs.

Standing back is not, however, a passive process. People are unlikely to simply grasp leadership in a laissez-faire climate; indeed the lack of structure and direction are as likely to create anxiety and factionalism, whereas by standing back and actively assessing the terrain, senior leaders are able to perceive where the most promising incipient leadership lies. A Seattle principal, speaking towards the end of the Carpe Vitam project, acknowledged shared leadership as a slow and pragmatic process, feeling out the strengths and weaknesses of staff, and learning the importance of flexibility and fluidity.

As a leader, you must be flexible and fluid... and [able to] go with the flow. Every day is different. It's important to involve everyone in leadership....to know the staff, recognize their strengths, build on their strengths, move them in a direction you want them to go or they want to go, in moving forward teaching and learning. We're on the right road....but still need more shared leadership. In some ways, I feel like we're just beginning.

For other principals the strategy was to identify the champions, staff with credibility among their colleagues, as this London-based head found:

Our experience is, if you want to make an initiative happen, you want to move something forward, you have got to create somebody within the institution who...for whom that is their priority. Because then, when it comes to deciding priorities, that doesn't drop off the bottom, because that's at the top. And I think we've found that in other things that we've done.

Implicit in this statement is a theory of change described as an epidemiological model (Gladwell, 2000, Hargreaves, 2003). The theory holds that it takes only one or two vital people within an organization to start doing something different which then spreads viral-like through the body politic. However, as in epidemics, spread does not occur unless conditions are propitious. Translating this into school context something innovative has to be made to 'stick' and to do so demands a quality of leadership prescient enough to recognize and nurture breakthroughs in practice.

It is now increasingly common for schools to institute a cross-disciplinary group of staff such as a school improvement group, a teaching and learning group, or school evaluation group, entrusted with the task of evaluating, planning for and/or implementing change. A group of six to eight staff may include learning support assistants and other school staff such as caretakers or catering staff. Such a group, representing different experiences and viewpoints can serve as a reservoir of expertise and a toolbox of evaluation strategies which provide the instruments of school improvement. The strength of powerful school improvement groups lie, like all great groups (Bennis, 1997; Surowieki, 2004) in their diversity and challenge to reach a consensus.

In one of the Danish schools in the project a meeting was held with seven elected parents, two teachers, the vice principal and the principal to discuss the future of the school and the contribution made by each of the potential leadership groups to a learning agenda. They arrived at the following working agreement:

Teachers will play the role of academic coaches, guiding students through learning situations, more than teaching in the more common sense of the word. They play a part in the upbringing of the child, helping him relate to the world around him, interpersonally, socially, culturally and politically, promoting wonder, seeking out problem solving methods in order to help them gain new knowledge.

The student is cast as academic explorer, learning in various contexts, dividing study time between knowledge centers, the home class and different study groups in accordance with the project he or she is investigating. The student navigates her way in an information-society, using knowledge to influence and take responsibility in the world around; locally as well as globally.

The parent helps a child meet the demands of participating in the group environment of school, participating actively in a cooperative spirit with the professional teaching team that coaches his child, co-responsible for the development of that child socially, academically and in interpersonal relations.

For each of these there were their own 'learning agendas' as well as leadership agendas embedded in a culture which respected the unique contributions these groups can make to the well-being of the school and its local community, so laying the groundwork for accountability (our fifth principle).

FROM EXTERNAL TO INTERNAL ACCOUNTABILITY

There is a dead hand of government-led accountability and there is 'rich accountability' (Robertson, 2005) which derives from a spontaneous recognition of what one owes to ones peers and to one's students, enhanced through mutual support and critique. It is this rich internal accountability that precedes and pre-empts external accountability, argues Elmore (2003:17):

Internal accountability is constructed as a deliberate contrast to external accountability. That is, internal accountability describes the conditions in a school that precede and shape the responses of schools to pressure that originates in policies outside the organization. The level or degree of internal accountability is measured by the degree of convergence among what individuals say they are responsible for (responsibility), what people say the organization is responsible for (expectations), and the internal norms and processes by which people literally account for their work (accountability structures).

The fifth principle was a late addition to our previous set of four, in part because in the form expressed by the English speaking countries it failed to resonate with the Greeks, Austrians and with the Nordic countries. Acceptance of the principle relied on spelling out the conditional clauses - taking account of political realities and exercising informed choice as to how the school tells its own story; developing a shared approach to internal accountability as a precondition of accountability to external agencies; maintaining a focus on evidence and its congruence with the core values of the school and reframing policy and practice when they conflict with core values.

In other words, accountability, like all else in the 'how' of learning and leadership, is value driven.

LEADERSHIP GROWS ORGANICALLY FROM A LEARNING FOCUS

The thesis of this chapter, and the findings of our Carpe Vitam project, is that when learning becomes a source of conversation, and takes on a vital life of its own in the culture of the school, grasping the learning moment and assuming leadership is hard to resist. Taking the lead, creative discontent and challenging inert ideas all require initiative and action. In this way leadership arises spontaneously and organically out of close encounters with learning. When this happens schools become, in David Green's (2002) words 'leaderful communities'. As a teacher in the Carpe Vitam project put it:

I have gained an understanding of the way of conceptualizing leadership with a focus on many people [who] can take part/initiate leadership in many contexts, and that leadership is focused on the core activities within the school, i.e. learning. Learning happens in the interaction, and that's why sharing is so important.

As we deepen our understanding of learning the nature of leadership becomes clearer. Like learning it is invested with emotion. It is highly context-related. It thrives on feedback. It arises informally and spontaneously in social contexts. It is alert and proactive. It engages with issues and dilemmas because it cares. It is restless and subversive and unaccepting of conventional wisdom or convenient truth. It makes the existential leap from the 'what' to the 'how' and when it fails it learns from failure and has another go.

NOTES

[1] http://www.humanevents.com/article.php?id=7591 last accessed 22/7/06
[2] Anecdote related by Richard Pring in his talk on Values in Education organized by the Center for the Study of Comprehensive Schools in November 2004

REFERENCES

Barker, R. G. (1986). Ecological Psychology: Concepts and methods for studying the environment of human behavior, Stanford University Press, Palo Alto, CA.

Bennis, W. (1997). Organizing Genius: the secrets of creative collaboration, London, Nicholas Brealey.

Billett, S. (2004). Learning through work: workplace participatory practices. In H. Rainbird, A.Fuller & A. Munro (Eds.), *Workplace learning in context* London: Routledge.

Czarniawska, B. (1997). *Narrating the Organization: Dramas of Institutional Identity*, Chicago: University of Chicago Press.

Elmore, R. (2005). *Agency, Reciprocity, and Accountability in Democratic Education:* Boston, MA: Consortium for Policy Research in Education

Frost, D. (2005). Resisting the Juggernaut: building capacity through teacher leadership in spite of it all, *Leading and managing, 10*(2), 83.

Fuller, A. & Unwin, L. (2004). Expansive learning environments: integrating organizational and personal development. In H. Rainbird, A. Fuller, & A. Munro (Eds.), *Workplace learning in context* London: Routledge.

Galbraith, J. K. (2004). The Economics of Innocent Fraud: truth for our times. New York: Houghton Mifflin.

Giroux, H. (1992). Border Crossings. London: Routledge.

Gladwell, M. (2000). The Tipping Point: how little things can make a big difference. London: Abacus.

Green, D. (2002). Unpublished contribution to the Carpe Vitam Leadership for Learning conference, Cambridge, May 22–24

Hargreaves, D. (2003). Education Epidemic: transforming secondary schools through innovation networks. London: Demos.

Heschel, A. (1962) *The Prophets*, London: Prince Press.

Johnson J. (2004) A Capacity building approach to school improvement: using learning preference profiling as a focus. Unpublished M.Ed Thesis, University of Cambridge.

Kennedy, M. M. (1999) 'The role of preservice teacher education'. In L. Darling-Hammond & G. Sykes (Eds.), *Teaching as the Learning Profession: Handbook of Teaching and Policy*. San Francisco: Jossey Bass.

Knapp, M., Copeland, M., & Talbert, J. E. (2003). *Leading for Learning: Reflective tools for School and District Leaders*, University of Washington.

MacBeath, J., Oduro, G., & Waterhouse, J. (2004). *Distributed Leadership in Schools*, (Nottingham: National College of School Leadership).

Moos, L. (2002). Cultural Isomorphs in Theories and Practice of School Leadership. In: Leithwood, K. & Hallinger, P. (Eds.), *Second International Handbook of Educational leadership and Administration* (pp. 359–394). Dordrecht: Kluver Academic Publishers.

Moos, L., & Moller, J. (2003). Schools and Leadership in Transition: the case of Scandinavia, in Cambridge *Journal of Education*, (*2003*), 33:3: 353–371.

Perkins, D. (2003). *Making Thinking Visible*, Harvard Graduate School of Education.

Qvortrup, Lars (2001). *Det lærende samfund. København*: Gyldendal. [The learning society]

Richards, A. (1992). 'Adventure-based experiential learning'. In J. Mulligan & C. Griffin (Eds.), *Empowerment through Experiential Learning*. London: Kogan Page.

Ritchhart, R. & Perkins, D. N. (2003). *Learning to Think: The Challenges of Teaching Thinking*, Project Zero, Harvard Graduate School of Education.

Robertson, J. (2005). Dimensions of Leadership: Principles, practice and paradoxes, (http://www.nationalpriorities.org.uk/Resources/Miscellaneous/NCSL/Voxpop.html)

Rudduck, J., & Flutter, J. (2004). How to Improve Your School: Giving pupils a voice. London: Continuum.

Sandal, R. (2001). The Culture Cult, Boulder, CO: Westview Press.

Surowiecki, J. (2004). *The Wisdom of Crowds*. New York: Random House.

Spillane, J. P., Halverson, J., & Diamond, J. B. (2004). Towards a theory of leadership practice: a distributed perspective, *Journal of Curriculum Studies*, *36*(1), 3–34.

Whitehead, J. W. Inavsion of the Body Snatchers: A tale for our times http://www.gadflyonline.com/11-26-01/film-snatchers.html

Woodhead, C. (2002). *Class Wars*. London: Little Brown.

9. SCHOOL CULTURE: DOES IT MATTER?

INTRODUCTION

School culture is often described as the 'social glue' that holds everyone and all organisational aspects together (Seihl, 1985; Stoll, 1999). Others use the metaphor of an 'umbrella' (Martin, 1985), under which the inter-related sub-cultures co-exist, and thus together they create a single identity. Some argue (Preedy, 1993; Bulach *et al*, 1995) that school culture is something we tend to understand intuitively. But what happens when we intuitively pick up some aspects of school culture and are totally ignorant of others? What happens when we don't make any effort at all to understand the concept or its influence on learning? In Chapter Three, the concept of school culture was broken down into specific components and the various comprising factors were highlighted. This chapter illustrates how our understanding and awareness about the concept shape various teaching and learning cultures in schools that may or may not be desirable at times.

WHAT IS A DESIRABLE TEACHING AND LEARNING CULTURE?

Although some general statements such as 'our goal is to create a safe and secure learning environment for children' are found in many school handbooks, in reality the actual or 'lived' learning environments vary according to different approaches to fostering cultures in schools. For example, some schools have regimented structures of rules and norms. Their practices project similar patterns of strict codes of conduct. Others have a more 'relaxed' attitude, fostering the same values to create a sense of responsibility in pupils through assignments requiring mutual trust. The appropriateness of such practices depends on the needs of the children coming from different socio-economic, religious or cultural backgrounds. Some other schools may be so complacent about their existing practices that they simply decide not to experiment with new initiatives as they feel threatened by the possibility of accommodating changes. This situation can give birth to a 'stagnant' school culture. Sometimes the shaping of such a culture can be done deliberately to foster a different sense of security by practising old norms and values, in which case the type of school is often

T. Townsend and I. Bogotch (eds.), The Elusive What and the Problematic How: The Essential Leadership Questions for School Leaders and Educational Researchers, 135–149.

called 'traditional'. Here, maintaining stability is the primary goal. The potential danger in these situations is that ultimately pupils who are educated in very traditional schools may lack skills to adapt to the wider world once they finish education, especially where there is a conflict of values between the school and the wider society. Ironically, on closer analysis, it is not unlikely to find that, in the handbooks, these schools like others also claim, as an objective, to help children to become 'independent lifelong learners'. It is how we approach this goal, in other words, how we decide to act upon it, that becomes important in relation to its outcome. This is where school culture plays a crucial role in manifesting the different styles of approach, according to our conscious or sub-conscious choice of guiding values. The differences create uniqueness even between two schools with very similar socio-economic background or pupil intake.

FOUR PRIMARY SCHOOLS

Case Study One (pilot study) – School A (CS1) Enrolment – 470, 3% free school meal entitlement* Case Study Two – School B (CS2) Enrolment – 190, 31% free school meal entitlement Case Study Three – School C (CS3) Enrolment – 343, 32% free school meal entitlement Case Study Four – School D (CS4) Enrolment – 117, 71% free school meal entitlement

Figure 1: The Series of Case Studies

* In the UK, 'free school meal entitlement' (FSM) is used as a socio-economic background indicator. Aberdeen City schools' average FSM rate is 20% and Scotland's school' average FSM rate is 20.5%.

WHAT MAKE SCHOOL CULTURES UNIQUE?

More or less similar sets of factors (see Chapter 6) are involved in shaping any school culture and yet they are all unique. What is it that makes them unique? Is it the same factors handled differently or different factors handled differently or a combination of some common and some different factors handled differently, that contribute to creating different traits of school cultures? The following section illustrates these various permutations.

Same factors, different components, different approaches, different outcomes

Emergent themes from the data sets in Schools A, C and D highlighted the fact that all three schools focused on their past history and tradition in guiding certain activities in the school. But the ways the schools dealt with the factors, and the particular components within the factors they decided to focus on were different.

For example, School A's approach to making use of their history and tradition focuses on 'what made us' and 'what has changed'. During the course of the study the annual picnic day was observed as an occasion to invite former pupils to the school (of different ages) and to publish booklets to emphasise how much the school had changed over the years. In interview the Headteacher mentioned how old practices were left behind with the passage of time. Some values from the past, such as maintaining a code of discipline, are still fostered but the approach has changed. Nowadays the pupils have a say in deciding how best they can maintain discipline in the school. School A made a subconscious choice of using reflective thinking in the course of initiating change in their practices.

School C also used the history of the area and the establishment of the school as an important component to focus on creating a sense of identity amongst the pupils. They organised co-curricular activities such as project work around relevant themes to highlight who they are. Unlike School A, however, School C gave priority to maintaining a strict code of discipline rather than establishing a democratic teaching and learning atmosphere where pupils have a say in making decisions. Some years previously, the school needed to take measures to control behaviour problems amongst the pupils, and currently this strict code is still practised without any modification over the years. This school consciously decided to maintain stability through strict discipline even at the cost of practising democratic values.

School D had a completely different approach to dealing with their history. They recently celebrated their 50th anniversary, when photographs from the past and the invitees' speeches highlighted 'what it was like before' and 'what is happening now' without much reflection on the process of change.

Pupils in all three schools mentioned above are learning about their history and tradition in one way or another but the learning outcomes may be different in each case. In School A the focus is on being open-minded and reflective. In School C, however, history is celebrated and tradition is maintained by holding on to practices which were considered a necessity for survival. With regard to discipline, in this school pupils do not have a choice: in most cases choices are made for them. In School D, the celebration of the anniversary was used mainly to involve pupils in extra-curricular activities and to create a sense of identity, without reflecting on why the changes occurred over the years or how history played an active role in creating the school's current identity. Creating a sense of identity was a part of all three schools' hidden goals behind the activities but each of them adopted different approaches to achieving the goals and consequently produced different outcomes.

Same goal, different approaches, different outcomes

School B, School C and School D all want to focus on creating a sense of identity and belonging amongst the pupils. This paragraph illustrates how they approached the goal in different ways. For example School B had a system of helping pupils through a 'Sunny Squad' team. This team is made up of elected members of pupils from each class and their role is mainly to help other pupils in the playground. The values that are emphasised during the 'Sunny Squad' meetings are 'sharing', 'caring', 'friendship' and being a 'team player'. The active team members in the field wear a cap, which carries the school logo on the front. The conscious choice of fostering specific values through practices contributed to shaping particular traits in School B's culture. School C in contrast to School B (as mentioned in the previous section) has a more traditional way of creating an identity through project work in history lessons. Both schools have similar aims but the 'Sunny Squad' initiative in School B has added implications for pupils' social skills development with regard to building relationships with peers. Unlike these two schools, School D focuses mainly on the after-school football club to create this sense of identity. But, as not all the age groups of pupils are involved in this club, this activity offers only limited opportunity for establishing an identity.

Different focus, same goals, different outcomes

Both School A and School D stated in their school handbook that they aim to achieve a 'secure and happy environment' for the pupils in the school. One of the ways School A focuses on achieving this goal is by creating opportunities to build relationships among pupils through both curricular and cross-curricular activities. Pair work and group work are emphasised during lessons throughout the day, as is a 'buddy system' in the playground. A range of after-school activities is offered for the pupils to learn additional skills as well as creating opportunities to build friendships with peers. The focus is consistent with their goal. This indicates awareness amongst the members of staff about how school culture influence children's learning.

In School D the emphasis is more on the co-curricular activities and even there the range is limited. During lessons in the classrooms observed, only a few were particularly encouraging of creative or co-operative activities with the peers in a group or in pairs. Despite the fact that the members of staff have a close relationship with the pupils in School D, in general pupils appeared to be happier and more confident in School A than School D. The dimension of 'pupil-pupil relationship' is neglected in School D where the focus is more on 'staff-pupil relationship'.

Same focus, different approaches, different outcomes

Building good relationships with colleagues is considered an important focus in establishing an 'effective' school culture in both School C and School D. To some extent, they both have established this goal but their approaches are different. Since School C is a much bigger school than School D, it is easier to build harmonious relationships amongst the members of staff in School D. The members of staff here generally work in small groups (infant, junior and upper stages) and make decisions about matters accordingly. The groups are closely monitored by one senior member of staff heading each team. Most of the time this arrangement works well, except on certain matters where the whole school is concerned; sometimes staff feel that decisions are being made at another end of the school without much scope for discussion. Relationships amongst the staff at a social level somehow work well, in that generally people are cordial to each other in the staff-room. But, on professional matters, sometimes disputes take place due to lack of proper communication.

In School D, the staff (a relatively small group) work together all the time. Their efforts are well coordinated and a supportive network contributes to a strong sense of security. However, the negative side is that School D seems to have forgotten to question their own practices. Most of the time the members of the school community are so convinced about following a certain code of practice that the thought of probing into the reasons behind such practices does not occur to them. As a result, long-standing practices such as using specific strategies to teach mixed-ability groups of pupils have not been evaluated and updated for some years. The school community is unaware of how a collaborative culture can produce a less effective learning outcome without the right approaches to practising it.

Sense of security

A sense of security amongst the members of staff is an essential component in an effective school culture. The Senior Management Team (SMT) in

School A provides the staff with such a feeling by being supportive in different ways. They believe in a democratic approach to resolving any problem. Impartial judgements on matters handled by the SMT are appreciated by the members of staff in general. Senior members of staff also are very helpful to the junior members in other ways. They are happy to pass on the benefit of their experience to their colleagues. When it comes to resolving a problem situation with the involvement of the parents, a senior member of staff is often present during the meeting between parent and teacher. They also investigate the matter thoroughly prior to lending a supporting hand. This kind of support system is capable of producing harmonious relationships amongst the members of staff as well as a steady level of academic performance in schools.

School B portrays a slightly different scenario. The Headteacher had joined the school only recently, before which the staff were accustomed to working with an authoritarian approach to management. Currently, most of the staff seem to like the open and democratic approach of the new Headteacher but at the same time they appeared to be confused at times. Some of the senior members of staff are still inclined to hold on to the previous ways of doing things in a hierarchical manner, whereas in staff meetings the new Headteacher encourages differing voices of opinion. School B is going through a process of transition but in the meantime, while they are adapting to the new style of management, their classroom practices have implications for pupils' learning. Some are quite structured and formal classroom cultures were observed along with less structured and semi-formal classroom environments (Das, 2006). The 'adjusting' sense of security amongst the members of staff in School B appeared to be influencing classroom practices in the form of various manifestations of 'power'. Since all members of staff are not fully aware of how the transformation of school culture is affecting pupils' learning, discrepancies in classroom practices remain largely unchanged.

Relationships with parents

The evidence from interviews indicates that all four case study schools had different views and approaches to parental involvement. School A found their middle-class parents often to be quite 'pushy'. Many parents want their children to perform at a higher level than they are presently achieving. Teachers in this school on occasions found themselves advising parents against this kind of pressure as possibly harmful to the development of the children's overall skills.

School B had a 'love-hate' relationship with the parents. Parents in this school are often vocal about their rights and they are not hesitant to organise a 'group petition'. However, they are also happy to offer their help for school activities. The school appreciate their contribution and tries to keep a clear channel of communication between the parents and the school.

School C values parental support as an essential element in educating pupils in school. They make an effort to communicate with them on a regular basis. However, there was little evidence of encouraging parental involvement in school activities. Teachers also complained that, although parents are supportive and are 'grateful' for what the school is doing for their children, they are inclined to bestow the sole responsibility for educating their children wholly to the school. Moreover, all that parents want from the school is for their children to be happy. In the opinion of the teachers, if the parents were a 'little more ambitious' and had higher expectation from their children, then the pupils' learning would benefit more. A key factor here is the socio-economic background. School C caters for pupils coming from predominantly working-class families. Academic aspiration is perhaps a secondary focus to survival in the wider community around this school.

School D finds their parents to be generally supportive, especially when the school was threatened with closure and the parents organised petitions against the action. Being a small school, the school is perceived as an island in the centre of the surrounding community. However, parental support is a 'grey area': strong indirect support from parents in the community is always present but the school seems reluctant at times to encourage active parental involvement. Nevertheless, School D had set up a 'home-school partnership unit' which was reported to have made efforts to work with parents on different occasions, but the initiatives failed to generate enthusiasm amongst them, which proved disappointing.

Different approaches to and different perceptions of handling matters in these case study schools produced different shapes of school cultures. Even though often they were found to have the same institutional goals, the choices of acting on them in various ways resulted in different learning outcomes for the pupils. This resonates with previous findings from studies on 'effective schools' (Rutter et al, 1979). Hopkins (1987) states:

> ...differences in outcome are systematically related to variations in the schools' climate, culture or ethos... (p. 3)

Different sets of values preferred and practised by the members of the school community in each case study school influenced the approaches to dealing with the factors that constituted their respective cultures. Not surprisingly, various patterns of practices emerged as a result.

An important point emerging from these case studies is that a cause of fundamental difference between cultures is the level of awareness (amongst those who live in it) of school culture and its effect on learning.

HOW DOES SCHOOL CULTURE AFFECT LEARNING IN SCHOOLS?

An awareness of school culture amongst all those who shape it can make a difference to how or what children learn in schools (Das, 2006). If the school community does not act upon the culture consciously or subconsciously, they are left at the mercy of ignorance, facing the implication of children's learning unfolding unexpectedly over a period of time. Donnelly (2004), for example, in her paper discussing the problem of 'integrated' schools in Northern Ireland, where there is a long-standing religious conflict, highlights an important issue. In her study, a lack of shared subjective ideas about 'integrated culture' amongst teachers carried implications for what children were learning in history lessons. Teachers' personal preferences influenced the prescribed curriculum. As a result, children in the same year were learning different things in two different schools. Individual teachers' personal values and religious orientation led the children to learn about the politically sensitive story of the Irish Famine in one school and the non-political story of Vikings in another. Instead of creating an integrated identity, different practices were taking the school communities away from the targeted goal of achieving integrated school ethos or culture. Following Dalin's (1993) argument, this situation could be considered as the 'sub-rational' level of organisational culture, where *values are based on personal preferences, experiences and biases...* (cited in MacBeath and Mortimore, 2001, p. 105). According to Dalin, culture at this level has a powerful role in the school at any point in time, both present and future. Situations such as this illustrate a problem which is not always easy to notice because often we are too accustomed to our own school culture of 'what goes on around here'.

If we agree on this as a problem, then who is to act on it? People in the school community, who are constantly shaping the culture through a conscious or sub-conscious process, are in an unique position to take measures towards solving problems such as this. Therefore, their awareness of this process becomes crucial to having a choice of nurturing children in an ideal learning environment.

Considering how adults' behaviour can influence children's learning in schools suggests another dimension of 'school culture'. The members of staff in schools contribute to shaping their culture by not only creating specific learning contexts and opportunities for pupils in the classrooms but also by passing on values through practices, while interacting with each other, throughout the school. From a sociological perspective Ballantine (1983) states:

> Learning is a necessary part of cultural transmission; learning involves developing cognitive orientations, values, objectives, and interests. In school, learning is a social activity involving others. (p. 36)

Following Vygotsky's (1978) view of social cognition, the cultural context provides children with essential support for learning. He argues that initially children gather the contents of their knowledge from their surroundings, and then they learn how to process the information through problem solving. This process of intellectual adaptation is also guided by the environment or culture in which their learning takes place (Cole and Cole, 2001).

According to Torrington and Weightman (1993), teachers generally accept that pupils' emotional and intellectual development should be nurtured in an ideal holistic environment in the school. This kind of environment is created and maintained by the 'ethos', 'the spirit', or in other words 'the culture' of the school. The concept appears to be abstract when we attempt to describe it through subjective interpretations. However, school culture is shaped and maintained by human attitudes and interactions (Nias *et al,* 1989). Handy and Aitken (1986) express this appropriately:

> ...organizations are living things, each with its own history and traditions and environment and its own ability to shape its destiny. (p. 83)

School as an organisation becomes a living entity when it involves the people responsible for creating a teaching and learning culture for pupils. The way to reach this goal is different for each individual school community but with conscious effort and informed judgement, it can become a productive process of enhanced learning.

THE LINK BETWEEN SCHOOL-CULTURE, COMMUNITY AND LEADERSHIP

School culture is not a static element. It develops, re-shapes and changes direction. If we consider the sociological perspective, according to Schein (1985), culture is 'invented, discovered and developed' by a group of people who learn to cope with change through the process of adaptation and integration. This argument implies the presence of a set of active agents, who carry the power to influence and change their culture. Applying the idea to school culture means that there are existing aspects of the culture, within which one finds oneself, that are waiting to be 'discovered'. Some new characteristics can potentially be invented through new initiatives and practices, and thus, through this entire process of organisation and re-organisation, a school's culture is developed and changed.

The culture-shaping process involves organisational dynamics within which people play individual roles. Undoubtedly, school leadership plays a significant part in it. Nias *et al,* (1989) argue that leaders are 'culture founders', whose job is to initiate change based on their expert judgement of a given situation. Alvesson (1993) reinforces the idea that understanding school culture is an essential requirement for school leadership as it enables the leaders to 'manipulate' culture according to the need of a particular time. These arguments may be valid with respect to leadership roles but nevertheless put less emphasis on the need for working collaboratively as a school community. A different approach is noted in Macneil and Maclin (2005):

> Principals who desire to improve a school's culture must foster an atmosphere that helps teachers, students, and parents know where they fit in and how they can work as a community to support teaching and learning. (p. 2)

According to the authors it is not only enough for the leaders to develop and articulate clearly a shared vision amongst the school community, but also they must create a learning environment that encourages shared authority and responsibility towards the collective goals.

The leaders' role is to guide the members of the community and be aware of the 'overall picture' at all times (Deal and Peterson, 1999). People involved in senior management in schools are responsible for managing and guiding the members of the school community. But at the same time the leaders must acknowledge that the school community is not made of 'passive agents', who can simply be 'manipulated' by using positions of authority. Sparks (1991) asserts:

> ...teachers should not be viewed as passive and unreflective vessels into which culture is 'poured', rather they are active in defining and redefining any given culture and their circumstances within it. (p. 10)

All individuals involved in the process of shaping a culture have the ability to make judgements about matters based on their very own professional, and in some cases personal, value systems. If it is an 'imposed' notion by the authority, the judgement of the individual is more likely to take place at a personal level; and if it is a collective decision, then opportunities for discussion on preferred professional values can be negotiated. The possible danger of creating low staff morale, and consequently less effective learning in pupils, is hidden in the former approach. The concept of *distributed leadership* (National College for School Leadership, 2001, Marks and Printy, 2003, Earley and Weindling, 2004) can be used effectively in such situations. Deal and Peterson's (1999) phrase of 'shaping school culture' (as opposed to manipulating it) is probably a more suitable alternative when it comes to discussing the role of leadership in the context of school culture. What is crucial for the leaders is to choose the appropriate style of management according to the particular need of a school community at particular points of time. Different management styles provide different 'role models' and express specific values and assumptions about the relationships amongst the members of staff.

Four different styles of management were observed in the four case study schools. The preferred styles of management in these schools are discussed here in the light of Bush's (1995) models of educational management and Bolman and Deal's (1991) organisational frameworks. According to Bush (1995), there are six different models for educational management – formal, collegial, political, subjective, ambiguity and cultural. The *formal model* emphasises the official and structural elements in an organisation. The *collegial model* highlights the necessity of exercising 'power' and the 'decision-making process' as a shared activity amongst the members of the organisation or in the case of a school, the school community. The central theme of the *political model* is to treat decision-making as a bargaining process, with power negotiation between different interest groups characterising this model. The *subjective model* focuses on the individuals rather than the organisation as a whole or its sub-units. The approaches adopted in this model regard schools as a social construct or sum total of the individual perspectives of the members of the school community. The *ambiguity model* highlights uncertainty and unpredictability in an organisation. It emphasises the complex nature of the organisational dynamics and uses it to analyse the outcomes of efforts or initiatives. The *cultural model,* to some extent extends the idea of subjective interpretations of the subjective model into a strong focus on the behavioural aspects of an organisation based on values, customs and beliefs, in which symbols and rituals are more important than the formal structure of the organisation. Bolman and Deal (1991) suggests four basic frameworks of organisations within which the various styles of management can be described. These are: a *political frame,* a *human resource frame,* a *structural frame* and a *symbolic frame.* Although all these frameworks carry elements of collaboration, the focuses on various organisational aspects and approaches differ from each other. These are discussed below in describing the different styles of management practised in the case study schools.

The style of management in School A portrayed characteristics of the *cultural model*. Decisions here are made at an institutional level as opposed to the level of the individual. These decisions and practices reflect a shared sense of values. School A also follows a rational process of decision-making. Here, elements of both the 'symbolic' as well as the 'structural' frame are exhibited. The norms of behaviour in the form of codes of conduct emphasise specific values through practices. In School A, events such as the annual picnic day are used to create shared meanings through collective effort. These aspects reflect the symbolic frame, whereas a focus on the democratic process of decision-making, rigorous planning and encouraging open communication highlights aspects of the structural frame.

School B's practices reflected a predominantly *political model*. Here, the members of the school community are going through a phase of transition from an era of an autocratic style of management to a democratic one. Although decisions are currently made at the institutional level (unlike in the political model), conflicts are taking place in the process of determining the goals or deciding how to achieve them. The Headteacher in these situations acts as both a participant and a mediator. The school management exhibited characteristics of a 'political' framework. The new Headteacher encourages open discussion and power sharing and consensus on issues is now sought through agreed notions of the majority. A participatory decision-making process is being emphasised. In some cases, 'authoritarian status influence' is still used to diffuse conflict. The style of management currently is transformational. The members of School B's community were not familiar with the new approach to working with colleagues previously.

School C's practices, to a large extent, demonstrated a *formal model*. The decisions here are made at the institutional level. Sometimes the members of the Senior Management Team (SMT) decide through which process a decision should be made: for example, whether a matter should be resolved through discussions held within the sub-unit team meetings where the representatives of the SMT are present, or in a whole school staff meeting or through informal chats in the staff-room. A focus on the hierarchical structure of the management was noticed in this school. Interestingly, despite the fact that School C practised a formal model of management, the members of the school community in interviews described the model within the 'human resource' framework (instead of the more compatible 'structural frame'). A strong sense of community prevails in this school. The staff's professional development is regarded as an essential aspect for future progress. Being a big school, the members of staff work in smaller sub-units. Building a supportive network to share resources and expertise between people is emphasised through practices.

School D followed a *collegial model* of mangement. In this school, the decisions made at the institutional level are based on agreement. The Headteacher usually takes the initiative to seek consensus on matters. Sometimes accountability is not a priority: instead, a strong focus on shared decision-making process is highlighted. School D exhibited elements of both the 'political' and 'human resource' frameworks of an organisation. Here, the absence of hierarchy is apparent, power is shared, sub-groups are lenient, frank communication is encouraged and people seem to enjoy working within the comfort zone of supportive network of colleagues. These are elements of a political frame. School D also projected a strong sense of community, mutual trust and acceptance and overall staff cohesion, which highlighted the human resource framework.

The illustrations of all four schools' styles of management are different from each other. They all exhibited evidence of collaborative work and yet their approaches to handling matters and dealing with the members of the school community varied in complex and subtle ways. These aspects of management to a large extent reflect the underlying traits of school culture. Mainly in the form of formal and informal codes of conducts, the organisational dynamics can be described as a part of both *behavioural* and *organisational* factors of school culture (as listed in Figure 1, Chapter 6). It is important for school leaders not only to be aware of the overall school culture but also to treat their style of management as intrinsically and intricately related to the shaping process of a desirable learning culture in schools. Unless the leadership is conscious of how the style of management affects various aspects of school culture, they are not in a position to initiate any change in it.

CONCLUSION

Culture, in general, is an abstract, powerful and complex concept. It is also a malleable, which implies that 'active agents' in the shaping process of culture, determine the nature of power dynamics at the outset as well as during the period of its formation. This issue involves a danger: in schools, if we do not exercise power carefully (to shape an effective school culture), the consequences can, in a worst-case scenario, can diminish children's individuality. Ideally a school's culture should encourage creativity and room for innovation within appropriate boundaries set by the wider national and global value systems.

Depending on the choices made and the level of consciousness of the culture-shaping process amongst the members of the school community, every school culture takes different shape or form. This is a subtle process and often takes place over a gradual period of time, resulting in unique school cultures. Differing approaches to dealing with various factors, contribute to the characteristic of uniqueness. School culture can be broadly categorised but even within the categories, 'individuality' remains.

The shaping process of culture is sometimes conscious. At other times, it is sub-conscious or even unconscious. Dalin's (1993) typology of organisational culture captures in essence the various levels of rationality in the culture-shaping process. Focusing exclusively on the locus of values in a school community, he argues that the 'rational' level of culture requires 'collective justification' of values, as opposed to the 'sub-rational' which is based on personal preferences and biases. However, as discussed and illustrated earlier, even though values are possibly at the centre of any discourse on culture, there are other factors (see Chapter 6) which also contribute to the various patterns of culture in schools. Moreover, although the ideal scenario of shaping an effective school culture requires effort and understanding of the existing culture of a school, in reality the effectiveness of most school cultures depends highly on the varied level of **awareness** of the culture's influence on learning amongst the members of the school community. This is where the 'unconscious' process of living a culture comes in.

In the case study series, School D's cultural practices raise a dilemma. In this school, people have a 'collective justification' for following certain practices, which categorises their culture as being at a 'rational' level (Dalin, 1993). Yet the school community lacks awareness of the cultural influence on their learning outcomes. Since School D follows collaborative practices primarily to 'work together for survival' (being under threat of closure), the school community forgets to question each other's opinions or viewpoints. What has happened here is that the main goal stated in the handbook regarding the schooling process, to help pupils 'achieve full potential', has become a focus secondary to that of survival. It is at this level when the culture of a school could be described as 'unconscious'. The question is: do we want to leave it at that or do we want to focus on the main goal with increased level of awareness about school culture? The choice is ours.

REFERENCES

Alvesson, M. (1993). *Cultural Perspectives on Organisations.* Cambridge: Cambridge University Press.
Ballantine, J. H. (1983). *The Sociology of Education: a systematic analysis.* London: Prentice-Hall.
Bolman, L. & Deal, T. (1991). *Reframing Organizations.* San. Francisco: Jossey-Bass.
Bulach, C. R., Malone, B., & Castleman, C. (1995). An investigation of variables related to student achievement, *Mid-Western Educational Researcher, 8*(2), 23–29.
Bush, T. (1995). *Theories of Educational Management,* London: Paul Chapman Publishing.
Cole, M., & Cole, S. (2001). *The Development of Children,* New York: Scientific American Books.

Dalin, P. (1993). *Changing the School Culture*, London: Cassell.

Dalin, P. (2001). In MacBeath, J. & Mortimore, P. (Eds.) *Improving School Effectiveness*. Buckingham: Open University Press.

Das, S. (2006). School culture: The evolving design of a study. *International Learning Journal, 12*(8), 193–202.

Das, S. (2006). *School Culture: exploring a concept,* University of Aberdeen.

Das, S. (2007). Should power dynamics embedded in school culture be treated as a threat or an opportunity to create collective knowledge? *International Learning Journal, 14*(7), 1–8.

Deal, T. E., & Peterson, K. D. (1999). *Shaping School Culture*. San Francisco: Jossey-Bass.

Donnelly, C. (2004). Defining the integrated ethos: perspectives from two integrated primary schools in Northern Ireland. *Education in the North,* 11, 27–35.

Earley, P., & Weindling, D. (2004). *Understanding School Leadership*. London: Paul Chapman.

Fullan, M. (1991). *The New Meaning of Educational Change,* London: Cassell.

Glaser, B. G., & Strauss, A. L. (1980). *The Discovery of Grounded Theory: strategies for qualitative research*. Chicago: Aldine Publications.

Handy, C., & Aitken, R. (1986). *Understanding Schools as Organizations*. Middlesex: Penguin Books.

Hopkins, D. (Ed.) (1987). *Improving the Quality of Schooling*. London: The Falmer Press.

MacBeath, J., & Mortimore, P. (Eds.) (2001). *Improving School Effectiveness*. Buckingham: Open University Press.

Macneil A., & Maclin V. (2005). Building a learning community: The culture and climate of schools. Retrieved from Connexions website: http://cnx.org/content/m12922/latest/

Marks, H., & Printy, S. (2003). Principal leadership and school performance: an integration of transformational and instructional leadership. *Educational Administration Quarterly, 39,* 370–397.

Martin, J. (1985). Can organisational culture be managed?, In Frost P., Moore, L., Louise M., Lundberg, C., & Martin J. (Eds.) *Organisational Culture*. Beverly Hills: Sage.

National College for School Leadership (2001). *Leadership Development Framework*. Nottingham: NCSL.

Nias, J., Southworth, G., & Yeomans, R. (1989). *Staff Relationships in the Primary School*. London: Cassell.

Preedy, M. (Ed.) (1993). *Managing the Effective School*. London: Paul Chapman Publishing.

Prosser, J. (Ed.) (1999). *School Culture*. London: Paul Chapman Publishing Ltd.

Rutter, M., Maughan, B., Mortimore, P., & Ouston, J. (1979). *Fifteen Thousand Hours*. London: Open Books Publishing.

Schein, E. H. (1985). *Organizational Culture and Leadership*. San Francisco: Jossey-Bass.

Seihl, C. (1985). After the founder: an opportunity to manage culture. In Frost P., Moore, L., Louise M., Lundberg, C., & Martin J. (Eds.), *Organisational Culture*. Beverly Hills: Sage.

Senge, P. M. (1999). *The Fifth Discipline*. London: Random House and Business Books.

Sparks, A. C. (1991). The culture of teaching critical reflection and change: possibilities and problems. *Educational Management and Administration, 19, 1,* 4–19.

Stoll, L. (1999). School culture: Black hole or fertile garden for school improvement? In J. Prosser (Ed.), *School Culture* (pp. 30–47). London: Paul Chapman.

Thacker V. J. (1998). *Using Cooperative Enquiry to Raise Awareness of the Leadership and Organizational Culture in an English Primary School*. Lewiston: The Edwin Mellen Press.

Torrington, D., & Weightman, J. (1993). The culture and ethos of the school. In M. Preedy (Ed.), *Managing the Effective School* (pp. 44–55). London: Paul Chapman.

Vygotsky, L. S. (1962). *Thought and Language*. USA: MIT Press.

Vygotsky, L. S. (1978). *Mind in Society: the development of higher psychological processes*. Boston: Harvard University Press.

Yin, R. K. (1994). *Case Study Research: design and methods*, London: Sage Publications.

10. HOW DISTRIBUTED LEADERSHIP EMERGES WITHIN DANISH SCHOOLS - EXPERIENCES WITH NEW SYSTEMS OF GOVERNANCE

The International Successful School Principal Project, (ISSPP[1]) takes as its point of departure that successful leadership implies a clear view of strategies on how to set directions, to develop people and to redesign/maintain the organization (Leithwood & Riehl 2005, Spillane et al. 2004). Day furthermore mentions a number of tensions that must be considered and balanced continuously in order to evaluate success in schools and their leadership: leadership versus management, development versus maintenance, autocracy versus autonomy, personal values versus institutional imperatives (Day 2005). This calls attention to the key elements in exercising leadership, which has to do with the appropriate distribution of power to stakeholders within the organization. In addition, it is important to understand relations in organizations within the broader tendencies in society that shape how public organizations may work. Individualisation, neo-liberally inspired market-oriented reforms of public services and organizational management concepts like the learning organization and so forth have all contributed to shaping new systems of governance that penetrate in profound ways how relations can be staged in public organizations (Krejsler 2005).

Schools were selected for the ISSPP project if they had received a positive external and independent inspection report by OFSTED (The English 'Office of Standards in Education') or the like, particularly with regard to the leadership and management of principals; if the results on "league tables" of tests and examination results could be shown to be improving and sustaining performance over time more than the "value added" local and national means; and if school principals were widely acknowledged by their professional peers as being successful principals. In Denmark we had problems with these criteria, because there is no inspection of schools on a national or systematic scale. There was also no national testing where results were made public at the time we were selecting schools. Therefore we had to find another way: We asked the superintendents of the municipal school systems (school districts) to select the most successful principal,

T. Townsend and I. Bogotch (eds.), The Elusive What and the Problematic How: The Essential Leadership Questions for School Leaders and Educational Researchers, 151–163.

taking into account what they knew about schools' outcomes and general status plus the peer acknowledgements of principals.

Therefore our approach to studying the success of principalship in Danish comprehensive schools has assumed that the conditions for non-coercive rational communication are crucial for the development of cultures that lead to success. We find justification for this approach and our data have disclosed essential aspects of what constitutes success. Students in both Danish case schools stress that their principals listen to them and that they thrive. Teachers also emphasize this feature as an important principalship trait.

Principals tended to distribute tasks to middle leaders and to teachers. We often see that they are active and eager in establishing and maintaining teacher teams of different kinds. It seems that very often the distribution can be labelled democratic rather than delegation (Gronn 2002, Spillane 2006, Woods 2004). The difference between these is that in the former, a democratic distribution, tasks are accompanied by responsibility and trust, in the latter, a technical delegation, there is no delegation of responsibility, interpretation and choice. The Danish experiences show principals distribute responsibilities together with tasks and thus give room for democratic manoeuvre in the teams and in classroom practice.

We know from research how pivotal relations between teaching content and teaching methods are and also how important the relations and communication between teachers and students and between students themselves are. This project begins to show us how important relations between principals and teachers and students are for the holistic education and learning of students and not only in how far schools are able to demonstrate high performances in tests.

THE DANISH EDUCATIONAL CULTURE IN TRANSITION

Since the beginning of the 90s, the Danish comprehensive education system has been undergoing a process of thorough transformation under the influence of strong international currents: a neo-liberal current has linked educational thinking closely to the economy through a push to make the school cognizant of the parents' demands, to more subject-oriented teaching, to a re-introduction of testing at all levels of primary school, pressure to harmonize within the European Union, inspiration from and fear of the OECD PISA program (Program for International Student Assessment), and individualization. (Krejsler 2005, Moos 2003c, Moos (Eds.) 2006).

For example the responsibility for finances and administration of the 'Folkeskole' (primary and lower secondary school, students aged 6-16) was devolved to municipalities and from there to schools. The traditional site-based management was redefined when schools were made financially autonomous and accountable. The school leader now manages very large parts of the budget in collaboration with School Boards, which have a parental majority membership. The Acts, and therefore the overall responsibility for objectives of the schools, remain in the hands of Parliament/the Ministry of Education but the interpretations and administration of the curriculum – which is fairly broad in its demands – is given to municipalities, which very often leave it unattended, and to the schools themselves.

The New Public Management (NPM) movement that pushes towards focusing on outcomes and on accountability and away from focusing on processes is gaining momentum. In Denmark since 2002 schools must post the results of school leaving tests on the Ministry's website. The government issues binding national 'goals', usually every two years, that are much tighter and more prescriptive than the curriculum used to be and has also introduced plans for more testing of students in grades 2, 4 and 6, in addition to the end of school test in grade 9. There is also a focus on economic incentives like merit pay for teachers and principals. In addition there is a focus on top-down management, and at the same time on decentralization. Administrators and politicians look to the private sector for inspiration. As an illustration one could mention a new postgraduate diploma in leadership that is intended to be relevant to leaders in industry and public service, as well as in education.

This development means that the meaning of leadership, professionals, and learning are under profound change. School leaders, it seems, (Moos et al. 2000) are caught in the cross-fire between first, the national objectives for schools, which focus on liberal education, i.e. the 'Bildung/Dannelse' of children to become citizens in a democratic society; second, the local authorities' demands for financial accountability; and third, the school culture - teachers are used to being very autonomous and are therefore not eager to be managed or led by the 'new, strong, visible' school leaders described by Government and the National Association of Local Authorities that is a major player in schooling politics.

CASE STUDY ANALYSIS OF DANISH SCHOOLS

In the following sections we demonstrate how case analysis captures the unique experiences of school leaders in Danish Schools. We emphasize how Danish principals are manoeuvring between demands for several kinds of accountability and the demand for "Democratic Bildung". Core concepts in our analysis are that leadership is enacted in interactions and that sense making is at the core of leading at all levels in schools.

Relations in distributed leadership

Managing relations and finding the right balance of how to distribute power to stakeholders within the organization are key elements in exercising leadership. In doing so a clear view of strategies on how to set directions, to develop people and to redesign/maintain the organization is crucial to successful leadership (Leithwood & Riehl 2005). Day draws attention to a number of tensions that must be considered and balanced continuously in order to proceed successfully with managing relations: leadership versus management, development versus maintenance, autocracy versus autonomy, personal values versus institutional imperatives (Day 2005).

In our empirical studies we found that a majority of the principals were inspired by approaches like the learning organization and distributed leadership, in the issue of management of relations. It is typical of most of the Danish schools of the cohort that the principal was setting direction by demanding commitment from all stakeholders in order to accomplish the purpose of the school. The vision of one of the schools was explicitly moulded upon the theoretical framework of the learning organization (Senge 1990), and her vision for developing people was built on a firm conviction that the exercise of one's professional role in a modern society cannot be disconnected from sincere personal commitment. This vision is implemented in a variety of technologies to manage relations that make up a version of distributed leadership that is on one hand participatory and on the other hand forces the employees to a high level of personal commitment, at times at an almost confessional level.

There are a number of internal, social technologies that firmly integrate all subjects within the organization that are continuously under further development and elaboration. At the Danish ISSLP schools all teaching and administrative staff participate in educational days that help to create a mutually shared language about the purpose and targets of the school and to foster a framework for interpreting the vision in the 'right' ways (Weick 1995, 2001c). The schools have action plans where school values and key priority areas are formulated. At a team level meetings are held continuously to create shared ways of operationalizing the vision. The principals keep up to date with team plans by having at intervals group appraisal interviews, where they get feed-back from, listen to, approve, and enter into dialogue with school teams in order to be part of the process. At some of the schools the meeting structure helps the Senior Management Teams (SMT) have the opportunity to influence teaching, the pedagogical principles and to keep informed about what is going on in the schools. At an individual level the principals make sure that the employees are committed by having individual appraisal interviews with each and every one. Here the issue of developing people is at the center. The appraisal interviews are opportunities for both principal and employee to evaluate the preceding period and to express expectations and wishes for the time to come. It is also an opportunity for the principal to ensure that the employee is committed to the school vision by asking the employee to justify how the school's vision is operationalized by him/her. Whereas the focus in some schools is on the individual teacher, as described above, it is on groups of teachers, like teams, in other schools.

All the principals stretch the network of managing relations much further by being very active with external stakeholders, being part of a principals' network in the municipality, holding information meetings, using the school web-site, and making public the school action plan. They furthermore encourage teaching staff to keep a high information level in relation to students and parents.

There are variations among the schools and principals, but most of the principals to a large extent are the driving force at the school. At some schools the principals are keen to ensure that a certain vision of the learning organization is employed. At still other schools a much larger portion of relation management is distributed to the teams, and the principals look more upon themselves as the one casting the bullets, and expects the employees to fire them themselves with a large degree of autonomy. Even if there are differences in the details the tendency is that the principals have a clear vision of the school, take initiatives to set directions, develop people, and design the organization; and they all invest a great deal of energy and trust in their staff.

The school organization

The Danish ISSLP schools are increasingly organized around division of the school into three levels, and departments: the introduction level 0 to 3rd form, middle level 4th to 6th form, and 7th to 9th form. Some of them are in the beginning of the process whereas others have fulfilled the process and have a full department structure. Corresponding to this there has been in some of the schools rebuilding activities so that the school architecture corresponds with this form of organising with the classes in the three levels concentrated in separate architectural units.

The organising of the teachers accordingly means that at each of the three levels the education is organized around self-governing teams of teachers that mainly do their teaching within the team. The teachers choose typically their teams by themselves, and the choice is obligatory for some years at some of the schools whereas it is possible to swap teams yearly at other schools. That structure means that students are swapping department three times during their stay at the school. Again there is a difference as to how long the schools have come in this change process, but all of the participating schools have in various degrees begun a reorganising process toward departmentalisation and team structuring.

This way of organising is basically found to be working well. Work in permanent teams implies that the teachers become "expert or researchers of their respective levels," as one principal puts it. As a consequence of this new structure some of the teachers feel that the cohesiveness among the staff has been damaged, a development they deplore, because the division of the school into three levels with their respective "home areas" and the collaboration in teams atomizes the staff.

This structure, with team organising, reflects an organization of the school's pedagogical staff of professionals and as such they tend to be self-governed to a large extent (Hansbøl & Krejsler 2004, Klausen 2001) through coordination via mutual adjustment. The organization is in consequence organized as a professional bureaucracy (Mintzberg 1983). In this kind of organization much discretion is left to the staff. The principal's influence is enacted through the meeting structures, through work with the vision for the school that is being developed together with the staff at project days, and through the planning processes. At the team level the principal's influence is exercised mainly through meetings with team-coordinators/department leaders, and through the scheduled meetings with the members of the teaching teams. At the individual level the principal can exercise his/her influence through the regular appraisal conversations with each teacher.

Power in the organization

The Senior Management Team (SMT) and/or the principal and/or the vice principal are represented in almost all of the meetings. That is to say that the SMT are the continuity figures in these meetings, and therefore they have the overall information of what is going on at the school. This privileged access to information of course gives them a special power, not necessarily in the form of exercise of direct power but in a more indirect way as agenda setting power (Barach & Baratz 1962), consciousness controlling power (Lukes 1974, Weick 1995) or structural power (Foucault 1976/1994); but both the way the organization is structured and the way the meeting structure is organized gives the management team rich possibilities to use both indirect, agenda setting power, conscience controlling and structural power. This is well demonstrated in the account from our observations.

Concerning the distribution of power, it is not a simple matter to decide which groups in the school have power over whom. As professionals working in self governing teams these teams have considerable power over how to perform their work. In all the participating schools it is typical that the management does not interfere in daily teaching matters as long as things are going right due to the decentralized organization. But as shown elsewhere professionals have acquired specific powers vis-à-vis the management (Hansbøl & Krejsler 2004). It is not possible for a management team of a professional organization to present effective leadership of Danish "Folkeskole" if they do not have a minimum of trust from their professionals. It is in reality possible for the staff to "sack" the management (Kofod 2005), if the staff lose trust in the management in such professional organizations.

Power relations in professional organizations are working in various ways – not only from top to bottom but also from the bottom upwards and horizontally. In the end the most important way the power relations in the school works is through the structure and through the conscience controlling power (Christensen & Jensen 1986a, 1986b, Foucault 1976/1994) that one may call the professional ethos. In the Danish ISSLP schools the organization, the team structure, and the meeting structure leave room for all three kinds of power to be exercised.

Couplings in the organization

We have here chosen to look on only one part of the organization, namely the staff and teachers' relations with the SMT. The school has almost as many other members of the staff as it has teachers employed. But for the sake of simplicity we concentrate on the relations between the management and the teachers.

When looking at the school's organization and meeting structure it is characteristic that it has both loose and tight couplings. The decentralized structure with semiautonomous departments and self-governing teams of teachers points in the direction of loose couplings between departments, and between departments and SMT. Taking into account that the complexity of the organization is high with this type of organising the solution of using loose couplings is a clever way to reduce this complexity (Weick 2001b). The SMT's control over what is going on in the classrooms is indirect and is exercised among other things through the meeting structure, and coordination is carried out through mutual adjustment and input of skills (Mintzberg 1983). At the same time the firmer structures such as the meeting structures are a sign of tight couplings. To be able to cope with fluid systems where parts work together in various constellations as in the

Danish ISSLP schools the organization must have an element of loose coupling to be able to act as a self designing system (Weick 2001a). The move towards decentralisation and delegation of competences makes it appropriate to have a loosening of the couplings (Weick 1976). In order to have secured feed-back mechanisms to make sure that the organization has the necessary robustness there must also be tight couplings.

The Danish ISSLP schools are thus at the same time characterized by tight and loose couplings. However, there are different couplings between the SMT and departments and between departments, depending of the degree of decentralisation in the single school.

DISCUSSION

In the Danish case schools there is a tendency to distribute leadership in various degrees from the school's leadership to teachers, and in some cases to the students in specific areas: "The school used to be an 'ask for permission school' – now it is a 'make your own decision school'… It does imply a lot of responsibility to delegate the full management of a department including economic affairs and so forth," says the principal at one of the schools.

At almost all Danish schools there is a leadership team and teacher teams. In some schools decision powers are distributed to the teacher teams, which not only plan their own teaching, but also decide on parts of the budget. The distributed structure of schools seems to resonate with the traditional educational rhetoric of education for 'democratic citizenship' and at the same time it seems to be an answer to the New Public Management (NPM) trend of decentralisation.

The purpose of schools has for many years been described in the Act on the Folkeskole (Act on Folkeskole 1995) in rather broad terms that were left to schools and to individual teachers to interpret and to act upon. In recent years the government has formulated more detailed goals and along with the local authorities has demanded more rigorous forms of accountability from schools. Therefore, principals are now beginning to describe directions for the school and to discuss them with teachers in order to develop a shared set of goals. Most schools strive to accomplish high outcomes within a broad range of academic, social and personal competencies, which all contribute to building the participatory democratic citizenship competences.

We find robust signs of what Beane and Apple (1999) have labelled participatory democratic communities, i.e., the open flow of ideas, critical reflection and analysis, concern for the welfare of others and the 'common good' as well as the concern for the dignity and rights of individuals and minorities. In many ways we see schools that are striving to be good communities for the broad and comprehensive development of students' cognitive, personal and social competencies.

The schools and their leaders have different interpretations of how to lead in a democratic way (Blase et al. 1995), but they can all be said to encourage teachers' involvement in decision-making. Teachers on their part encourage students to involve themselves in decision-making at the classroom level. Leaders are all child-centered and committed towards improving teaching and learning. They all have trust in teachers' motives, and they are all able to listen and to communicate openly.

One aspect of democratic or shared leadership in these schools is making sure that the people who are to make decisions are able to do so in a competent way. The principals and the rest of the leadership teams show great trust in teachers' teaching competence, and principals show great trust in the competence and commitment of deputy and department leaders. As found one could interpret meetings where strategies are discussed as the principal's way of making sure the teachers are living up to demands and that they do so in ways with which he/she can agree. In this way the principal is educating the department leaders into becoming capable and intelligent leaders in their own right. In one instance it was said that when heads of departments have learned to make the right decisions in the same way as he does, then they are competent to assume responsibility for those decisions. In fact this is a form of power exercise that has been called pastoral power, (Foucault 1976/1994) where the principal acts as the herdsman seeing that the herd, the teachers or the middle leaders, act in the principal's "Dorian Grey" picture (Wilde 1998/1891).

Another aspect that that was observed and heard is that many teachers and heads of departments asked for the principal's advice or acceptance of their ideas. They often wanted a 'father's or mother's nod' before they carried their ideas out in practice. It was often ideas or actions that they themselves were authorized to carry out on their own and therefore the request for acceptance can be seen as feedback from the principal, asking for acceptance of the action as being within the norms of the professional community or the school's value base. The communication in these situations was often clear, transparent and elaborated, so both parties knew what was agreed upon and on what premises. On the other hand there seemed to be a tendency for teachers and department leaders to ask for acceptance from the principal as an authority and at the same time for reassurance from the principal as a person. This can be interpreted in a way that even if the principal is renowned for a democratic disposition and willingness to delegate the staff members are apparently not able to decide on their own without the approval of the principal with his "fatherly nod." This kind of dependence on the principal is often seen with very charismatic leaders. The risk is that teachers leave the organization irresolute when the leader disappears. (Yukl 2002) As such these charismatic leaders make "their" organizations vulnerable.

The observations made in the schools we studied led us to ask if there is a trend towards building relations in schools on affective rather than on cognitive sources (Moos 2003c, Warren 1999). If this trend increases one could ask if it eventually is going to undermine the rational community and the democratic relations and leave too much power in the hands of a charismatic leader?

Generally there seems to be a tendency for empowered employees to seek reassurance and acceptance from their leaders. Poul Poder (2004) has found that many employees have grown dependent also on the emotional support of their leaders. The trend is a result of the decentralisation of power within value-led enterprises and institutions that rely heavily on the commitment of employees' willingness to work according to the values of the institutions and not according to rules. The case schools are in many ways examples of value-led institutions or communities, and the principals are seen to be both good rational communicators of insights and ideas, but are also beginning to grow into 'paternalistic/maternalistic dependency leaders' (Baumannn 1999) because the teachers and department leaders draw them into that position. It could lead to the question of 'How can staff be led and empowered in ways that enable them to become autonomous professionals and co-leaders?' (Moos 2003a) It is, however, important not to reduce this to a psychological issue. Of even greater importance is to understand how staff's dependence upon the principal's reassurance that they do things in the right way can be attributed to structural features that have accompanied recent changes in the governance of complex organizations. The learning organization, new public management and other modern organizational technologies are thus characterized by considerable tension between on the one hand a need to develop committed staff that can take initiative and work flexibly, individually and in self-governing teams, and on the other hand increasing the focus on strong leaders that have detailed knowledge of what happens in all corners in order to be able to set directions in accordance with the organization's vision. This is happening when the SMT is represented in almost all regular meetings according to the meeting structures where they are the only persons that are given privileged access to the organizational knowledge. It is stated in the present Danish coalition government's internal political agreement on the government's joint policy that "the schools that function best are those with a strong and visible leadership...". (Government 2005)

This means that the leader(s) cannot and shall not plan out in detail what s/he expects, partially because s/he cannot in a complex value-based organization predict all that will happen, partially because an attempt to do so would most likely inhibit and hamper staff initiative. Therefore these complex school organizations are both loose and tight coupled to reduce the complexity and to make the value-based principalship work, because the staff knows what is expected of them from the school's identified values, and therefore ought to know how to act accordingly. This means, inversely, that staff as they take initiatives will often need feedback from leadership as to whether what they do might cause objections (Krejsler et al. 2004). Staff are thus under increasing pressure to be able to guess which set of interpretations of organizational values that will be accepted. Therefore, we see that they seek the so-called fatherly or motherly nod which becomes a simultaneous tightening of the couplings. When their interpretative skills are not good enough or when the values perhaps are not sufficiently internalized; one needs to consider the use of social technologies. Principals declare their democratic disposition and the rhetoric of the self-governing position is that they ensure teams' autonomy. The teachers also claim the need for professional autonomy. Nevertheless it seems that the more or less hidden use of the technologies could be rather efficient steering mechanisms that ensure the principals keep a firm grip of the power even if the rhetoric is that schools are democratic systems where decisions are taken after a power free conversation in a Habermasian sense. (Habermas 1981/1996)

NOTES

[1] The International Successful School Principalship Project (ISSPP) has participation from the US, UK, Australia, China, Canada, Sweden, Norway and Denmark. Part of the data presented here are included in Moos, L., Krejsler, J. & Kofod, K. (2006): Communicative Strategies among Successful Danish School Principals, in: Leithwood, K. and Day, C. (Eds.) (2006): Successful School Principals: International Perspectives. Dordrecht, Springer

REFERENCES

Act on Folkeskole 1995. Consolidation Act No. 55 of 17 January.
Barach, P., & Morton, S. B. (1962). The Two Faces of Power. *American Political Science Review*.
Baumannn, Z. (1999). *In Search of Politics*. Stanford University Press.
Beane, J. A., & Michael, W. A. (1999). The Case for democratic schools. In M. W. Apple & J. A. Beane (Eds.), *Democratic Schools, Lessons from Chalk Face*. Open University Press.
Begley, P. (2000). Cultural Isomorphs of Educational Administration. *The Asia Pacific Journal of Education*.

Blase, J., Jo, B., Gary, L. A., & Sherry, D. 1995. *Democratic Principals in Action. Eight Pioneers.* Corwin Press.

Christensen, S., & Poul-Erik, D. J. (1986b). *Kontrol i det stille - om magt og deltagelse* [Controle in Silence - on power and participation]. Samfundslitteratur.

Day, C. (2005). Sustaining Schools in Challenging Contexts: Leadership in English Schools. *Journal of Educational Administration, 43*(6), 573–583.

Day, C., Alma, H., Mark, H., Harry, T., & John, B. (2000). *Leading Schools in Time of Change.* Open University Press.

Foucault, M. (1976/1994). *Viljen til viden. Seksualitetens historie 1,* Samlerens Bogklub ed. Det Lille Forlag.

Gronn, P. (2002). Distributed Leadership. In K. Leithwood & P. Hallinger (Eds.), *Second International Handbook of Educational Leadership and Administration* (pp. 653–696). Kluver Academic Publishers.

Habermas, J. (1981/1996). *Teorien om den kommunikative handlen* [The Theory of the Communicative Action]. Ålborg Universitetsforlag og Institut for pædagogik og uddannelsesforskning, Danmarks Lærerhøjskole.

Hansbøl, G., & Krejsler, J. (2004). Konstruktion af professionel identitet - en kulturkamp mellem styring og autonomi i et markedssamfund. in *Relationsprofessioner - lærere, pædagoger, sygeplejersker, sundhedsplejere, socialrådgivere og mellemledere,* edited by L. Moos, J. Krejsler, and P. F. Lauersen.

Jacobson, S. L., Christopher, D., & Kenneth, L. (2005a). The international successful school principal project. *Journal of Educational Administration 43*(6), 532–629.

Jacobson, S. L., Christopher, W. D., & Kenneth, L. (Eds.). (2005b). The international successful School Principal project. *Journal of Educational Administration.*

Klausen, K. K. 2001. *Skulle det være noget særligt? - organization og ledelse i det offentlige* [Is it supposed to be something special? - Organization and leadership in the public sector], 1st ed. Børsens Forlag A/S.

Kofod, K. K. (2005). På sporet af ledelse - ledelse i spor. En analyse af ledelse i socialpædagogiske institutioner. [On the track of leadership - leadership in tracks. An analysis of leadership in social pedagogical institutions]. in *Institut for Pædagogisk Sociologi.* Danmarks Pædagogiske Universitet.

Krejsler, J., Per, F. L., & Birte, R. (2004). Folkeskolelærernes professionalizering. in *Relationsprofessioner,* edited by Lejf Moos, John Krejsler, and Per Fibæk Laursen. Danmarks Pædagogiske Universitets Forlag.

Leithwood, K., Doris, J., & Roseanne, S.. (1999). *Changing Leadership for Changing Times.* Open University Press.

Leithwood, K., & Carolyn, R. (2005). What we know about successful school leadership. In W. Firestone & C. Riehl (Eds.), *A new agenda: Directions for research on educational leadership.* Teacher College Press.

Lukes, S. (1974). *Power. A Radical View.* McMIllan.

Mintzberg, H. (1983). Structure in Fives. Designing effective Organizations. Prentice Hall.

Moos, L. (2003b). Leadership for/as 'Dannelse'? In L. Moos (Ed.), *Educational Leadership.* Danish University of Education Press.

Moos, L. (2003c). *Pædagogisk ledelse - om ledelsesopgaven og relationerne i uddannelsesinstitutioner* [Educational Leadership - On the leadership assignment and the relations in educational institutions]. Børsen.

Moos, L., Stephen, C., Olaf, J., & Jill, M. (2000). *Skoleledelse i Norden.* Nordisk Ministerråd.

Moos, L. (Eds.). (2006). What kinds of democracy in education are facilitated by supra- and transnational agencies? *European Educational Research Journal Special Issue* (forthcoming).

Poder, P. (2004). Feelings of power and the power of feeling: handling emotion in organizational change. Pp. 274 in *Institute of Sociology.* Copenhagen University.

Government: The Govenment Agreement 2005. February 2005. The VK government II: New goals.

Senge, P. (1990). *The Fifth Discipline.* Century Business.

Spillane, J. P. (2006). *Distributed Leadership*. Jossey-Bass.

Spillane, J. P., Richard, H., & John, B. D. (2004). Towards a theory of leadership practice; a distributed perspective. *Journal of Curriculum Studies, 36*(1), 3–34.

Starrat, R. J. (2001). Democratic leadership theory in late modernity: an oxymoron or ironic possibility? *International Journal of Leadership in Education, 4*(4), 333–354.

Warren, M. E. (1999). Democratic theory and trust. In M. E. Warren (Ed.), *Democracy & Trust*. Cambridge University Press.

Weick, K. E. (1976). Educational Organizations as Loosely Coupled Systems. *Administrative Quarterly* 21.

Weick, K. E. (2001a). Organizational Design: Organizations as Selfdesigning Systems. In *Making Sense of the Organization*. Blackwell Publishers Ltd.

Weick, K. E. (2001b). Sources of Order in Underorganised Systems: Themes in Recent Organizational Theory. in *Making Sense of the Organization*. Blackwell Publishers Ltd.

Weick, K. E. (1995). *Sensemaking in Organizations*. Sage.

Weick, K. E. (2001c). *Making Sense of the Organization*. Blackwell.

Wenger, E. (1999). Communities of Practice. Learning, Meaning and Identity. Cambridge University Press.

Wilde, O. (1998/1891). *The Picture of Dorian Grey*. Oxford Paperbacks.

Woods, P. A. (2004). Democratic leadership: drawing distinctions with distributed leadership. *International Journal of Leadership in Education, 7*(1), 3–26.

Yukl, G. (2002). *Leadership in Organizations*. Prentice Hall.

11. LEADING SCHOOLS IN POOR COMMUNITIES: HOW DO WE KNOW?

INTRODUCTION

The consequences of growing up 'poor' affect the educational aspirations and achievement of millions of young people worldwide (Rainwater & Smeeding, 2003). It is clear that poverty presents a substantial barrier to educational attainment and achievement. It remains the case that certain groups of pupils consistently fail to reach their potential while other groups of pupils succeed and that children from low income families do not on average overcome the hurdle of lower initial attainment (Power et al., 2003). The odds, it would seem, are 'still stacked against schools in poorer areas' and the social class differential remains a powerful indicator of subsequent educational achievement (Gray, 2001:1). Research also shows the cumulative effect on underachievement of attending less effective schools. As Gray (2004:306) summarizes, 'part of being disadvantaged is having the misfortune to end up attending 'poorer' institutions rather than chance would predict'. In short, the more socially disadvantaged the community served by the school; it would seem more likely it is that the school will underachieve.

Many schools labelled as 'failing' or 'low performing' serve highly diverse student populations with multiple cultures, languages, religions and economic circumstances. Such diversity presents two problems, firstly, the sheer range of learning needs that schools must take into account, and secondly, the presence of significant numbers of children whose needs typically exceed the capacities of many schools to adequately address. These powerful, interlocking variables render the teaching and learning processes, normally accepted and expected in the majority of schools, much more difficult to achieve in schools in high poverty contexts.

The extent to which any pattern of underachievement is due to the influence of the school, the community or the individual is inherently complex, making any attempt at intervention at only one level questionable. Those close to schools in challenging circumstances understand only too well that there are no 'quick fixes' to the problems that they face (Myers and Stoll, 1998). However the research evidence consistently demonstrates

T. Townsend and I. Bogotch (eds.), The Elusive What and the Problematic How: The Essential Leadership Questions for School Leaders and Educational Researchers, 165–179.

that the quality of leadership determines the motivation of teachers and the quality of teaching in the classroom (Hallinger & Heck, 1998). It shows that effective leaders exercise an indirect but powerful influence on the effectiveness of the school and on the achievement of students (Leithwood and Steinbach 2002). The contemporary school improvement literature shows that leadership is a major contributory factor to raising achievement (Reynolds, 2001 and Hopkins 2001b; Harris et al. 2006). Consequently, this chapter goes beyond what we know about leadership in poor communities and considers how we know it.

LEADING SCHOOLS IN POOR COMMUNITIES: WHAT DO WE KNOW?

The collective research evidence suggests that principals who work in schools in poor communities often originate from similar socio-economic backgrounds. Generally, they have deliberately chosen to work in schools in disadvantaged communities and have a strong commitment to making a difference to the life chances of the young people who live there. They have a strong moral purpose but often wrestle with idealism/pessimism about how much this is possible in practice. Very often they spend long hours at work to the detriment of their health and family life (Blackmore, 1999). While this is not an uncommon feature of principals in other school contexts (Day, Harris, Hadfield, Tolley, & Beresford, 2000), it tends to be more prevalent in schools in challenging circumstances thus negatively affecting recruitment and retention in the areas of greatest need (Thomson, Blackmore, Sachs, & Tregenza, 2003). Principals who work in this context are often prepared to buck the system when necessary, and are willing to resist external interference where they feel it is detrimental to students and staff (Harris et al. 2003). They do however also attend to those systemic issues which are potentially threatening and those which can be mobilized to the school's advantage. Their prime accountability is first and foremost to the students and their families.

When first appointed, principals in these schools generally look for some 'quick' but important changes. These often mean improvements to the physical environment (painting and carpeting plant, attending to amenities such as toilets and staff rooms, and purchasing equipment and new furniture), changes to the schools' symbolic systems (e.g. assemblies, logos, uniforms) and interventions in basic management practices (ranging from communication and decision making to administrative procedures related to money, records etc). Such interruptions in the ongoing trajectory of school not only signal change, but change which improves the things that matter most to people – the everyday infrastructure that supports the work of teaching and learning. Intermediate strategies often involve strengthening relationships with families and introducing systematic CPD allied to understanding the local area and families, and also planning for change. Change in these schools is slow (Myers and Stoll, 1998; Tyack & Cuban, 1995) and principals are often frustrated by the continual policy churn of governments as with their ongoing commitments to social justice (Gewirtz, Dickson, & Power, 2002).

Several research projects reported that to be most effective, a leader's style needs to be attuned to the specific context experienced by a particular school (Carter and Jackson, 2002) and/or to the stage in a school's development (Harris, 2002; Stark, 1998; Andrews and Morefield, 1991). For example, Crawford (2004) argued that, while a charismatic leader may be effective in the early stages of turning a school round, as time goes on staff may begin to feel a lack of ownership of the school's development. At this stage, she argued, a more distributed or 'shared' style of management might be more effective in helping to implement the necessary changes. Stark (1998), in a review of the first three years of special measures, questioned the view that principals best suited to the task of turning around a failing school were likely to have an animated, dynamic, charismatic approach. In Stark's (1998) view a calmer, organizational approach could work most successfully for both failing and successful schools.

THE WORK OF THE PRINCIPALS

Accurate diagnosis of the problems faced by the school and the causes of those problems is identified in the literature as a key part of the leader's role. Sanders (1999) argues that the urban principal must develop a comprehensive understanding of the culture that exists in the urban community, identify the strengths and weaknesses of the school and district and focus on what needs to be accomplished. It was also considered important to consult others in the community in order to determine the school's priorities and precise needs (Barber, 1996; Englefield, 2001). Several writers (for example: Franey, 2002; Barber, 1996; Harris, 2002) noted the importance of ensuring that all teaching and support staff shared the principal's vision for the school.

The evidence suggests that successful principals who work in these schools invest primarily in relationship building and survive the daily demands by sharing leadership through an extended leadership team and through distributing key responsibilities to teachers (Harris & Chapman, 2002; Thomson, 1999). They find resources (time and money) to allow teachers to take up the vital work of professional knowledge production. They work to build up a staff of like-minded teachers and they often develop strong out-of-school friendships with them – particularly those in

the SMT. Qualities of the effective leader identified in a summary of the literature (NCSL, 2005) are listed below.
- Accessibility (Sebring and Bryk, 2000; Andrews and Morefield, 1991)
- High visibility (Andrews and Morefield, 1991)
- Consistency (Reynolds et al., 2001; Ofsted, 2000)
- Integrity and an ability to engender trust (Hopkins, 2001; Sebring and Bryk, 2000)
- Creating a common sense of purpose (Stark, 1998)

The work of leading and managing in challenging school contexts relies heavily on trust and reciprocity. Evidence suggests however that these principals are often caught in a double bind where systemic emphasis is placed on individual performance of schools and the individual leadership of the principal rather than collective performance or collective leadership (Blackmore & Thomson, 2004). Some writers (Franey, 2002; Carlson et al., 1999; Sanders, 1999) have noted that effective school leaders spread leadership responsibility school-wide by building teams throughout the staff of the school. Franey (2002), describing her own experiences as a new principal of an urban school, reported that she had established small teams that included both teaching and support staff. These teams were supported by continuing professional development, and it was intended that they would provide opportunities for flexible, creative, project-specific working.

A clear focus on a limited number of goals has been identified as a key characteristic of effective and improving schools (Hopkins, 2001; Reynolds et al., 2001). Connell (1996) studying schools that had moved from the category of poorly performing schools in New York found that a common denominator of success was a focus on students' academic achievement, and that all had developed new instructional strategies. Teddlie & Stringfield (1993) likewise found that in ineffective schools in Louisiana heads focused less on core instructional policies than in effective schools. Other researchers have similarly stressed that a focus on teaching and learning is crucial, something which can be encouraged by training staff in specific teaching methods at the start of the school's improvement effort (Hopkins, 2001; Johnson, 1999).

The importance of setting and demonstrating high standards of teaching is also emphasized in several studies (Andrews and Morefield, 1991; Englefield, 2001; Harris, 2001). In their discussion paper, Andrews and Morefield (1991) pointed out that effective principals made themselves available to staff as an instructional resource, and in this way set expectations for the continual improvement of teaching and learning across the school. Several other writers have also highlighted that effective principals focus on raising pupil achievement (Ofsted, 2000; Carlson et al., 1999;

Carter, 1999). For example, when summarizing the common features of leadership in schools that were more effective than others in similarly disadvantaged areas, Ofsted (2000.) noted the importance of identifying raising achievement as the school's central purpose in school plans. Effective headteachers in challenging circumstances were also found to monitor and evaluate pupils' achievement effectively (Englefield, 2001; Carlson et al., 1999; Carter, 1999).

COMMENTARY

The research evidence consistently points to the fact that leading and managing in high poverty locations is qualitatively different from leading in more advantaged contexts. Although these schools may share certain external pressures and operational issues this is where the similarity ends. Unlike 'effective' or 'improving' schools which consistently share similar characteristics (Sammons et al., 2000) the inherent complexity of schools in poor neighborhoods means that they do not readily share common conditions or features. As Hargreaves (2004, p. 30) has recently argued 'underperforming schools are not all alike, the reasons for or nature of their underperformance vary greatly'. Thomson (2000; 2002) has developed a framework for analyzing how macro social and economic changes, national, state and local education policies and ongoing local school trajectories come together and illustrates how this delimits what it is that principals can accomplish (Smulyan, 2000).

In short, each school in challenging circumstances is unique and has its own particular histories, issues and possibilities. This points towards the need for differentiation of leadership approaches and school improvement strategies (Chapman & Harris, 2004; Stoll, 2004) as each school requires its own specific combination of interventions, resources and directions. But these schools also share some common issues: they are under scrutiny from policy makers and school systems; and in some parts of the world (USA, UK, Australia and some Canadian provinces) they have suffered significantly as a result of neoliberal reform policies that have marketized schooling and polarized still further geographically and socially divided societies (Pacione, 1997a, 1997b)[5]. As a consequence of the nature of the communities they serve, they need to have closer connections with other public services such as health and welfare; they often have difficulty attracting and retaining well qualified staff; and they are very often enrolled in multiple policy projects which steer what they do (Johnson, 1999; Riddell, 2003). This requires greater systemic recognition and action than is the case at present (Thomson, in press).

At their best, schools that are improving in difficult circumstances are marked by high degrees of innovation, strong staff cultures of support and inquiry-based collaboration, with opportunities for students, teachers and parents to develop strong leadership roles. An unintended consequence of developing teachers in such a culture is that they are likely to be attractive to other schools, thus causing staff turnover and destabilizing progress (Reynolds, Clarke, & Harris, 2004). When these schools are working well, there is a strong and demonstrated commitment to the view that all students can learn and that their learning must be accelerated, at the same time as practices that cater for difference are investigated and developed. This professional activity is accompanied by a sense of 'realism' through which the impact of social, economic and political processes is acknowledged and recognized.

LEADING IN SCHOOLS IN POOR COMMUNITIES: HOW DO WE KNOW IT?

An overview of the literature reveals that there are four major strands of research that have focused upon issues of leading and managing schools in high poverty contexts. The first strand seeks to answer the question **"what works?"** particularly in relation to the type of leadership and school improvement identified (Carter, 2002; Chapman, 2002; Franey, 2002; Harris, 2002; Harris & Chapman, 2002; Potter, Reynolds, & Chapman, 2002). This research highlights the challenges faced by those who lead and manage the schools which serve the poorest neighborhoods and communities (Harris & Chapman, 2002; Henchley, 2001; Keys, Sharp, Greene, & Grayson, 2003; Leithwood & Steinbach, 2002). Data have been largely drawn from interviews with 'effective/successful/outstanding heads'. This body of work seeks some generalisable principles to inform the field and practice. The evidence from this group of studies points towards leadership as a shared or distributed entity. Recent evidence highlights however that not all schools in challenging circumstances have the internal capacity to support leadership in this form (Harris & Chapman, 2004). We see this work as primarily producing information from leadership 'cases'.

The second strand comprises accounts and stories by individual heads, sometimes written by successful or outstanding heads themselves as a memoir **"I did it my way"** (Hampton & Jones, 2000; Meier, 1995; Monroe, 1997; Stubbs, 2003; Tompkins, 1998; Winkley, 2002; Harris et al. 2006). Some of these accounts reinforce leadership as being primarily an individual endeavor despite references to empowerment of staff. Others are life histories written by researchers and tend to be more theorized but essentially they are based on first person accounts of leading schools in difficulty (Rizeborough, 1993; Tomlinson, Gunter, & Smith, 1999). Both narrative approaches seek to tell an exemplary theory-building narrative from which others might gain insights about the process and practice of leading schools in difficulty.

The third strand of work uses ethnographic approaches to ask "**What is going on here?**" by in depth explorations of schools in disadvantaged neighborhoods. Some of these studies focus specifically on leadership, (Lingard, Christie, Hayes, & Mills, 2003; Thomson, 2003), while some chart the life of particular disadvantaged schools and consider leadership as part of the equation (Gewirtz, Ball, & Bowe, 1995; Lipman, 1998; O'Connor, Hales, Davies, & Tomlinson, 1999; Tittle, 1995). Other studies take a city or 'area' approach in which leadership activity is highlighted (Thomson, 2002). This group of work seeks to contribute to the analysis of the (re)production of inequality and disadvantage. It takes a socio-political and critical stance on the structural and cultural factors that continue to impinge upon and constrain schools in disadvantaged communities.

This strand of research also seeks to ask' **What might schools/leaders do to help all children succeed**? Shields (2003) and Edwards (Shields & Edwards, 2005) take the view that heads must develop cultural expertise that is both intellectual and lived and practice dialogue. Ryan (2003; 2005) argues not for distributed leadership but for anti-hierarchical schools in which the different contributions of people with different skills and perspectives are honored. *The Sage Handbook of Educational Leadership* (English, 2003) contains several chapters that outline alternative approaches to leading and managing schools in high poverty locations. Lyman and Villani (2004) stress the importance of understanding the economic and political causes of poverty, their imbrications with localities and race, and the need for heads to become advocates for democracy and human rights. Miron and Lauria (2005) suggest that schools in inner cities need to focus on the political identities of their students and how these are formed in and through schooling. These writings draw on a range of critical, feminist and postcolonial theorists as well as empirical research.

The final strand of enquiry consists of action research studies undertaken by schools themselves, sometimes in partnership with university researchers. Here schools ask **How can we find out how to do better for all students and in so doing, make it happen?** Such reports are often unpublished, appear in professional journals or official education system publications.

The strengths and weaknesses of each research strand are summarized in appendix 1. In this analysis we are not making a case for one of these strands of research over another as we see each as important but each requiring further development and interconnection. The main thrust of our argument is that the research base about leading in schools in poor communities is atomized and that there is a need for more multi-method and multi-disciplinary approaches to exploring leadership practice in all contexts.

FILLING THE RESEARCH GAPS

There remain important areas which none of the four research trends addresses adequately. There are nine points which we wish to highlight, although clearly this is not an exhaustive list:

(1) Too little of the research 'comes clean' about the everyday reality of principals in disadvantaged schools and tends not to explore the compositional impact of dealing with:
– Variable teaching quality and proficiency
– Ongoing crises that require continual management (illness, death, violence, abuse etc)
– Constant external interference
– Doing more with less
– Unfavorable social mix of students and how this is produced
– Managing truancy and retention issues
– Negative effects of competition and choice and ethically managing cooperation and competition with neighboring schools
– Unrealistic expectations about raising performance
– Developing community involvement
– Working with multiple agencies whether one thinks this is a good idea or not
– Working beyond the school through systemic and professional organizations to advocate for the needs of disadvantaged schools and their communities

(2) Too little of the research examines the particular curriculum and pedagogical knowledge required of principals e.g.
– Literacy is a major barrier to educational attainment and heads need specific educational expertise in this area
– Dealing with diverse school populations is an ongoing curriculum, pedagogical and policy issue and heads need to be expert in inclusive pedagogies

(3) More research is needed that looks more deeply at the practices of leaders other than the disadvantaged school principal i.e. students, governors, district personnel and parents. The relationships principals establish with parents, local government, local community leaders and organizations is also a comparatively blank research canvas.

(4) More research is needed not only into how to manage and lead in hostile and managerial cultures/structures, and how leaders can influence

others to change these circumstances. While the case has been made for teachers as leaders, we need more research into how teachers can effectively lead change.

Specifically, we suggest that:

(5) A stronger set of research in each of the four strands needs to be developed, viz.

– to cover different locations, including schools in diverse national contexts

– include longitudinal studies that use multiple data sources and modes of analyses

– represent the diversity of leadership practice and the diverse gender, ethnicity and race 'identities' of principals

– compare work in high poverty schools with those in more affluent localities

– examines questions of recruitment, selection and induction of heads in urban schools

(6) Research which brings each leadership strand together with other related literature in the same tradition e.g 'what works' in leadership in disadvantaged schools with 'what works' in pedagogy and curriculum

(7) Research which is more empirically explicit, methodologically sophisticated and better theorized and which produces more reflexive accounts of the research process, and

(8) Research which has a specific focus on the specific CPD and training needed for principals working in areas of rural and inner city disadvantage (c.f. Wallace & Rogers, 2001). Given the current interest in the US on specific training for inner-city principals, it is perhaps surprising that so little in this area currently exists. We note however the development of urban leader standards within the NCSL (Brighouse, 2005; National College for School Leadership, 2005a, 2005b) and the prospect of more focus on this area.

Finally

(9) It has been argued that researchers in separate paradigms too often lack both the desire and language to speak with each other because of their different understandings about knowledge (Rhodes 2000). We suggest that researchers from different strands, disciplines and theoretical traditions urgently need to work together to address some of the gaps identified in the research literature. In the first instance, more reading across the traditions would be useful. Cherryholmes (1999) proposes that it is useful for researchers to break out from the grip of the framework they most frequently use. Cherryholmes (1999:8) suggests that a 'reading' rather than a 'researching' approach takes researchers outside the paradigms that lock

them into mutually exclusive ways of viewing a research issue. He argues that all research reports can be read differently from various theoretical perspectives. This 'multiple' T approach requires people to drop preconceived positions and to deliberately attempt to work across various knowledge and methodological standpoints. There is little precedent for this type of approach in education, which is not so much mixed methods as mixed methodologies/epistemologies, let alone in the educational administration field. Some examples can be found within gender/race research (e.g. Honan, Knobel, Baker, & Davies, 2000; Lather, 1991).

We propose that future leadership research needs to be longitudinal, empirically explicit in design, multi-method in orientation. It should embrace the diversity of leadership practice use multiple data sources and modes of analyses, be comparative and ultimately theory building. A comprehensive review of the leadership literature (Hallinger and Heck, 1999) identified certain 'blank spots' (i.e. shortcomings in the leadership research) and 'blind spots' (i.e. areas that have been overlooked because of theoretical and epistemological biases) within the field. Many of these 'blank' and 'blind' spots remain as researchers adopt methodologies that simply cannot penetrate the complexity of leadership practice in schools in all communities but especially in the poorest communities. If we are to have a more complete and sophisticated understanding of leadership in schools in the most disadvantaged settings we urgently need new ways of knowing and new methodologies to take us there.

REFERENCES

Andrews, R. L., & Morefield, J. (1991). Effective leadership for effective urban schools, *Education and Urban Society, 23*(3), 270–278.

Barber, M. (1996). Creating a framework for success in urban areas. In M. Barber & R. Dann (Eds.), *Raising Educational Standards in the Inner Cities*. London: Cassell.

Blackmore, J. (1999). Troubling women. Feminism, leadership and educational change. Buckingham: Open University Press.

Blackmore, J., & Thomson, P. (2004). Just 'good and bad news'? Disciplinary imaginaries of head teachers in Australian and English print media. *Journal of Education Policy.*

Carlson, K. G., Shagle-Shah, S., & Ramirez, M. D. (1999). *Leave No Child Behind: a Baker's Dozen Strategies to Increase Academic Achievement.* Chicago: Chicago Board of Education.

Carter, K., & Jackson, D. (2002). Introduction – leadership in urban and challenging contexts: perspectives from the National College for School Leadership, School Leadership & Management, *22*(1), 7–13.

Carter, S. C. (1999). No Excuses - Seven Principals of Low-Income Schools Who Set the Standard for High Achievement. Washington, DC: The Heritage Foundation.

Carter, K. (2002). Leadership in urban and challenging contexts: investigating EAZ policy in practice. *School Leadership and Management, 22*(1), 41–59.

Chapman, C. (2002). Introduction- schools in challenging and urban contexts. *School Leadership and Management, 22*(3), 239–241.

Chapman, C., & Harris, A. (2004). Strategies for school improvement in schools facing challenging circumstances. *School Leadership and Management, 22*(3), 41–59.

Cherryholmes, C. (1993). Reading research. *Journal of Curriculum Studies, 25*(1), 1–32.

Cherryholmes, C. (1999). *Reading pragmatism.* New York: Teachers College Press.

Crawford, M. (forthcoming). Challenging circumstances: the role of distributed and intensified leadership. In R. Bennett & L. Anderson (Eds.), *Rethinking Educational Leadership: Challenging the Conventions.* London: Sage/Paul Chapman.

Day, C., Harris, A., Hadfield, M., Tolley, H., & Beresford, J. (2000). *Leading schools in times of change.* Buckingham: Open University Press.

Englefield, S. (2001). *Leading to Success: Judging Success in Primary Schools in Challenging Contexts.* Nottingham: National College for School Leadership.

English, F. (Ed.). (2003). The SAGE handbook of educational leadership. *Advances in theory, research and practice.* Thousand Oaks: Sage.

Franey, T. (2002). The "Smart Story": the challenge of leadership in the urban school, *School Leadership & Management, 22*(1), 27–39.

Gewirtz, S., Dickson, M., & Power, S. (2002, September 11-14). Governance by spin: the case of new Labour and Education Action Zones in England. Article presented at the European Conference for Educational Research, Lisbon.

Gray, J. (2001). *Causing Concern but Improving: a Review of Schools' Experiences* (DfEE Research Report 188). London: DfEE.

Greene, K., Keys, W., & Sharp, C. (2002). *Successful Leadership of Schools in Urban and Challenging Schools: a Review of the Literature.* Annotated Bibliography. Unpublished report.

Gray, J. (2004). Frames of reference and traditions of interpretation: Some issues in the identification of 'under-achieving' schools. *British Journal of Educational Studies, 52*(3), 293-309.

Hallinger, P., & Heck, R. (1996) Reassessing the principal's role in school effectiveness: a critical review of empirical research 1980-1995 *Educational Administration Quarterly, 32*(1), 5–4.

Hampton, G., & Jones, J. (2000). *Transforming Northcote school. The reality of school improvement.* London: RoutledgeFalmer.

Hargreaves, A. (2004). Distinction and disgust: The emotional politics of school failure. *International Journal of Leadership in Education,* 27–43.

Harris, A. (2002). Effective leadership in schools facing challenging contexts. *School Leadership and Management, 22*(1), 15–26.

Harris, A., & Chapman, C. (2002). Effective leadership in schools facing challenging circumstances. Nottingham: National College for School Leadership. Retrieved from http//www.ncsl.org.uk/research.

Harris, A., & Chapman, C. (2004). Towards differentiated improvement for schools in challenging circumstances. *British Journal of Educational Studies, 52*(4).

Harris, A., Muijs, D., Chapman, C., Stoll, L., & Russ, J. (2003). *Raising attainment in the former coalfield areas.* Moorfoot: Department for Education and Skills.

Harris, A. (2002). Effective leadership in schools facing challenging contexts, *School Leadership & Management, 22*(1), 15–26.

Hopkins, D. (2001). *Meeting the Challenge: an Improvement Guide for Schools Facing Challenging Circumstances.* London: DfEE.

Honan, E., Knobel, M., Baker, C., & Davies, B. (2000). Producing possible Hannahs: theory and the subject of research. *Qualitative Inquiry, 6*(1), 9–32.

Johnson, M. (1999). *Failing school, failing city.* Oxfordshire: Jon Carpenter Publishing.

Keys, W., Sharp, C., Greene, K., & Grayson, H. (2003). *Successful leadership of schools in urban and challenging contexts.* Nottingham: National College for School Leadership.

Lather, P. (1991). *Feminist research: with/against.* Geelong: Deakin University Press.

Leithwood, K., & Steinbach, R. (2002). Successful leadership for especially challenging schools. In *International handbook of school leadership.*

Lingard, B., Christie, P., Hayes, D., & Mills, M. (2003). *Leading learning: making hope practical in schools*. Buckingham: Open University Press.

Lyman, L., & Villani, C. (2004). *Best leadership practices for high-poverty schools*. Lanham, Maryland: Scarecrow.

Meier, D. (1995). *The power of their ideas. Lessons for America from a small school in Harlem*. Boston: Beacon Press.

Miron, L., & Lauria, M. (2005). *Urban schools: the new social spaces of resistance*. New York: Peter Lang.

Monroe, L. (1997). *Nothing's impossible. Leadership lessons from inside and outside the classroom*. New York: Public Affairs.

National College for School Leadership. (2005a). *Chartered urban leader status. Guidance for governors, headteachers and aspiring school leaders*. Notitngham, UK: National College for School Leadership.

National College for School Leadership. (2005b). *A model of school leadership in challenging urban environments*. Nottingham: National College for School Leadership.

Office for Standards in Education (2000). *Improving City Schools*. London: Author.

Office for Standards in Education (2002). *The Annual Report of Her Majesty's Chief Inspector of Schools 2000/01*: Standards and Quality in Education. London: Author.

Pacione, M. (1997a). The geography of educational disadvantage in Glasgow. *Applied Geography*, *17*(3), 169–192.

Pacione, M. (Ed.). (1997b). Britain's cities. Geographies of division in urban Britain. London: Routledge.

Power, S., Warren, S., Gillbourn, D., Clark, A., Thomas, S., & Kelly, C. (2003). *Education in deprived areas. Outcomes, inputs and processes*. London: Institute of Education, University of London.

Rainwater, L., & Smeeding, T. (2003). *Poor kids in a rich country. America's children in comparative perspective*. New York: Russell Sage Foundation.

Reynolds, D., Hopkins, D., Potter, D. and Chapman, C. (2001). *School Improvement for Schools Facing Challenging Circumstances: a Review of Research and Practice*. London: DfEE.

Rhodes, C. (2000). Reading and writing organisational lives. Organization. *Speaking Out, 7*(1), 7–29.

Riddell, R. (2003). *Schools for our cities. Urban learning in the 21st century*. Stoke on Trent: Trentham.

Riseborough, G. (1993). Primary headship, State policy and the challenge of the 1990s: An exceptional story that disproves total hegemonic rule. *Journal of Education Policy, 8*(2), 155–173.

Sanders, E.T.W. (1999). *Urban School Leadership: Issues and Strategies*. Larchmont,

Ryan, J. (2003). *Leading diverse schools*. Dordrecht: Kluwer.

Ryan, J. (2005). *Inclusive leadership*. San Francisco: Jossey Bass.

Sebring, P. B., & Bryk, A. S. (2000). 'School leadership and the bottom line in Chicago', *Phi Delta Kappan, 81*(6), 440–3.

Shields, C. (2003). *Good intentions are not enough. Transformative leadership for communities of difference*. Lanham, Maryland: Scarecrow Press.

Shields, C., & Edwards, M. (2005). *Dialogue is not just talk. A new ground for educational leadership*. New York: Peter Lang.

Stark, M. (1998). 'No slow fixes either: how failing schools in England are being restored to health.' In: L. Stoll & K. Myers (Eds.), *No Quick Fixes: Perspectives on Schools in Difficulty*. London: Falmer Press.

Smulyan, L. (2000). *Balancing acts. Women principals at work*. New York: State University of New York Press.

Stoll, L. (2004, October 21–23). Failing schools: Towards more differentiated understanding and approaches to improvement. Article presented at the Jacob Foundation Conference on Educational Influences.

Stoll, L., & Myers, K. (Eds.). (1998). *No quick fixes. Perspectives on schools in difficulty*. London: Falmer.

Stubbs, M. (2003). *Ahead of the class. How an inspiring headmistress gave children back their future*. London: John Murray.

Thomson, P. (1999). Against the odds: developing school programs that make a difference for students and families in communities placed 'at risk'. *Children's Issues*, *3*(1), 7–13.

Thomson, P. (2000). Like schools, educational disadvantage and 'thisness'. *Australian Educational Researcher*, *27*(3), 151–166.

Thomson, P. (2002). *Schooling the rustbelt kids. Making the difference in changing times.* Sydney: Allen & Unwin Trentham Books UK.

Thomson, P. (2003). No more Managers-R-Us! Researching/teaching about head teachers and 'schools in challenging circumstances'. *Journal of Education Policy*, *18*(3), 333–345.

Thomson, P. (in press). Leading schools in high poverty neighbourhoods: an encounter with the National College for School Leadership. In G. Whitty & C. Vincent (Eds.), *The international handbook of urban education*. Dordrecht: Kluwer.

Thomson, P., Blackmore, J., Sachs, J., & Tregenza, K. (2003). High stakes principalship: sleepless nights, heart attacks and sudden death accountabilities. Reading media representations of the US principal shortage. *Australian Journal of Education*.

Tittle, D. (1995). *Welcome to Heights High. The crippling politics of restructuring America's public schools.* Columbus: Ohio State University Press.

Tomlinson, H., Gunter, H., & Smith, P. (Eds.). (1999). *Living headship. Voices, values and vision.* London: Paul Chapman Publishing.

Tompkins, J. (1998). *Teaching in a cold and windy place. Change in an Inuit school.* Toronto: University of Toronto Press.

Tyack, D., & Cuban, L. (1995). *Tinkering toward utopia. A century of public school reform.* San Francisco: Jossey Bass.

Wallace, M., & Rogers, G. (2001). Potentially aspiring headteachers in small Welsh primary schools: educational professionals that policy forgot? *School Leadership and Management*, *21*(4), 441–461.

Winkley, D. (2002). *Handsworth revolution. The odyssey of a school.* London: Giles De La Mare.

APPENDIX 1

	Case study	Life story	Ethnography	Action Research
Strengths	Precise descriptions of practice Accessible to practitioners Useful in CPD	Produces nuanced situated standpoint narrative which can be of interest to leaders/managers particularly neophytes Useful for CPD Stories have historical importance	In depth, rich accounts of practice Of interest to policy practitioners and scholars Shows ecology of school in context – rich description. Connects strongly with other accounts of poverty e.g area studies (Lupton, 2003; Peel, 1995) Of historical interest May produce strong policy recommendations	Produces real change in schools. Creates ownership among school community. Works from and with the particularities of the situation Follows timeline of the project rather than imposed deadlines. Stories of use to other schools.
Methodological Issues	Interview basis depends on informants' veracity. Multiple informants would produce more robust data. Snapshot data has inbuilt weakness, need for more fine grained longitudinal studies. Studies which use multiple sources of data, including observation, and also which consist of multiple visits over time are needed. Need to build up multiple studies of different schools in different locations	Based on multiple interviews over time which shows change May not include taken for granted issues unknown to interviewers Does not seek other views Could include documentary and photographic evidence and structured memory work, but rarely does	Time consuming to undertake Delay may render implications redundant as events overtake study Can use multiple and mixed methods 'Going native' and ethical paradoxes are perennial problems	May be methodologically sloppy e.g. May generate more date than can be handled, may use wrong research tools to produce data. reflection stages may be rushed, may not have access to all data required for reconnaissance. May be inadequately resourced May disrupt the very teaching and learning it seeks to improve. May not be documented. Lack of generalisability
Critique	Critique is made of positivist format – this is "truth"	Takes interview data as truth Critique is also	May work both too finely and too abstractly for	Lack of criticality and research know-how can produce research

	List of generalizations homogenize and contradict claims to uniqueness and difference Furthermore, some practitioners find the lists of practices alienating (Baskwill, 2003) Can reinforce the stand-alone school as the unit of change	of its hermeneutic nature – and in the case of autobiography, subjectivism and narcissism Can reinforce the centrality of the single heroic leader	findings to be of use to schools May not produce useful generalizations Can dodge the agency of the school to focus on structural and policy issues	which appears 'pragmatic' but is in reality a mélange of approaches which fails to dig into the epistemological and methodological issues: it may simply reproduce a positivist approach
Influence issues	Research becomes quickly dated as the educational and political world shifts Funders are not yet prepared to support longer and more in depth projects Doe not have broader policy take	May be too specific and singular to be of intended use Not of interest to funders No policy take	Critical stance is not acceptable to all funders, particularly governments May focus on policy to the detriment of the everyday	Not taken seriously by academy. Knowledge created rarely enters scholarly literatures. Seen by policy makers as a domesticated form of research useful to meet predetemined outcomes.

12. THE POSSIBILITIES FOR EDUCATIONAL RESEARCH AND ACTIVISM IN POST-KATRINA NEW ORLEANS

INTRODUCTION

In today's world, certain events, such as 9-11 or the post-Katrina flooding of New Orleans, rise to another level. More precisely, in such instances, we are confronted by two events, the image event and the real event (Baudrillard, 2002).

> The role of images is highly ambiguous. For, at the same time as they exalt the event, they also take it hostage. They serve to multiply it to infinity and, at the same time, they are a diversion and a neutralization.... The image consumes the event, in the sense that it absorbs it and offers it for consumption. Admittedly, it gives it unprecedented impact, but impact as image event (p. 27).

Where modern philosophers have contrasted the differences between appearances and reality (for example, Plato's Allegory of the Cave), under extraordinary conditions, Baudrillard (2002) describes the image and the real as inseparable, feeding one off the other so that the borders of image and reality are indistinguishable, and essentially become fictional. Baudrillard (2002) continues:

> We try retrospectively to impose some kind of meaning on it, to find some kind of interpretation. But there is none... And, against this immoral fascination (even if it unleashes a universal moral reaction), the political order can do nothing (p. 30).

What Baudrillard (2002) attributes to the 9-11 acts of terrorism and its insidious relationship to political and moral systems governing the world is relevant, too, to the image event of the natural disaster, Hurricane Katrina. In New Orleans, there were the images of poor, American Blacks trapped inside of the Superdome and the Convention Center, prior sites for spectacles of sport and global business. Given the realities of the educational and economic systems, not just in New Orleans, the post-Katrina image events were from the beginning being interpreted as a failure

T. Townsend and I. Bogotch (eds.), The Elusive What and the Problematic How: The Essential Leadership Questions for School Leaders and Educational Researchers, 181–194.

of the nation politically, socially, racially, economically and educationally. As people waited for their government to rescue them, their hopelessness was already seeded in the absence of mindful political and educational leadership which failed the people.

Where were the institutions of society that might allow these others, life-long residents of New Orleans, to have the capabilities to consider alternatives that were certainly not beyond anyone's imagination? That is, the flooding of New Orleans was a known-reality of science, history, and fiction. Yet, watching the people trapped in New Orleans demonstrated how empty and powerless the post hoc interpretations were. Therefore, for Baudrillard (2002), among the many interpretations are those which identify the event – 9-11 or Katrina - as self-determined, self-inflicted, as if the residents brought the flood waters to their attics. The existence of New Orleans within an antiquated system of levees and pumps become the

... enforced regulation as a product of absolute disorder, but a regulation it imposes on itself - internalizing, as it were, its own defeat (pp. 32-33).

Viewers of television or the internet were ready to believe the best and the worst, but mostly the worst, that is, news reports of looting, raping, and dying – real realities that in many instances were not confirmed then or up-to-now. In addition, the response to the event led to what Baudrillard called a substitution - that is, substituting an understandable pseudo-event, such as evacuating residents and then the rebuilding of the city by the same powers whose policies and practices had led to the city's own destruction. The need to make sense of this event or, at least establish blame for the events, while still trapped within already established model-dependent thinking was and still is the primary human responses to understanding and interpretation of the events. To Baudrillard, this thinking and acting is inadequate.

Throughout this event, the mass media was in New Orleans providing real time images through on-the-ground reporting of thousands of still photographs and video clips. Within weeks, CNN had published Katrina: State of Emergency (2005). For all who saw the event as it unfolded, the book retold the story as "a small easterly wave, forming off the coast of Africa" (p. 9), a full 11 days before it became a tropical storm over the Bahamas, before on August 25th, it became a Category 1 hurricane hitting North Miami Beaches, and, ultimately, before it became a Category 5 hurricane on August 28th in the Gulf of Mexico. There were pictures of evacuees fleeing New Orleans under a mandatory evacuation ordered by Mayor Ray Nagin. The march to the Superdome as a shelter followed by Katrina hitting landfall slightly east of New Orleans at 6:10 AM as a

Category 4 storm. Then came the devastation from Grand Isle, Louisiana to Pascagoula, Mississippi to Mobile Alabama to Pensacola, Florida. Images of flooding all along the gulf coast, caused primarily by 20 feet storm surges battering the coast and traveling 40 miles inland were shown over and over again.

Then, another imaginable and already predicted worst case scenario: the breeches in the levees surrounding New Orleans. All of which were already captured at the very moments by not-so-anonymous AP photographers named John Bazemore, Eric Gay, Dave Martin, William Colgin, Peter Cosgrove, Mari Darr-Welch, and Ben Sklar (CNN Reports, 2005). There were CNN, AP, Reuters, the local *Times-Picayune* reporters and photographers, all there and capturing the images for newspapers, television, and the world-wide web. For most in the audience, the pictures told stories of New Orleans that had nothing to do with the French Quarter, Bourbon Street, the street cars along St. Charles, Mardi Gras, or Jazzfest. Only the name Superdome was as prominent in the news, now as it was then. But the differences in the two Superdome meanings only heightened people's knowledge of the city and the disaster itself.

THE ROLE OF EDUCATIONAL RESEARCH

Within the city, within this media event, the question of doing educational research takes root. How do we as educational researchers in post-Katrina New Orleans justify the realities of the causes of destruction and the rebuilding described in a previous chapter on school reform? If the analysis is grounded in traditional theories, for example, effective schools research, and traditional methods of research have proven to be inadequate in instances that do not require rebuilding, then what new educational theories or research methods must we try to create to meet the present and ongoing situations?

Which research questions matter most? How do educational researchers link the rebuilding of New Orleans as a city to the rebuilding of schools as both immediate and long-term concerns? What does rebuilding mean? How does rebuilding differ from school effectiveness or improvement? How do we identify leadership, formally or informally? Who is really in charge? Whose plans should be followed? Is there a plan or a theory?

Even in Years 2 and 3, post-Katrina, one of the most prominent educators in the city told the *Times-Picayune*, "The state has told us that we don't have a philosophy of education. I told them, 'You're right.' We haven't had the time to sit around and theorize. We're trying to get schools open" (Riedlinger, June 4, 2006). Why is it okay for the National Hurricane Center to state that there is no science yet to predict the number, the locations, the intensities, and the directions of hurricanes, – the natural cause of this disaster – while educational policymakers and the public demand that educators state a priori educational theories while trying to open more and more schools after the storm? Everyone understands the realities that research is being conducted in order to learn about hurricanes - apart from the images of the hurricanes themselves. Yet, when it comes to educational research, educators are asked to recite yesterday's theories in order to justify today's educational leadership actions. In science, we look for new evidence and hopefully new predictive theories. In education, why have we been trapped by the dominant ideology of educational research that has created a cause and effect mindset such that the political and pedagogical demands on education are inconsistent with scientific discoveries?

The paradox between science and education is striking. That is, New Orleans and the nation ignored already existing scientific research provided to the media, the Army Corp of Engineers, academics, etc. about the dangers of a hurricane, the inadequacies of the canal pumping systems, and the levees themselves. Likewise, there have been numerous studies, many published by the authors of this chapter documenting both the successes and failures of New Orleans' schools for over two decades. In other words, research – when available – is not only ignored in education, but it is also ignored in public policy as well. We know that neither the Hurricane Center nor the Army Corps of Engineers nor the New Orleans school system was adequately funded for many years prior to Katrina: coincidence or policy? Given these realities, how should educational researchers proceed in the on-going study and rebuilding of New Orleans schools?

In education, policymakers and educational leaders demand research-based innovations. For researchers, this mantra appears to be good news, justifying the painstaking data collection and analysis procedures that go into all research projects. However, the facts tell a very different story: how relevant were previous research studies? In New Orleans, would prior research now be used to rebuild the cities' schools? If so, how? If not, then why should educational researchers repeat the same research questions tested by traditional methods? Should we not begin to seek alterative methods of research not only in this unique event-environment, but also as a matter of professionalism?

THE HOW OF TRADITIONAL RESEARCH

Traditional methods of research, not just educational research, are well known, albeit extremely technical. Research is a profession practiced by every academic discipline and many practical fields in society. Research methods range from the scientific method to phenomenological interviews, ethnographies, symbolic interactionism, etc. Frequently, the research design makes explicit a conceptual framework taken from a priori theory or, more naturalistically, the conceptual framework emerges as grounded theory based on the methods and findings themselves. Similarly, it is up to the researcher to decide on a particular unit of analysis, be it individuals, social groups, etc. The focus of the study may be limited to behaviors, communication, culture, practice, processes, etc., all of which comprise important decisions for researchers who do their work systematically. That is, words or numbers or observations become categories which are connected to other categories until the researcher arrives at a conclusion. The researcher is NOT content with telling the obvious or giving the answers to specific questions as findings. Research is not journalism. Research is analysis and interpretations. So again, the question here is how to proceed as an educational researcher inside an environment that needs desperately to be researched, archived, and remembered for all of the unprecedented actions that the people of New Orleans, teachers, administrators, parents and children were engaged in.

At the same time, if Baudrillard (2002) is correct, the purpose is not about interpretation or understanding of the political or moral order. Those were shaken to the core by the event itself. What new methods are there to capture image events that are part of the postmodern condition of realities? Except for Douglas Brinkley (2006), Michael Dyson (2006), and Spike Lee (2007), the stories being told in New Orleans are not by academicians cum researchers, but rather by journalists and people on the ground. Will these stories be adequate for developing theories-in-practice so that the rebuilt schools do not look and feel like yesterday's pre-Katrina schools?

Context Matters Especially in Unprecedented Contexts

For over twenty years, pre-Katrina, the New Orleans public schools had been engaged in chronic educational reform, "over and over again." The widely held perception on behalf of informed citizens, practitioners in and out of the system, and researchers was that, on balance, school reform had failed. Worse the children of New Orleans had suffered as a result. By most measures of achievement data, the system had failed. Put differently, the question was no longer how to "fix" a system that was chronically "broken." From the perspective of elite groups in particular, and their educational leaders like Scott Cowen, President of Tulane University, the question was how to design a new system that would continually engage in sustained "transformation."

After dismissal of the pre-Katrina school superintendent for fiscal mismanagement, the question on the mind of the general citizenry was: could any measure—short of fundamental overhaul—salvage a deeply dysfunctional educational system. Katrina provided this opportunity, both as a result of human and natural disasters (Brinkley, 2006).

One hope lay in a new concept, for New Orleans, of charter schooling. Another hope rested on historical patterns of selective admission to public schools. The latter has a long history of promoting and realizing academic successes in the New Orleans' public schools. On the West Bank of New Orleans, a small cluster of schools came together in the Algiers Charter School District. In post-Katrina New Orleans, the schools would not operate via selective admissions; rather, they would enrol anyone if space allowed. This policy puts a great burden on public school educators as do any and all high educational expectations for the city. It also creates a tension and fear among educators that everyday practices might revert back to pre-Katrina school days, damaging significantly any vision for change and rebuilding. Thus, the high stakes of failure could conceivably work against the hopes for academic excellence and world class curricula. These were the dynamics locally, statewide, and nationally that educational researchers faced as they considered action steps to rebuild New Orleans schools.

Who we are and what we did

The event for rebuilding schools was labeled the educational summit. It was the first staff development session for new principals, their assistant principals, and the school leadership teams prior to opening of schools Post-Katrina. The researchers were independent and from out of town, having accepted an invitation from the Greater New Orleans School Leadership Center as well as the Algiers Charter School Association. The researchers, both the authors as well as a larger team of researchers invited to New Orleans, came from different geographical and philosophical locations. All invited had had close ties both to the new Director/Superintendent, Dr. Brian Riedlinger, and to the city itself. Three of the researchers, Scott Bauer, Ira Bogotch, and Luis Miron, were former professors at the University of New Orleans, where Dr. Riedlinger had received his graduate education. Dr. Bauer had also worked closely with Dr. Riedlinger on staff at the Greater New Orleans School Leadership Center. The other external consultant invited initially was Dr. Kenneth Leithwood, who had a longstanding contractual agreement with the School Leadership Center as its evaluator.

From the beginning, it was made clear to us that our presence was not to do research per se [there was no prohibition, however, on doing research], but rather to support and counsel Dr. Riedlinger in his own on-going work as an educational leader heading the Algiers Charter School Association. While we came as consultants, concerned friends, and professional development educators, our professional training and temperaments come from the profession of doing research. Nevertheless, the first task for all of us was to learn about what was happening on-the-ground. For this reason, we did not come with any predetermined research questions nor our institutions' Human Subjects' permission to collect data and conduct research. We did collect data, of course. And, in so doing, we followed the protocols of researchers. That is how we have been socialized and educated professionally to do no harm in the field.

Day One

Our initial group meetings were with Dr. Riedlinger. We listened to him as he described the establishment by the state of the Algiers Charter Schools Association. We listened more than we asked questions. When we did ask questions, they were more for our own clarification: what was the difference between the Algiers' charters and other charters under the titular authority of the Orleans' Parish School Board and the Louisiana State Department of Education? Dr. Riedlinger asked us to sit with him and listen to presentations by the turnaround consultants hired by the city and the mayor. We all took notes, again, for our own understanding of what was happening and what were the unique structures that had been established to control the city's schools. We learned of the State's takeover of what is still called the Recovery District – schools that had failed to meet the minimum standards established by the state for more than one year previously. We heard also of issues of past mismanagement. The words and examples were not fully explained. Nevertheless, the idea emerging was that the new system or more likely the many new systems would all be held fiscally and educationally accountable by the State through monitoring by external accounting firms such as the Boston Consulting Group and Alvarez and Marsal.

Subsequently, we met with the administrators of the newly established schools. To repeat, all of us had long histories in New Orleans and we had known many if not all of these school leaders – principals and assistant principals. The work in group settings was cordial and comforting. Again, we mostly listened. When asked what we thought, we spoke candidly. Individually, we offered ideas for how to proceed, primarily by supporting these leaders and in bringing together ideas around the concept of a World Class curriculum.

All of us took notes; all of us explored ways in which we could help. All of us returned in January for a second visit. At that time, the schools were up and running for about one month. Our first day, we spent with the principals and assistant principals; the next day with the schools' leadership teams comprised of selected teachers. As always, we debriefed with Dr. Riedlinger sharing our impressions of the day's events.

The research community

One consequence of Katrina was that it has become a metaphor used and appropriated by those who did not know [or care about New Orleans in particular] in a personal sense. A kind of post-Katrina cottage industry has emerged whereby scholars would drop the name Katrina and New Orleans or the word "turnaround" into their speeches or writings without first hand knowledge of what the actual people there felt, needed, or desired. Again, if Baudrillard (2002) is correct, such repositioning of the researcher as truthteller is inadequate for this image event. Nevertheless, future researchers will have to decide for themselves how to untangle the media images from realities.

Educational Research

Educational research traditionally comes after the fact, after actions have been taken. But when an event so catastrophic happens, there is no time for traditional research methods. As researchers, we are living in new circumstances and new times. Researchers need to rethink their traditional methods, their questions, their systematic analysis, and their so-called objectivity. In this particular case, there were no precedents that could even be used as analogies. This was not akin to school improvement, school restructuring, or school reform, but rather something called school rebuilding – a new and different concept for educators who had been accustomed to working inside of large, on-going, and very predictable systems, structurally, politically, and ideologically.

Words to describe the past system ranged from scandalous to the worst in the nation. Much of the language was hyperbole. Yet, the language gave opportunities to national, state, and local policymakers to follow their own ideological ideas regarding schools and rebuilding. As researchers with professional and personal connections to the people in the schools and the communities, for us, none of the past conditions of the city's schools, however bad, could be compared to the loss of lives and property in post-

Katrina New Orleans. Therefore, something new-as opposed to our sense of reform needed to happen out of necessity as well as professional desire. Specifically, the participants themselves were the story in a unique way. That is, the tragedies of New Orleans were not limited to communities from which the children came [so-called at risk students], but rather every teacher, every administrator had a personal story that involved losses to family and friends. It was a situation in which teachers and administrators who were ministering to others also needed ministering. In sum, everyone living and working in New Orleans is at risk on a daily basis. There is no pre-determined future for the schools or the city. At the same time, however, there were children in New Orleans and, for an educator that means just one primary thing: that is, educate the child. Get the child back into a school setting and begin teaching. The world outside of New Orleans was still in place and moving; these children, who were still there, had to be brought back to the routines of teaching and learning. The question for Dr. Riedlinger, the designated educational leader in Algiers, and the researchers was whether these routines would be the old routines or something different.

The Major Challenge to Understanding

There are tangible tensions across capturing stories, rebuilding on the fly, and writing results in a valid and reliable method so that the stories, data, practices could withstand external and often critical scrutiny. In some sense, therefore, the role of the researchers, too, was to minister, to validate, to report, to bring hope from the outside world to New Orleans. The decision to bring in "external" consultants who were themselves insiders in the lives of the people was an initial source of comfort to all. Even the administrators who had no past relationship with the consultants heard testimonies of past commitment to public school improvement in the city. But this history and our presence were at best symbolic. We were not living the at risk realities of the participants. At the end of the day, we would be flying home. Nevertheless, the power of symbols became important for all of us. Even the name given to our visits – Summit I and Summit II – had a symbolic meaning that was far greater than our contributions could actually be. But good leaders, and we found many in New Orleans, know well how to use symbols and symbolic meanings to carry forward.

Our educational research methods seem to be inadequate for three reasons: First, our research in New Orleans has been subsumed under the images of the media. Our written and spoken words cannot compete for public attention with Anderson Cooper, CNN's photo-essays, Time

Magazine articles, Douglas Brinkley's *The Great Deluge*, or Spike Lee's *Children of the Storm*. Secondly, we work under the scrutiny of university Institutional Review Boards, the ethical principal "to do no harm," and our profession's peer-reviews. Our objectives, however, go beyond this ethic as we actively strive "to do good," not just avoid doing harm. In instances involving social injustices, the harm has already affected the lives with whom we have a research relationship. Moreover, the institutional constraints on educational research seem to be even stricter than the legal and moral constraints placed on the media, who themselves are subject to scrutiny and legal action. Thirdly, in contrast to media, scientific and technological research, we have limited resources as educational researchers. Without extensive resources, we cannot compete with rock star professors, CNN, AP, Reuters, or non-academic book publishers. Thus, real events within public schools are subsumed by the image events recorded by others (Baudrillard, 2002; Boorstein, 1961/1987); thus, educational research has fewer opportunities, from conception to publication, of making a difference for the public good.

Have we made a difference?

On face value, educational leaders in New Orleans had little choice but to do something fundamentally different. Having charter schools district wide in a system where only one school had reopened by Thanksgiving, out of a total of 128, made the conditions for quick reform ideal. It did not hurt, moreover, that the federal government promised a grant of up to $20.9 million to launch the massive experiment in school reform (http://www. nola.com/newslogs/tporleans/index.ssf?/mtlogs/nola_tporleans/archives/20 05_10_08.html). In June, the school district faced a $35 million shortfall when the state entered into a Memorandum of Understanding with an accounting firm, Alvarez & Marsal, who had offices throughout the world as turnaround consultants (http://www.nops.k12.la.us/content/board/minutes/ 2005/bmin060905s.pdf.). The district was also in danger of failing a federal audit of its $300 million operating budget, as auditors had already disclaimed its 2004 financial statement.

Alvarez & Marsal's proposed to contract out non-instructional services such as cafeterias and food purchasing, payroll, and transportation. The services would be strengthened by the waving of union rules granted to the charter district, post-Katrina. Further, the charter school system's free market hiring process for teachers coupled with a curriculum unencumbered by interference from central office bureaucrats altered the educational landscape in New Orleans dramatically. Statements to the contrary would have to be examined critically.

Likewise, Scott Cowen's dual role as transformation architect and the leader of Tulane University's effort to restructure its institutional mission in the wake of Hurricane Katrina served him well. He had previously consolidated the partnership with Lusher Charter School Uptown and a nearby companion high school, Fortier, with a grant of $1.5 million to the school. Thus he appeared to embrace the movement to charter the district. However, the Orleans Parish had voted 4-2 in October to charter all 13 schools on the West Bank. This seemed markedly inconsistent with the stated process of the education subcommittee of the Bring Back New Orleans Commission (Nagin, 2005). This process on face value appeared to call for research, analysis, and evolutionary change leading to sustained transformation. Among other elements, these processes suggested the following:
- Conduct case studies of America's top performing schools
- Conduct an extensive literature review of best practices of high performing schools
- Conduct a thorough analysis of pre and post Katrina school performance and capacity

At the very least, the birth of the Algiers Charter School Association did not align well with the rapid fire pace of the opening of these reconfigured schools in December, and especially with the near overnight decision of the Orleans Parish School Board and the State to approve the charter licenses for the 13 schools. Moreover the rapidity of events may make achieving long term political legitimacy and institutionalization of governance arrangements problematic. From the perspective of critical social theory, we observed the inconsistencies between what appear clear moves toward a market-driven model for school reform embedded in the charter schools and the calls for sustained educational transformation from the chair of the education committee of the Bring Back New Orleans Commission, Tulane President Scott Cowen.

In the short term, it appears that the process of transformation embedded in the call for sustained change must embrace the disposition of research to slow down long enough to (1) maximize community, school and parental input and (2) make school demographics equitable.

A NEW RESEARCH PARADIGM: WITHIN-SCHOOL ACTIVISM

We do not advocate abandonment of traditional research methods including data collection methods. Data are necessary to making sound political and research judgments-even in image events. For this reason, we worked with the school leadership teams in Algiers to conduct surveys of their constituencies including students. Among the many dramatic stories happening in New Orleans, one stands out and is reflected in the initial data collected.

O. Perry Walker High School was considered one of the worst high schools in the city pre-Katrina. In rebuilding, its new principal, Mary Laurie, welcomed students back with an apology. "I apologize for every adult who said you couldn't learn and every school in chaos," she said at a first-day assembly. "We failed them. If we don't acknowledge that, we're never going to change . . . We've got to get it right. If not this time, when? We will never get this chance again." That message was not delivered just once and then forgotten. Laurie has repeated it again and again.

The results of such leadership appear promising. In the first ever customer satisfaction survey after Katrina, the following parental results came in regarding Walker High School.

As a parent, my input is sought after and valued at my child's school					
	Never	Sometimes	Often	Almost Always	Always
O.Perry Walker	10.9	20.2	6.4	11.6	50.9
Compared to last year-do you agree this year's school experience was better?					
	Don't Agree	Somewhat Agree	Agree	Mostly Agree	Always Agree
O.Perry Walker	1.5	1.9	2.7	36	57.9
Overall my child's school is doing a good job					
	Don't Agree	Somewhat Agree	Agree	Mostly Agree	Always Agree
O.Perry Walker	1.7	3.9	16.7	5.8	72

For comparative purposes, we do not have pre-Katrina data because parents were not asked these or similar survey questions – especially in schools with the kind of reputation of Walker High School. Post-Katrina is different. Principal Mary Laurie and others are bringing new leadership paradigms to New Orleans' public schools, for now.

CONCLUDING THOUGHTS:

How can educational research stay or become more relevant in today's media-oriented world? Without Douglas Brinkley, Anderson Cooper, or

Spike Lee, how often and effectively will the stories of school rebuilding be told? Will image event stories be more effective than research in the short and long-term? Or, will image events consume educational research, rendering the latter powerless? In Lee's *Children of the Storm*, Mary Laurie, the principal highlighted in the previous section was on camera for no more than five seconds, modestly acknowledging the featured student who was shooting the film. There was no context or appreciation of Ms. Laurie's leadership. That said, is educational research sufficient for telling on-the-ground stories of school rebuilding and educational struggles?[1] How many other educational leadership stories are being told? Being ignored? How can we learn from the everyday practices of school rebuilding and contrast them with school improvement efforts as we know them from our literature? What is the place and pace for systematic research methods in a world that has lost patience with the medium and texts of research writing and reading? How can educational research compete with image events? It cannot. What then is the future of educational research?

Nevertheless, we received feedback from the Algiers Schools' leadership teams regarding Year 1 post-Katrina professional development. Principals, APs, and teacher-leaders were asked to rank their professional development activities. "Native Eyes", the name given to the work described here and in Chapter 6, was ranked first or second by the participants (Reidlinger, personal communications, September, 2006). Again, what was it that we really did? We listened and the participants knew we heard them. As natives, too, we did not need to interpret what they themselves had experienced and knew intimately and better than we could ever know.

POSTSCRIPT

By the time this chapter is being read, New Orleans' schools will be in its fourth year of operation post-Katrina. There will have been more policies written by the State of Louisiana, more schools opened [hopefully] by either the Recovery District or the Orleans Parish School Board itself. There will be [hopefully] greater cooperation between communities and the schools. There will be more for-and not-for-profit proposals to open charter schools. But the question is whether the rebuilt schools will be substantively better than before. Regardless of research methods, the answer, hopefully, will be yes.

NOTES

[1] Bloggers, investigative news paper reporters, and concerned citizens such as Carl Bernofsky, April Capochino, and Steve Ritea report on-line and in print for Tulanelink.com, the Times-Picayune, LinkedIn and other sources. Their on-the-ground reporting has helped researchers like us who are not in New Orleans stay current with events.

REFERENCES

Baudrillard, J. (2002). *The spirit of terrorism*. London: Verso.
Boorstein, D. (1961/1987). *The image: A guide to pseudo-events in America*. New York: Vintage.
Brinkley, D. (2006). *The great deluge*. New York: HarperCollins.
CNN News (2005). *Katrina: State of emergency*. Atlanta: CNN.
Dyson, M. *Come hell or high water; Hurricane Katrina and the color of disaster*. New York: Basic Civitas Books.
Lauria, M., & Miron, L. (2004). *Urban Schools: The New Social Spaces of Resistance*. New York: Peter Lang Publishing, Inc.
Lee, S. (2007). Children of the Storm: Soledad O'Brien & Spike Lee *Tell Katrina Stories, Through Teens' Eyes*. CNN Productions.
Nagin, R. (2005). *Bring Back New Orleans Commission*. http://www.bringneworleansback.org/

13. FOSTERING CULTURAL COMPETENCE THROUGH SCHOOL-BASED ROUTINES

Mrs. Matthews has just called Mrs. Baker, a 5th grade teacher, into her office. Mrs. Matthews was standing in the doorway of a 2nd grade classroom when she overheard Mrs. Baker talking to another teacher two doors away. "I can't work with these kinds of students. They are overly confrontational, disrespectful, and most of them are significantly below grade level. Their parents never respond to my many invitations to visit the classroom to see how their children are doing. If I knew that teaching would be like this, I never would have gone into the profession." As Mrs. Baker sits down, Mrs. Matthews says, "I was in the hallway yesterday and heard your conversation. I didn't realize that you were having problems with some of the students."

Mrs. Matthews, a second year principal at Lennox Elementary, realizes that she has an awesome task ahead. Lennox Elementary, an urban school, serves over six hundred students. Sixty-five percent of the students are African American, 32% are Hispanic, and 3% are European American. In contrast, 75% of staff members are European American, 15% are African American, and 10% are Hispanic. Many of the students come from impoverished homes as evidenced by over ninety percent of the population qualifying for free or reduced lunch. The school has been continuously plagued with a significant student mobility rate (approximately 15% per year), an ever increasing teacher turn over rate (40%, 50% and 57% respectively for the last 3 years), failure to meet state testing standards (on the last state-wide testing an average of 70% of the population failed to met high standards in reading while an average of 59% of the population failed to met high standards in mathematics), and a lack of parental involvement (only 35% of parents regularly attend school functions).

Mrs. Matthews must develop and implement a plan to help move her school in a positive direction by improving teachers' cultural competence as they work with a very diverse population. What might Mrs. Matthews plan look at, and how could she ensure that it is implemented effectively?

T. Townsend and I. Bogotch (eds.), The Elusive What and the Problematic How: The Essential Leadership Questions for School Leaders and Educational Researchers, 195–214.
© *2008 Sense Publishers. All rights reserved.*

THE ADMINISTRATOR'S ROLE IN DEVELOPING TEACHERS' CULTURAL
COMPETENCE THROUGH SCHOOL ROUTINES

Culturally sensitive learning communities are schools where the leaders have intentionally shaped the culture and acted to ensure that all members, adults and students, are learners, and where teachers and other community members address challenges and issues, particularly those related to student learning (Taylor, 2002). The development of these culturally sensitive learning communities, where students feel welcome, safe, and important members of the school body, and where teachers feel confident in their abilities to bring about student success, is a deliberate process. When students feel valued as individuals and teachers know that their needs are important in the eyes of local administrators, each party will do their best to create a positive school environment. School administrators must realize that, as leaders of the school community, the environmental climate begins with them, is communicated to staff members, and significantly impacts students. Therefore, they must ask themselves these questions: "Do I help my teachers to feel empowered as they work with diverse students?" "Do my teachers have a positive outlook on all students' academic and social performance?" "Do my teachers feel that they have the necessary skills to succeed in a multicultural environment?"

Administrators can use the following three routines to foster cultural competence in teachers. The first step in this process is to make efforts to become aware of today's changing society. Awareness and acknowledgment of the changing school demographics serves as a starting point toward gaining an understanding of the impact of this change on teaching and learning. Then, administrators can share their newly developed belief and vision for a successful school to their staff. The next step in this process calls for administrators to ensure that staff professional development addresses issues of cultural diversity as an integral part of school procedures. Educators will need to develop a solid knowledge base of strategies that can be used to promote student achievement and administrators will need to facilitate this process. The final step in this process requires that administrators assign specialists who are experts in multicultural education to assist teachers in designing instruction. Educators will need additional support beyond the professional development sessions, to ensure appropriate implementation and use of the information.

Administrators should be aware of today's society, how it impacts schools, and shape their belief and vision for a successful school.

Administrators need to be aware that public school students are becoming more diverse, socially, economically, and linguistically. By 2012, the western

United States will no longer have any racial or ethnic majority. Changes in the demographics of cultural groups will continue to modify the face of U.S. schools from monoracial, monolingual environments to multiracial, multilingual, multicultural institutions. In fact, more than six million children in U.S. schools speak a language other than English at home, and more than 150 languages are spoken throughout the nation's public schools (Matczynski, Rogus, Lasley, & Joseph, 2000; Gay, 2004).

In addition to the changing faces of today's school populations, educational reforms focusing on the development of new standards for students have become more commonplace. Most states have begun to create standards for graduation, new curriculum frameworks to guide instruction, and new assessments to evaluate students' knowledge. However, the success of students from diverse backgrounds continues to be of great concern. For example, on national assessments in reading, writing, mathematics, and science, African-American students' performance continues to lag behind that of European American students, with no progress toward closing this gap.

Meanwhile, the organization and daily functions of schools are changing more slowly. Most schools are organized to only prepare about 20% of their students for "thinking work"—those students are tracked very early into gifted and talented, advanced, or honors courses. These opportunities are least available to African American, Latino, and Native American students. As a consequence of structural inequalities in access to knowledge and resources, students from racial and ethnic minority groups in the United States face persistent and profound barriers to educational opportunity (Darling-Hammond, 2000).

With these discrepancies between culturally diverse groups, educational achievement, and day-to-day school functioning, it is imperative that administrators develop a vision of success for their school, and effectively impart this belief and vision to their staff. In order to impart their belief and vision they first have to acknowledge cultural diversity in the school. Administrators need to recognize the impossibility of cultural neutrality among fellow administrators, staff, and students, because individuals make assumptions and base their expectations about others as a result of first language, and race, and the school environment is no different from the general population. Therefore, attempting to be color-blind in a school where diversity exists may impede the goal of providing the best education for all students. Administrators must use forums like professional development, faculty meetings, one-on-one conferences/conversations with teachers, and grade level learning team meetings to address diversity by raising questions about cultural dilemmas, including beliefs about linguistic, ethnic, and ability differences (Murtadha-Watts & Stoughton, 2004).

The academic growth of many diverse students oftentimes requires the tireless efforts of teachers. Administrators can take advantage of every opportunity to publicize and celebrate even the smallest incremental gains in student achievement, letting both the teachers and students know that their efforts and contributions are appreciated and recognized. Displays of public recognition can take place during daily morning or afternoon announcements and/or school assemblies. Before teachers begin to work with diverse students; they must know: (a) they will be held to high professional standards (e.g., treat all students with dignity and respect), (b) all teachers will be expected to meet high expectations in their professional work, and (c) all staff members will be expected to support and facilitate these expectations for the betterment of the entire school. In order for any of these expectations to begin to hold, administrators must be regularly seen around the school interacting with both teachers and students (Sather, 1999).

Administrators should ensure that staff (professional) development addresses the issues of cultural diversity as an integral part of school procedures.

Professional development for teachers, designed to raise their cultural awareness and better prepare them to differentiate instruction for diverse students, is crucial to teacher and subsequently student performance. Administrators should ensure that these professional development activities involve more than disseminating information or instructional strategies. It must be systematic and continual (White-Clark, 2005). Because school districts typically inform schools about when to conduct professional development activities, it is important that local administrators provide input into the kinds of training teachers receive to make sure that multicultural awareness is a regular part. One specific area of focus may include aspects of learning the English language and general conventions of communication. This will ensure that the achievement gap between English language learners and native English speakers will gradually become smaller as all students will be better prepared for high stakes testing (Thomas & Collier, 2003).

Professional development opportunities can influence how teachers think about the issue of addressing cultural differences in the classroom, and can expand their understanding of the diversity versus disability problem, and is therefore a critical component of teachers' professional growth. Administrators must make this practice an integral part of school procedures (Voltz, Brazil, & Scott, 2003; Klotz, 2006).

*Administrators should assign specialists who are experts in multicultural
education to assist teachers in designing instruction.*

It is essential for administrators to establish a support system for teachers as
they learn to work diverse students. By putting support systems in place,
they can establish a climate that embraces diversity and encourages
teachers to be more receptive to new ideas and instructional approaches to
meet the needs of their culturally diverse students (White-Clark, 2005). A
partial list of professional personnel who may provide support and their
roles includes: (a) behavioral specialists can observe children in the
classroom, prepare functional behavioral assessments, and work with the
teacher to develop behavior support plans (b) social workers can work with
families around problems that the child is experiencing at school, and in
some cases, develop behavior support plans for the home (c) instructional
specialists can be assigned to the classroom and to individual children as
needed. These individuals can model instructional strategies, co-teach
lessons, provide feedback to teachers, and provide extra instructional
support to students. They can also be helpful in implementing behavior
support plans and monitoring progress, and (d) a member from the child's
cultural background can be included in the Individualized Education Plan
(IEP) meeting, if it is determined that the student may be eligible for
special education services as a result of academic deficiencies or behavior
problems. These support systems provide additional perspectives and
approaches to the professional development process while teachers develop
their ability to work with students of different cultures (Warger & Burnette,
2000; Borko, Wolf, Simone, & Uchiyama, 2003; Boothe, 2000; Klingner &
Artiles, 2003; Smith-Davis, 2004). Along with the close support of experts
in the field of multicultural education, teachers' cultural competence can be
further enhanced when administrators establish a personal working
relationship with them, helping them to realize that they are a part of the
school's decision-making process and not mere recipients of its regulations.

BUILDING STRONG CULTURAL COMMUNITIES THROUGH ADMINISTRATOR AND TEACHER TEAMS

As stated earlier, one of the ways in which administrators impart their
belief and vision for a successful school environment is though dialogue
with staff members. Dialogue between administrators and teachers is
extremely important as it is the primary means by which both parties will
learn from each other about culturally competent practices. Before any
dialogue between administration and teachers can take place, however,
teachers must know that they can trust that their administrator is working in

the best interest of the students and the entire school staff. Therefore, administrators must strive to make the school environment a non-threatening place where staff members feel comfortable enough to voice their opinions, ideas and concerns (Taylor, 2002). Through culturally focused dialogue, they can begin to see how social and historical forces affect their own students, advantaging some and disadvantaging others. An example of a culturally focused dialogue would be one where school leaders recognized a deficit model of teaching and learning and brought it to the attention of faculty as a schoolwide, ongoing concern. Questions that could be raised during these dialogues include: (a) Are teachers and supervisors aware of diversity in learning styles? (b) Are a variety of approaches used to assess mastery and competence of standards? (c) How are people of color portrayed in the curriculum? (d) Are multicultural library and media materials available to support instruction? Concerns that could be raised include: (a) student attendance and behavior, and (b) gains in student learning (Murtadha-Watts & Stoughton, 2004; Williams, 2001; Gideon, 2002).

An important goal for administrators is to pose these types of questions and critical issues to teachers, work with them and as a result identify instructional practices that engage students' specific interests and prior knowledge. Such dialogue brings to light the problems inherent in teaching that avoids cultural responsiveness; the goal should be to draw attention to ways in which teachers can develop culturally responsive teaching practices. School leaders must work with teachers, observing and creating analytical self-reflective notes about their teaching and helping them to be honest about their assumptions about the curriculum. They must also work with teachers to provide learning that truly engages students and at the same time is authentic, rigorous, and thought provoking (Murtadha-Watts & Stoughton, 2004; Riehl, 2006). Learning communities enable administrators and teachers to learn from one another and expand knowledge and teaching strategies to increase their ability to effectively help students from diverse cultures. Some of these strategies involve daily routines that teachers can use to foster culturally competent pedagogy (Craig, Hull, Haggart, & Perez-Selles, 2000).

THE TEACHERS' ROLE IN DEVELOPING CULTURAL COMPETENCE THROUGH SCHOOL ROUTINES

Many teachers enter the workforce with inadequate preparation to implement culturally responsive pedagogy based on a sound foundation of cultural competence. This lack of preparation has resulted in a reliance on less effective methodology that may consist of minimal, fragmented content, such as discussing holidays, reading a limited amount of multicultural literature, or having international food fairs (White-Clark, 2005). The development of cultural competence that later translates into actual teacher practices cannot be limited to preservice course work, inservice training sessions, or community-based experiences. In addition, there must be a concerted effort by both teachers and administrators to bring multicultural concerns and issues to the "front and center." (Nieto, 2000, p. 81). The prospects of teachers developing cultural competence as a result of chance or a limited number of university courses or experiences that may or may not take place, make it vital for educators to take the responsibility to develop, implement, and maintain activities that are embedded in the existing routines of the school. Teachers can use the following ten routines to enhance their cultural competence as they teach students from diverse backgrounds. They can: (a) take an introspective look at your own culture along with your feelings toward culturally diverse students, (b) classroom meetings, (c) arrange classroom discussions that highlight cultural diversity, (d) engage in one-on-one conversations with students from diverse backgrounds, (e) use multicultural literature for personal and professional development, (f) use multicultural literature in the classroom, (g) find and use strategies that have been proven to work with minority students, (h) use culturally responsive classroom management strategies (i) seek the guidance of a mentor, and (j) establish sound parent relationships.

Taking an introspective look at culture

According to Pang (2001), teachers, who look introspectively, think seriously, critically, and honestly about their own views of cultural diversity and culturally diverse students (as cited in Ford & Trotman, 2001) improve the achievement levels for their students. During this time of self-reflection, teachers analyze their own feelings toward those who are culturally different, determine how it relates to the dominant culture, and think about what frame of reference influences these feelings. Two critical tasks exemplary teachers can undertake to develop cultural competence are (a) learn about each student, taking a personal interest in establishing a positive relationship and (b) consistently questioning one's self in order to clarify several salient issues (i.e., examining one's own biases, assumptions, and values) (Howard, 2003; Weinstein, Curran, & Tomlinson-Clarke, 2003). Introspection is a private activity that must be conducted on terms that each teacher finds personally comfortable. It is also possible to openly discuss some of the thoughts one may have after taking the time to "draw conclusions," about current knowledge, required knowledge, and future directions regarding culture. Thus, it is possible for teachers to conduct forums in which they, along with their students, openly talk about culture and its implications.

Minor and Sandler (2000), relate a story about Jenny, a fictitious Caucasian teacher on the road to developing cultural awareness, who realized, during her introspective moments, that she was perceiving others through her own cultural biases. Jenny interpreted the behavior of those around her using a narrow "cultural filter," that was informed by her own experiences and notions. It was difficult for her to "see past," this strict interpretation of behavior. Like Jenny, as teachers come to realize their biases, assumptions, and stereotypes, they begin to recognize how these assumptions influence their teaching and relationships with minority groups.

Self-analysis can be difficult and cause a great deal of discomfort. When teachers make an attempt to reflect on their own experiences and try to determine how these experiences may have played a part in shaping their professional practices, it can be helpful to use a guide. By using a guide, teachers can consider information from a broader view and be prompted to consider issues that may have been left uncovered without the assistance of an outside source. Bromley (1998), created a self-assessment tool that teachers can use to examine their assumptions and biases. Some of the questions included in the assessment are:
- What are my perceptions of students from different racial or ethnic groups?
- What are the sources of these perceptions (e.g., friends, relative, television, movies)?

After careful introspection, teachers must then try to find commonalities to connect the dominant with the minority culture(s) in their classrooms in order to build a global community (Corbin & Ledford, 2002).

In schools, teachers can engage in introspection as part of the planning or preparation period on a daily, weekly, or monthly basis. Teachers can examine the reliability of the self-assessment tool by comparing results on a regular basis. The results can be used for further self-reflection or shared with a mentor (described below) or even during classroom meetings (described below).

Classroom meetings

Classroom meetings are formal gatherings, when teachers designate time to interact with students and discuss issues pertaining to a host of "classroom issues." These issues may include, but are not limited to, (a) a new student entering the class, (b) a conflict among two or more peers, and (c) an upcoming social event. The meetings are intended to allow the classroom teacher and the students to understand the issue and agree upon a manner in which to "deal with the issue" (Edwards, & Mullis, 2003; Frey, & Hallie, 2001).

Classroom meetings can be scheduled on a regular basis or as-needed. The delicate nature of classroom meetings must also be mentioned here. Conducting discussions about student to student conflict and/or teacher to student conflict can be intimidating for any teacher in any classroom situation. Teachers must be prepared for discussions "going the wrong way," and have a distinct plan for dealing with such issues. This fact does not diminish the usefulness of classroom meetings, but rather highlights a cautionary note for teachers to understand the delicate nature of dealing with classroom interactions.

In schools, teachers can conduct classroom meetings at almost any time during the school day, as a morning exercise where the teacher chooses one day twice a month to directly discuss methods to effectively interact with others or an emergency meeting, when an unpleasant incidence between students takes place and the event is used as a catalyst to generate a discussion that requires students to reflect on what has taken place and identify possible actions for the future to promote harmony among classmates. In the beginning, classroom meetings require a systematic approach and teachers should have a thorough knowledge of themselves and their students. In addition, before the meetings can be used on a regular basis the classroom teacher must work with students and collaboratively establish discussion ground rules to maintain order and social decorum. Specifically, teachers should adhere to the following steps:
– Ask students to move into their discussion configuration (e.g. a circle or semi-circle with the teacher in the middle).
– Call the meeting to order and identify the purpose of the meeting.
– Identify the issue of the day
– Discuss considerations for the issue (e.g. the cause of the conflict, and students involved)
– Create positive solutions.
– Identify possible barriers to solutions
– Implement the solution
– Evaluate the usefulness of the solution

Arranging classroom discussions that celebrate cultural diversity.

A classroom discussion is a formal approach for students to learn content associated with different cultural groups and how this content contributes to a better understanding of all members in the school community. There are several ways in which to facilitate this approach. First, teachers can invite culturally diverse civic leaders, business leaders, artists, writers, members of the police and fire department, college professors, and academically successful high school students to the classroom to talk about their heritage and their road to success (Banks, 2001). These talks can then lead to an open discussion among the visitors, students, and teacher. Second, teachers can use popular literature-specifically, magazines and other periodicals, to supplement the curriculum. This type of literature not only serves to increase the knowledge base of teachers, but also serves as a resource for lesson planning. Supplementing the curriculum may also provide culturally diverse students with an opportunity to learn about high-achieving individuals who come from backgrounds similar to their own (Jairrels, Brazil, & Patton, 1999). If materials contain inaccuracies, omissions, or distortions, then teachers need to help students question the content in order to assist them in overcoming possible feelings of alienation (Villegas & Lucas, 2002). Third, teachers can simply arrange specific times for informal "show and tell" classroom discussions. Here, students are encouraged to share aspects of their culture, such as rituals, dress, and food through means by which they feel comfortable (Brownell & Walter-Thomas, 1997). They can relate stories their parents have told them, experiences they have had while visiting or living in their native countries, or books they have read about aspects of their culture. Also during this time teachers can ask questions to clarify misconceptions, ask for explanations, and gain suggestions from their students. Classroom discussions require the active participation of teachers and students. Oftentimes, teachers will ask students to "share experiences," without contributing to the conversation. Multicultural education is built on the contributions of all teachers and students regardless of background (Cruz-Janzen, 2000).

In schools, discussion forums help all students enhance self-esteem and gain pride in their culture when they see their backgrounds valued in classroom reading and other activities (Montgomery, 2001). Teachers who discuss these issues are saying to children that culture is important and must be represented accurately. It also communicates to students that they are respected and validated, which in turn, serves as the basis for a meaningful relationship between teachers and students (Villegas & Lucas, 2002).

Engaging in one-on-one conversations with students from diverse backgrounds

To further develop a deep understanding of diverse students, teachers can engage in private conversations with them. According to Ford and Trotman (2001), most teachers recognize that positive student-teacher relationships are the foundation for students' school success. Culturally responsive teachers make a conscious effort to connect with students on an interpersonal level.

Jenny (the fictitious teacher described in Minor & Sandler, 2000), related her experience of a one-on-one meeting with one of her students after she grossly overreacted to an incident between two African American students whom she thought were on the verge of fighting. Jenny's reaction to the "non-fight," was met with much criticism from her seventh grade class. In an effort to understand herself and why she had misunderstood the situation, she decided to ask for clarification. This was the conversation she had one afternoon after school.

> "Jenny, I was wondering, is there a difference between how kids act when they're just angry and how they act when they're going to fight?" "Of course," he said, looking at me as if I was crazy. "Like what? Will you show me?" Jenny explained that he could tell if an argument would become a fight by very specific phrases and gestures people would use. He instructed me that, "Some words are just arguing words, but other words are definitely fighting words. You have to be really careful what you say." I was really impressed by how adept he was at reading signs that were a mystery to me (p. 39).

Jenny realized that she was so busy teaching her students that she had not thought about what she might learn from them (Minor and Sandler, 2000). Not only will one-on-one conversations serve to edify the teacher, they will also communicate to the student that their ideas and opinions are valued, and important enough to receive the teacher's undivided attention. Private conversations will also help students to feel more comfortable expressing themselves openly to teachers, which will lead to improved classroom performance.

In schools, teachers can identify several opportunities throughout the day to engage in one-on-one interactions with students. They can arrange to talk with them before classes begin, eat lunch with them, meet with them for brief conversations during times of independent student practice activities, or talk with them as they wait for transportation home.

Using multicultural literature for personal and professional development

Using multicultural literature calls for the teacher to "engage with text on a personal and professional level." Reading and seeking to understand the profiles, experiences, and commentaries on different cultural groups introduces teachers to material that can help present similarities and differences. As teachers interact with multicultural literature on a personal and professional level, not only will their knowledge of cultural diversity increase, their students will also come to gain a greater understanding of individuals different from themselves. On a personal level, teachers can purchase or borrow books that are written by people of color, including history, literature, and education (Minor and Sandler, 2000). Some of these books include: *Song of Solomon* by Toni Morrison, Cry, the Beloved Country, by Alan Paton, and Women of Silk by Gail Tsukinama. On a professional level, teachers can ensure that books received during training sessions are not only read, but applied in classroom settings.

Using multicultural literature in the classroom

Multicultural literature helps children identify with their own culture, exposes them to other cultures, and opens the dialogue on issues regarding diversity (Colby & Lyon, 2004). Some of these materials include: children's books, international literature, and resources found via the internet. All materials require critical examination to ensure all groups are portrayed in an accurate manner. The use of children's books in the classroom provides opportunities to examine multiple perspectives. Students can compare and contrast the five versions of The *Three Little Pigs* (see http://www.media-awareness.ca/english/resources/educational/ lessons/elementary/stereotyping/ stereotyping_and_bias.cfm). Teachers can guide students through a con-versation about cultural differences, multiple perspectives, and how the needs of culturally different families affect the teacher/learner relationship (Corbin & Ledford, 2002).

Teachers who use multicultural literature in the classroom can create a connection between themselves and students in a quest to become culturally competent and gain insight into students' cultural backgrounds. Both teacher and students will "grow" as experiences from literature are shared and related to the realities of the classroom, homes, and the community. These efforts may ultimately help teachers cultivate personal cultural competence. It is necessary for teachers to collect materials that can serve as a "bank," to be used throughout the school year to avoid the "add-on" nature of some multicultural efforts.

In schools, the use of multicultural literature can occur on several occasions throughout the day. Teachers can use these materials during read aloud activities, alternate their use with the traditional basal text, encourage students to read them independently during silent reading periods while they also engage in independent reading, and assign homework from these materials.

Finding and using strategies that have been proven to work with diverse students.

Lispson and Wixson (1997) stated that "perhaps no single factor influences the instructional setting more than a teacher's knowledge and beliefs about teaching and learning" (p. 128). Teachers need to know and implement effective instructional strategies for the benefit of their students, supported with empirical evidence with replicated results. Cultural background can have a significant influence on the way in which students receive, respond, and produce information. It is important that students also support the strategies teachers choose and perceive these strategies as valid. It is difficult to utilize instructional methods that students do not view as appropriate, fair, and beneficial (Alder, 2002).

Several instructional strategies have been identified as having application for all students, regardless of cultural background or presence of disability. Students can benefit from, (a) cooperative learning strategies and the use of community resources when designing curriculum (Matczynski, Rogus, Lasley, & Joseph, 2000), (b) recognition of learning style (Young, Wright, Laster, 2005), and (c) recognition and documentation of students' background knowledge as a starting point for academic study (Lasley & Matczynski, 1997). Recognition of the learner is one of the most significant concepts underlying any instructional strategy. McMinn (2001) discussed different methods students use to process and apply the information they receive. Many students adopt a particular method of learning and rely on this method to complete their academic tasks (students may adopt this method regardless of its proven effectiveness). If teachers are unaware of the method which students use to process information, students may either reject a useful method or fail to identify a possibly effective one that does facilitate learning. In a classroom with students from various cultural backgrounds, it is essential that teachers help students understand themselves and their notions regarding effective methods used to learn and retain material. Several questions can be posed to help clarify a students' learning profile:

– Do they prefer to participate in group discussions or are they more inclined to speak to the teacher privately?
– Are they comfortable working in collaborative groups or do they work better alone?
– Do they have a competitive nature, or do they enjoy cooperative groups? (McMinn, 2001)

Montgomery (2001) highlighted two effective culturally sensitive instructional strategies, (a) think-aloud and (b) reciprocal questioning. The think-aloud method takes advantage of the benefits of modelling. When using the think-aloud, the teacher reads a passage and talks through the thought processes for students. This shows students how to generate questions as they read, leading to a greater comprehension of the text. The reciprocal questioning method requires that teachers and students engage in shared reading, discussion and questioning. The goal is to help students learn to self-question and gain an understanding of the meaning they are constructing as they read.

When culturally diverse students' perceptions about teaching methods are taken into account, teachers are better able to provide them with the necessary support. A study conducted by Diamantes in 2002, examined the impact of obtaining information about student perception of the learning environment in order to assist science teachers in multicultural classes. Using the My Class Inventory (MCI), discrepancies were found between students' perceptions of the actual and preferred classroom environment. These results were then used to guide improvements in classroom environment. In a related study conducted by Thompson in 2000, researchers identified instructional strategies that either helped or deterred students from learning. These tenth-grade culturally diverse students perceived literature-based activities, oral practice, individual help, peer interaction, games, and use of real objects as being most helpful to them in the classroom (as cited in Curtin, 2005). The connection between teacher and student goes beyond the social relationship, but is better understood as a comprehensive relationship involving social and academic interactions that are built on the foundation of understanding how each views the purpose of school, and the most effective and efficient manner in which one can accomplish these goals. Teachers and students must have an open line of communication in order to appreciate and benefit from the relationship previously described.

In schools, strategy selection is an on-going process that teachers undertake on a number of occasions. Some teachers consider new strategies at the beginning of an academic unit, while others make weekly decisions about new and possibly more effective instructional strategies. The teacher needs to know about student progress and why students are or are not making progress. This insight will enable teachers to continuously make the "right decision" regarding the selection and implementation of instructional strategies.

Using culturally responsive classroom management strategies

One of the most fundamental elements necessary for the success of any classroom is the behavior management techniques employed by the teacher. Being able to manage classroom behavior is crucial because, perfectly written lesson plans and excellent curriculum become irrelevant if students' behaviors prevent teaching and learning from taking place. Classroom management techniques become especially important when teachers are faced with students from diverse backgrounds, whose behavior patterns may vary from dominant culture. Since approximately 86% of teachers are European-American (Gay & Howard, 2000), they must develop and use culturally responsive classroom management techniques in order to build positive classroom interactions among diverse cultures in the classroom. Teachers can (a) establish expectations for behavior, (b) show patience and caring, (c) demonstrate assertiveness and show authority, (d) ensure equitable treatment of all students, and (e) teach students to think about setting and determine appropriate behaviors.

At the beginning of the year teachers should establish clear expectations for behavior. They need to be explicit about their expectations, engage students in discussions about the class norms, model the behavior they expect, and provide opportunities for students to extensively practice these appropriate behaviors. Effective teachers usually have six general rules of conduct, and they make sure that students understand what the norm means in terms of specific behavior (Weinstein, Curran, & Tomlinson-Clarke, 2003).

Personalized care and psychological safety are important for school success. For many children from diverse backgrounds their needs are sometimes unmet in the home. Dryfoos (1998) notes that at-risk urban adolescents "lack nurturance, attention, supervision, understanding, and caring," and may have inadequate communication processes with adults in their homes (p. 37). Therefore, students' need for care must be met at school if teachers expect students to focus on academic tasks during the day (Brown, 2003; Alder, 2002). Teachers can meet the care and psychological needs of their students by patting them on the back, giving them approving nods and smiles, pulling them aside for one-on-one attention/instruction, and showing an interest in the things they enjoy.

Research in culturally responsive teaching supports teachers adopting an assertive stance with urban students. Urban teachers must explicitly demonstrate assertiveness and establish authority through their verbal exchanges with students (Brown, 2003). Because urban students expect and respond to more direct verbal commands, teachers must use this method when communicating with them (Hemmings, 2003). For example, instead of saying, "Would you please stop doing that?" It would best serve the teacher to redirect the student by saying, "Stop doing that, please."

It is important for teachers to monitor their behaviors in terms of equitable treatment of all students. Teachers must ensure that cultural differences do not cause them to treat students unfairly. They must continually ask themselves: "Am I more encouraging with some students than I am with others?" "Do I more quickly chastise some students than I do others?" "Do I make stereotypical judgments about some of my students based on their dress and actions?" "Do I have different levels of expectations for students from the majority culture than I do for students from diverse backgrounds (Weinstein, Tomlinson-Clarke, & Curran, 2004)?" Until students feel like they are truly valued and equally respected by their teachers, teachers will be unable to impact these students academically or socially.

We all behave differently in different settings. For example, we behave more formally at official ceremonies than we do at social outings. Teaching students the differences between their home, school, and community settings can help them "switch" to the appropriate behavior for each context. For example, a teacher may talk about differences between conversations with friends in the community and adults at school, and discuss how each behavior is valued and useful in each setting. While some students adjust their behavior automatically, others must be taught and provided ample opportunities to practice (Burnett, 1999).

Seeking the guidance of a mentor

Many teachers coming into the classroom are unprepared for the students sitting before them. During preservice training many teachers were only exposed to a limited number of experiences directly intended to prepare them to teach and relate to students from diverse backgrounds. How are teachers supposed to make up for this shortfall, while meeting all the other challenges of teaching? Teachers, especially those new to the profession, can benefit from the expertise of those who truly understand the steps necessary to achieve success. When teachers seek the guidance of mentors, they ask for peers, as well as administrative assistance to help support them in the development of cultural competence and effective instructional methodology. Teachers can find mentors in several ways:
– Ask or wait for their administrators to pair them with teachers who truly understand the culture of the school and students.
– Seek the assistance of teachers whom they have observed as being successful in relating to students from diverse cultures.
– Use staff development settings, specifically geared towards multicultural and related issues, to voice their needs, questions, or concerns and learn from teachers in this forum; following up with teachers who show an interest in helping them or demonstrate expertise in these workshop discussions.

– Use small group or one-on-one collaborative settings to gain the support of other teachers versed in this area.

How does seeking the guidance of a mentor help teachers build cultural competence? A support system increases teachers' effectiveness and encourages them to initiate and implement effective strategies. A support system can alleviate the feeling of "going it alone." Teachers with this kind of help will be more receptive to new ideas and instructional approaches to meet the needs of their culturally diverse students (White-Clark, 2005). Mentors can identify issues of inequalities associated with teaching racially and linguistically diverse students, and help novices to rethink their practices (Achinstein & Barrett, 2004). Teachers who have the assistance of mentors face instructional and cultural diversity challenges with experienced educators who are there to help maintain a support system designed to help them be successful.

Establishing sound parent relationships

Public schools are often a source of alienation for low income and minority parents (as cited in Harris, 1999). With such a sobering statement, how can teachers truly develop cultural awareness if they do not understand the profound role that families play in their students' outlook on the schooling environment? According to Cobrin and Ledford (2002), teachers must understand the needs of culturally different families and how these affect the teacher/learner relationship. Knowledge and understanding of the variety of family structures and systems increase the professional's ability to respond to the family's needs. In turn, respect for the diverse systems of family organization enhances the professional's effectiveness (Bruns & Corso, 2001). In short, teachers must strive to help parents of culturally diverse students feel that they are an essential part of the school environment by making sure that these parents feel comfortable enough to communicate with faculty and staff, and participate in classroom and other school-wide activities and events. How can this be done? Teachers can:
– Establish regular communication through the use of home/school notebooks, planners, newsletters, or utilize the medium of telephone calls depending on the family's preference; ensuring that written material for linguistically diverse families is in the native language. If parents cannot utilize the aforementioned modes of communication, it is also helpful to use alternatives (e.g., providing information to churches for distribution or broadcasting school information on local radio). Teachers may have to "tap into" local resources to make information accessible and widely available.

- Use respected individuals from the community and school system, such as counselors, principals, ministers, and parent liaisons, to deliver special invitations to school activities or events (Harris, 1999).
- Ensure that an interpreter is available, for linguistically diverse families, at general school or private classroom meetings to explain and or clarify information related to their child's needs.
- Ask parents to share pictures, family recipes, dramatic play props, family experiences, books, and other print materials, stories and other artifacts that reflect their cultures (Swick, Boutee & Van Scoy, 1995-1996).
- Invite grandparent to serve as assistants in their grandchildren's classrooms.
- Involve parents...in multicultural social and educational activities (Boutee & McCormick, 1992).
- Visit community cultural events (Boutee & McCormick, 1992).
- Suggest, or help to start parent education workshops and academic evening classes (Cobrin & Ledford, 2002).

When efforts are made to show parents that teachers want what is best for them and their children, the barriers impeding teacher/family relationships is removed and a new appreciation for diversity is established. Only when teachers truly understand and value their diverse classroom population will they be able to effectively teach, interact, and appreciate their students and communities.

SUMMARY

Establishing a community in which the development of cultural competence is a priority requires the joint effort of administrators, staff members, and outside entities. Each group must know that their ideas and contributions are significant to the positive growth of the multicultural environment in order for significant participation and cooperation to take place. Administrators must recognize that they are key players in the establishment of culturally competent school-based routines because the environmental climate begins with them, is communicated to staff members, and is subsequently felt by students. Therefore, they must ensure that culturally competent practices can be clearly identified in daily routines, and systems such as individual and grade-level teacher/administrator conferences, inter- and intra-departmental sharing sessions and school-wide forums.

Moreover, administrators should institute school-relevant questionnaires to evaluate the effectiveness of these practices. Only when cultural competence is fostered in schools, will diverse student populations reach their maximum potential.

REFERENCES

Achinstein, B., & Barrett, A. (2004). (Re)Framing Classroom Contexts: How New Teachers and Mentors View Diverse Learners and Challenges of Practice. *Teachers College Record, 106*(4), 716–746.

Alder, N. (2002). Interpretations of the meaning of care: Creating caring relationships in urban middle school classrooms. *Urban Education, 37*(2), 241–266.

Banks, J. A. (2001). *Cultural diversity and education: Foundations, curriculum, and teaching.* (4th ed.) Boston, MA: Allyn & Bacon.

Boothe, D. (2000). How to support a multiethnic school community. *Principal Leadership* (High School Ed.), *1*(4), 81–82.

Borko, H., Wolf, S., Simone, G., & Uchiyama, K. (2003). Schools in transition: Reform efforts and school capacity in washington state. *Educational Evaluation and Policy Analysis, 25*(2), 171–201.

Boutee, G., & McCormick, C. (1992). Authentic multicultural activities: Avoiding pseudomulticulturalism. *Childhood Education, 68*, 140–144.

Bromley, K. D. (1998). *Language art: Exploring connections.* Needham, MA: Allyn & Bacon.

Brown, D. (2003). Urban teachers' use of culturally responsive management strategies. *Theory into Practice, 42*(4), 277–282.

Brownell, M., & Walter-Thomas, C. (1997). An Interview With ...James M. Patton: Helping Teachers Understand Cultural Diversity. *Intervention in School and Clinic, 33*, 119–122.

Bruns, D., & Corso, R. (2001). *Working with Culturally & Linguistically Diverse Families.* ERIC Clearinghouse on Elementary and Early Childhood Education. Champaign IL, 1–7.

Burnette, J. (1999). *Critical behaviors and strategies for teaching culturally diverse students.* ERIC Clearinghouse on Disabilities and Gifted Education. Reston VA, 1–6.

Colby, S., & Lyon, A. (2004). Heightening awareness about the importance of using multicultural literature. *Multicultural Education, 11*(3), 24–28.

Corbin, M., & Ledford, C. (2002). Building Global Community: Connecting Cultures in the Classroom. *Delta Kappa Gamma, 69*(1), 27–31.

Craig, S., Hull, K., Haggart, A. G., Perez-Selles, M. (2000). Promoting cultural competence through teacher assistance teams. *Teaching Exceptional Children, 32*(3), 6–12.

Cruz-Janzen, M. I. (2000). From our readers: preparing preservice teacher candidates for leadership in equity. *Equity and Excellence, 33*(1), 94–101.

Curtin, E. (2005). Teaching Practices for ESL Students. *Multicultural Education, 12*(3), 22–27.

Darling-Hammond, L. (2000). New standards and old inequalities: School reform and the education of african american students. *Journal of Negro Education, 69*(4), 263–286.

Diamantes, T. (2002). Improving Instruction in Multicultural Classes Using Classroom Learning Environment. *Journal of Instructional Psychology, 29*(4), 277–282.

Edwards, D., & Mullis, F. (2003). Classroom meetings: Encouraging a climate of cooperation. *Professional School Counseling, 7*(1), 20–28.

Ford, D., & Trotman, M. (2001). Teachers of Gifted Students: Suggested Multicultural Characteristics and Competencies. *Roeper Review, 23*(4), 235–239.

Frey, A., & Hallie, D. (2001). Classroom meetings: A program model. *Children & Schools, 23*(4), 212–222.

Gay, G. (2004). The importance of multicultural education. *Educational Leadership, 61*(4), 30–35.

Geneva, G., & Howard, T. (2000). Multicultural teacher education for the 21st century. *The Teacher Educator, 36*(1) 1–16.

Gideon, B. (2002). Supporting a collaborative culture. *Principal Leadership* (High School Ed.), *3*(1), 41–44.

Harris, H. (1999). School Counselors and Administrators: Collaboratively Promoting Cultural Diversity. *NASSP Bulletin, 83*(603), 54–61.

Hemmings, A. (2003). Fighting for respect in urban high schools. *Teachers College Record, 105*(3), 416–437.

Howard, T. C. (2003). Culturally relevant pedagogy: Ingredients for critical teacher reflection. *Theory into Practice, 42*(3), 195–202.

Jairrels, V., Brazil, N., & Patton, J. (1999). Incorporating popular literature into the curriculum for diverse learners. Intervention in *School and Clinic, 28*(1), 49–66.

Klingner, J., & Artiles, A. (2003). When should bilingual students be in special education? *Educational Leadership, 61*(2), 66–71.

Klotz, M. (2006). Culturally competent schools: Guidelines for secondary school principals. *Principal Leadership* (High School Ed.), *6*(7), 11–14.

Lasley, T. J., & Matczynski, T. J. (1997). *Strategies for teaching in a diverse society: Instructional models.* New York: Wadsworth Publishing Company.

Matczynski, T. J., Rogus, J. F., Lasley, T. J., & Joseph, E. A. (2000). Culturally relevant instruction: using traditional and progressive strategies in schools. *The Educational Forum, 64*(4), 350–357.

McMinn, P. (2001). Preparing the Way for Student Cognitive Development. *Multicultural Education, 9*(1), 13–15.

Minor, V., & Sandler, S. (2000). Jenny Evans on a Journey Toward Her Students. *Multicultural Education, 8*(2), 38–39.

Montgomery, W. (2001). Creating Culturally Responsive, Inclusive Classrooms. *Teaching Exceptional Children, 33*(4), 4–9.

Murtadha-Watts, K., & Stoughton, E. (2004). Critical cultural knowledge in special education. *Focus on Exceptional Children, 37*(2), 1–8.

Nieto, S. (2000). Placing equity front and center: Some thoughts on transforming teacher education for a new century. *The Journal of Teacher Education, 51*(3), 180–187.

Pang, V. O. (2001). Why do we need this class? *Phi Delta Kappan, 76,* 289–292.

Riehl, C. (2000). The principal's role in creating inclusive schools for diverse students: A review of normative, empirical, and critical literature on the practice of educational administration. *Review of Educational Research, 70*(1), 55–81.

Sather, S. (1999). Leading, lauding, and learning: leadership in secondary schools serving diverse populations. *Journal of Negro Education, 68*(4), 511–528.

Smith-Davis, J. (2004). The world of immigrant students. *Principal Leadership* (High School Ed.), *4*(7), 44–49

Swick, K., Boutee, G., & Van Scoy (1995-1996). Families and Schools Building Multicultural Values Together. *Childhood Education, 72,* 75–79.

Taylor, R. (2002). Shaping the culture of learning communities. *Principal Leadership, 3*(4), 42–45.

Thomas, W., & Collier, V. (2003). The multiple benefits of dual language. *Educational Leadership, 61*(2), 61–64.

Villegas, M., & Lucas, T. (2002). Fostering culturally responsive teaching. In *Educating Culturally Responsive Teachers,* (pp. 65–111). Albany, NY: State University of New York Press.

Voltz, D., Brazil, N., & Scott, R. (2003). Professional development for culturally responsive instruction: A promising practice for addressing the disproportionate representation of students of color in special education. *Teacher Education and Special Education, 26*(1), 63–73.

Warger, C., & Burnette, J. (2000). Five strategies to reduce overrepresentation of culturally and linguistically diverse students in special education. ERIC Clearinghouse on Disabilities and Gifted Education. Arlington VA, 3–4.

Weinstein, C., Curran, M., & Tomlinson-Clarke. (2003). Culturally responsive classroom management: Awareness into action. *Theory into Practice, 42*(4), 269–276.

Weinstein, C., Tomlinson-Clarke, S., & Curran, M. (2004). Toward a conception of culturally responsive classroom management. *Journal of Teacher Education, 55*(1), 25–38.

White-Clark, R. (2005). Training Teachers to Succeed in a Multicultural Classroom. *Education Digest, 70*(8), 23–26.

White-Clark, R. (2005). Training Teachers to Succeed in a Multicultural Climate. *Principal, 84*(4), 40–44.

Williams, B. (2001). Ethical leadership in schools servicing African American children and youth. *Teacher Education and Special Education, 24*(1), 38–47.

Young, C. Y., Wright, J. V., Laster, J. (2005). Instructing African American students. *Education, 125*(3), 516–524.

14. CONCLUSION: 'WHAT' + 'HOW' EQUALS 'WHOW'

WHAT + HOW = WHOW!

In our Introduction, we argued that it was important to embark on a discussion that would bring educational leadership theories and practices closer together to benefit leadership activities both within schools and universities. Within schools, leadership activities bring theories to life through our actions. Within universities, leadership activities pertain to instructing future leaders and conducting better research.

Now as we come to the end of the book, we ask whether we have made our point; that is, have we brought the heretofore disparate leadership activities, the 'what' [to do] and the 'how' [to do it] closer together? Have we made it clear that when state mandates, educational laws, leadership standards, ministerial pronouncements, curricular designs and professional development programs are presented as ready-made answers to be delivered by school administrators to teachers and students that we are failing to make education come alive in ourselves and in others. We are not advocating for any specific 'what' or any specific 'how,' but rather we are calling for the explicit integration of the what and the how in terms of developing educational theories and practices. As such, the authors have demonstrated a meta-knowledge base for school leaders, for educational leadership professors, and for educational leadership researchers.

Variations of the what-how questions are central to all our studies and practices in school leadership. In today's era of accountability, the 'what' question is phrased as 'What can school leaders and teachers do to increase student achievement?' Not surprisingly, the authors here responded that while we have a great deal of knowledge, and even an emerging consensus of the 'what,' our knowledge base as both leaders and researchers is still insufficient.

THE ELUSIVE WHAT AND THE PROBLEMATIC HOW

In Part I, the authors address two related questions:
- **What do we know** about school leadership and school improvement?
- **What can we do** as leaders and researchers?

T. Townsend and I. Bogotch (eds.), The Elusive What and the Problematic How: The Essential Leadership Questions for School Leaders and Educational Researchers, 215–229.
© 2008 Sense Publishers. All rights reserved.

- In Part II, the authors addressed two different related questions:
- **How do** we know it?
- **How should** we do it?

These two sets of related 'what + how' questions build upon current knowledge and demonstrate how to create a meta-knowledge base for school leaders. In so doing, we are looking for the power of education, the 'whow!' of leadership and school improvement. This pedagogical power can come only through deeper understandings and more explicit explanations of educational aims and processes. We have three goals: to improve practice, to better instruct future leaders, and to conduct research that makes a difference for schools and universities.

KNOWING-WHAT

Harris and Thomson identified five dimensions of the 'what': vision and values, leading learning, investing in professional development, distributing leadership and community building. MacBeath focused on leading learning and how that has and will dramatically change our notions of school leadership. Das settled upon culture. Dukes and Ming called their 'what' cultural competence. Moos, Krejsler, and Koford explored the contextual meanings of leadership success, while Bogotch, Miron, and Biesta searched for school rebuilding in an unprecedented context, namely New Orleans. What is the what? Is it culture, organization, resources, vision, purpose, communications, or outreach – singularly, collectively, or in some as yet to be discovered sequence? Will the dialogic shadowing methods described by MacBeath reveal the invisible and also challenge conventional wisdom? Or, as Das says of the construct of culture, the 'what' is an 'abstract, elusive, composite.' Moos et al. question whether success can have the same meaning across nations and cultures. Bogotch et al. struggle, as empirical researchers, to distinguish reality from images and pseudo/media-events. The elusive 'what' leads us to ask: How do we know the what? Harris and Thomson take us from empirical studies to memoirs and ethnographies. Across the board, case study research designs predominate throughout this text. Why? Why have we arrived at a method that emphasizes on-the-ground, close-up views of leadership and school improvement? Is our abstract conceptions of 'what + how = whow!' premature because our knowledge base is insufficient? Do we, in fact, need to also know when, where, and why in addition to the what + how? Are we ready for equations? How can our findings compete with CNN images?

KNOWING-HOW

Elmore (2007, p. 2) has argued that 'schools improve by investing thoughtfully and coherently in the knowledge and skill of educators'. Such a view is consistent with our thesis that knowledge is the 'what' and skills are the 'how'. We argue that school leaders also need a knowledge-how. A recent OECD report (2007, p. 4) indicates:

> As countries struggle to transform their educational systems to prepare all young people with the knowledge and skills needed to function in a rapidly changing world, the roles and expectations for school leaders have changed radically. They are no longer expected to be merely good managers but leaders of schools as learning organizations. Effective school leadership is increasingly viewed as key to large-scale education reform and to improved educational outcomes.

However, Richard Elmore offers a deeper analysis of why a school leader's knowledge-how may be insufficient. He wrote (2007, p. 1):

> The problems of school quality and performance are *systemic* in nature – that is, they stem from a constellation of social, organizational, cultural, and technical factors within schools that reinforce each other to hold the system in a powerful state of equilibrium well below its potential. Complex systems produce exactly what they are designed to produce; in this sense they are highly functional at maintaining themselves, regardless of whether they are functional in terms of achieving larger social purpose.

How then are we to prepare our school leaders in ways that will not only lead to a new generation of high level student achievement, but at the same time move towards a reorganization of the complex system known as school? Standing in the way of this transformation is the accountability movement, which was purported to have been set up as a mechanism for improving student achievement, but might also be seen as a mechanism for justifying government inaction in the areas that count. Elmore further states (2007, p. 2)

> In many other systems, including all state accountability systems in the U.S. and the U.S. national policy (*No Child Left Behind*), accountability for performance is considered to be the leading instrument of policy and human investment is considered to be a collateral responsibility of states and localities, which can be exercised according to their preference. In the U.S. this situation has resulted in a disastrous gap between capacity and performance – the states and the federal government exert increasing pressure on schools to

perform, but have essentially defaulted on their responsibility for human investment, leading to an increasingly large number of low-performing schools that continue to operate at low capacity.

What Elmore is saying is that expectations have been raised (the 'what' of school improvement) without there being any consideration of building the capacity of the people expected to perform the miracles now directed at them (the 'how' of school improvement). It is clear that improving the capability of school leaders, in a range of ways and developing a new set of values, attitudes and dispositions towards the task ahead, needs to be a priority of education systems around the world. However, what is happening in too many education systems is the continued focus on the 'what' components related to school management, even though there is an imperative to start looking at the 'how' components of school leadership and school improvement.

As this final chapter is being written, the two chapter authors have been coming to grips with a new set of standards and a new set of priorities that are attached to state accreditation of school leadership programs in the state of Florida. On the other side of the world, there have been two instructive reports on education in the state of Victoria, Australia. The first (Elmore, August 2007) looks at the strategic nature of educational improvement implemented by the state government, and the second (OECD, December 2007) looks at the specific undertaking of building leadership capacity within the school system.

Given the concerns that have been expressed throughout this book, related to the delicate balance required by school leaders in terms of managing state agendas for accountability and leading local communities in ways that educate the children of those communities, it may be instructive to look in some detail at these two examples of what people involved in the education of school leaders are currently facing.

THE CASE OF VICTORIA

The first and perhaps most important thing that needs to be said about leadership development in Victoria is that it is part of a comprehensive strategic plan designed to transform the whole system. Thus, the nature of transformation has to be in line with our understanding of complex systems. Elmore (p. 1) argues

Improvement strategies have to be complex and simple at the same time—*complex* in the sense that they have to operate across a number of social, organizational, cultural and technical dimensions simultaneously, *simple* in the sense that they have to embody a clear storyline, or narrative, that everyone in the system can understand and use to give purpose to their work. Systemic strategies work to the degree that they change not only the visible features of the system, but also the values, beliefs, and expectations of the people who work in the system and their daily practice.

Elmore further argues that one of the things that 'distinguishes the Victorian approach among its peers, is the presence of a *strategic* view of school improvement'. Another is its focus on capacity building (p. 2).

From the ministerial level, through the department level, to the operating level of the public schools office, into the regions and then into the schools, there is broad agreement on the essential message that the strategy is fundamentally about investing in the knowledge and skill of people.

The starting point for this comprehensive reform was the State Government's *Blueprint for Government Schools* (DEECD, 2003) that identified both circumstances and directions for public education in the state of Victoria. After substantial discussions at state, department and school levels, three priorities for reform were identified:
– Recognizing and responding to diverse student needs;
– Building the skills of the education workforce to enhance the teaching-learning relationship; and
– Continuously improving schools.
In order to address these three priorities a series of seven 'flagship strategies' became the comprehensive action plan for moving forward. They outlined a series of actions to be taken within each strategy.

Flagship strategy 1: Student learning

– Identify a framework of 'essential learnings' for all students
– Develop the principles of learning and teaching for prep to year 12
– Improve reporting on student achievement
– Develop broad assessment processes against which defined standards of learning at key points of schooling can be measured
– Develop a knowledge bank that documents exemplary practices in schools

Flagship strategy 2: Developing a new resource allocation model

– Replace the school global budget with a new resource allocation model

Flagship strategy 3: Building leadership capacity

- Improved principal selection process
- Mentoring programme for first-time principals and a coaching support programme for experienced principals
- A balanced scorecard approach to principal performance management
- An accelerated development programme for high potential leaders
- A development programme for high performing principals
- Local administrative bureaus for networks of small schools

Flagship strategy 4: Creating and supporting a performance and development culture

- Accreditation scheme for performance and development culture in schools

Flagship strategy 5: Teacher professional development

- 60 teachers to undertake teacher professional leave ranging from 4 to 10 weeks
- Induction programme for beginning teachers, complemented by
- Mentoring programmes for beginning teachers

Flagship strategy 6: School improvement

- A differential model of school review
- Schools with student performance outcomes above expected levels to: indicate plans to expand horizons; propose alternative models of review; act as mentor schools and share good practice.
- Support for schools where student performance is satisfactory but where indicators suggest there is scope for improvement;
- Improvement strategy for schools where student performance outcomes are below the expected levels
- A range of interventions and support strategies.
- Schools to prepare single planning and accountability document
- Schools to be provided with parent, teacher and student opinion data
- Performance and development culture

Flagship strategy 7: Leading schools fund

- Provision of a Leading Schools Fund

The Office of Government School Education (OGSE) 'recognised that a precondition for implementing the school improvement strategy was for teachers, principals, and staff of the education office to "understand and engage in the core work of school improvement'" (Fraser and Petch, 2007, cited in OECD, 2007). An evidence-based model, the Effective Schools Model, based on a review of school effectiveness research (Sammons, Hillman and Mortimore, 1995) was used as a basis for building capacity in the system, and this became the basis for navigating the departmental website dedicated to the transformation process (http://www.sofweb.vic. edu.au/blueprint/)

One aspect where the Victorian system differs from that of our other case, Florida (or even more broadly, the USA), is in the area of terminology. Whereas the American terminology identifies standards, the Victorian system uses the word capabilities. The word 'standard' is similar to the word 'competence'. Both measure something that people can do or demonstrate. Cairns (1998) suggests that competence measures something learned in the past that can be measured today. He argues "Modern Teachers need to be developed as capable which is seen as moving 'beyond' initial competencies. The Capable Teacher is what we should be seeking to develop, encourage and honour as the hallmark of our profession" (1998, p. 1). Capability on the other hand, looks at what you have today that will assist you to make good judgments in the future. Stephenson (1993) describes capability as

...having justified confidence in your ability to:
- take appropriate and effective action
- communicate effectively
- collaborate with others
- learn from experiences
...in changing and unfamiliar circumstances.

The critical point is the last one, where changing and unfamiliar circumstances now are part and parcel of school leaders' and teachers' daily lives.

The Victorian framework of leadership capabilities uses Sergiovanni's Model of Transformational Leadership (Sergiovanni, 1984, 2005) as the basis for the leadership domains identified and within each domain a series of specific capabilities are also identified. Each domain has been developed into five different levels of leadership performance that forms a continuum of school leadership that encompasses teachers, middle level managers, new principals and principals with some years of experience.

This enables all people within the system to see themselves as leaders, to interpret where they are on the continuum, and to identify what they need to know or be able to do in order to move to the next level of capability. These capabilities are addressed by a range of programs offered by the state, or in conjunction with universities, that may result in a qualification in some cases, but in many cases do not. Many different programs are offered to aspirant school leaders and people who are already in leadership positions. Some involve mentoring and coaching, others are for principals who have been in the system for some years. Some involve teacher leave from the normal place of work so that they can research and report on practices elsewhere that might improve the capacity of their own school.

The OECD report argues (2007, p. 28) that 'the improvement strategy has also found ways of reconciling accountability and development' and that the

> ...Victorian leadership programme is an outstanding example of effective large-scale reform. Its rigorous, systematic process is projected out over several years in a carefully calibrated sequence with ample political support. No promise of a quick fix is made; but deep belief in the chosen course and its ultimate success characterize this programme...The Department has created professional learning opportunities for leaders at all levels in the system to seize, and the increasing numbers that have done so inject further knowledge and vitality into the system. This results in building human as well as knowledge capital on a large scale.

THE CASE OF FLORIDA

The nature and practice of school leadership and preparation programs have been under more intense scrutiny in the United States. Nationally, the Council of Chief State Superintendents commissioned the development of standards titled the *Interstate school leaders licensure consortium: Standards for school leaders* (1996). Almost without exception, individual states moved to adapt the ISLLC standards or develop their own state standards using ISLLC as a template. Florida, which had been a pioneer in using leadership research to develop principalship competencies as early as 1983, was one of the last states in the U.S. to develop its own set of state standards, nine years after ISLLC, in 2005. Earlier that same year, 2005, the field of educational leadership was shaken by the publication of the Levine report, *Educating School Leaders* (March, 2005). While many of the criticisms could have been predicted and were already being addressed, the tone of the Levine report was unequivocally negative. Part IV of the Report was subtitled 'A Race to the Bottom,' with sections including 'An Irrelevant Curriculum,' 'Low Admission and Graduation Standards,' 'A Weak Faculty,' 'Inadequate Clinical Instruction,' 'Inappropriate Degrees,' and 'Poor Research.' The report also identified nine criteria for judging the quality of leadership programs:

– Purpose,
– Curricular coherence,
– Curricular balance,
– Faculty composition,
– Admissions,
– Degrees,
– Research,
– Finances, and
– Assessment.

Many of these nine factors, however, are controlled by decisions made outside of university departments of educational leadership; yet departments of educational leadership are being held accountable for things they do not control. For instance, the number and quality of faculty depends on decisions made at the next level up (i.e., the College); admissions policies (and the quality of students enrolled), especially in state universities, are determined by university administrations that are more concerned with maintaining student numbers than they are about the background capabilities of those entrants; the quality of research undertaken depends on the College and University workload policies; and the resources available to a department are limited to those the state provides to the university, the university provides to the college and the college provides to the department. Unfortunately, many of these criteria in present day Florida are not at the level that one would hope for.

The Levine report (2005) generated substantial criticism from people within and outside the field. In Florida, the response was top down. Although educational leadership programs were assessed under the overall College of Education accreditation, National Association of Colleges of Teacher Education (NCATE), in 2008, another state mandated review of educational leadership programs offered at state universities was conducted. Now, in addition to a new set of ten statewide leadership standards, specific criteria [91 indicators total] were linked directly to a revised Florida Educational Leadership Examination (FELE) and were mandated for program reviews. The State Department of Education further asserted that new levels of partnership between universities and school districts would be required, thus changing the nature of leadership preparation.

In the past, there had been two levels of certification for Florida school leaders, the first level aligned with having undertaken an approved master's degree in educational leadership combined with having successfully passed the state certification test, the Florida Educational Leadership Examination (FELE). The second level of certification was school district based. The districts were charged with providing newly qualified school leaders with the specific knowledge required for working within that particular district.

The new Florida school leadership reforms seem to have amalgamated these two levels in ways that have created a range of difficulties for departments of educational leadership. In many cases the program being offered previously was general in the sense that it provided graduates with the knowledge in a non-district specific way, thus allowing departments to service a number of districts simultaneously. Specific knowledge was then supplied by the various districts in their own way and in their own time. Now, departments of educational leadership are obliged to provide documentation that their programs meet the needs of the districts they serve in very specific ways. This has created a situation whereby university departments that serve many school districts may now have to develop different programs to meet the different needs of various districts which may have totally different requirements than the districts geographically next to them. This makes for additional stresses on departments that serve multiple districts at a time when the resources available to university departments of educational leadership are at an all time low.

In theory, all of the new criteria and indicators of performance seem to be appropriate to developing programs that are focused on preparing leaders to high levels of competence. But in practice, there are a number of difficulties associated with this task. We have pointed out that departments of educational leadership are already accredited by two other agencies, one national (National Association of Colleges of Teacher Education – NCATE) and one regional (in Florida's case it is the Southern Association of Colleges and Schools – SACS) which may or may not require a different set of criteria for gaining accreditation. So much faculty time is now devoted to the various accreditation exercises that there is virtually no time left over to conduct leadership research on how schools might be improved. In this context of multiple accountability routines, which – unlike the case in Victoria is not comprehensive – the enormity of the discrete tasks can be seen.

A further concern arises when one considers that now university faculty is required to incorporate specific elements of state mandated programs as part of its own program curriculum. In Florida, the *William Cecil Golden Program for School Leaders,* directs its participants to particular books and expects faculty to undertake particular activities, thus usurping the professor's right to determine what curriculum he or she wishes to provide in addressing the specific skills, attitudes and dispositions that are associated with the course. The state is not only directing university departments on the 'what' to learn, but is also directing them on 'how' it should be learned.

Yet, even if this level of direction by the state was not considered unacceptable, the complexity involved reveals the magnitude and direction of the task.

It should be quite clear that the Florida Department of Education has a very specific agenda for university education of school leaders: that is, universities are expected to educate students specifically for employment by the state of Florida. This in itself is not such a bad thing and one might expect that graduates of a leadership program in Florida should be employable in Florida. But when one looks at the skills and competencies identified in detail, one might wonder exactly what being an educational leader in Florida entails.

Of the 91 specific skills identified as part of the new statewide FELE examination, 44 of them (48%) refer to a knowledge and understanding of state or federal legislature. Of the 16 skills that are identified under the standard of Managing the Learning Environment, 15 refer to state legislation or standards and of the 13 skills related to Human Resource Development, 12 refer to Federal or state laws or regulations. All 4 of the ethical leadership skills do the same. Clearly, an ethical leader is one that obeys the local rules. Four of the 6 skills related to Community School Partnerships can likewise be accomplished through memorizing state statutes.

It is telling that all of the skills under Vision focus more on communication of the vision than actually developing one, that the two skills under Diversity involve following the law and state communications and that only two of the ninety one skills (under Decision-Making Strategies) make any mention of leadership at all.
– Apply current concepts of leadership (e.g., systems theory, change theory, situational leadership, visionary leadership, transformational leadership, learning organizations).
– Select examples of organizational conditions or leadership actions that create positive attitudes toward change.

Therefore, it is clear to us that the notion of leadership as an art form is not required or wanted in the State of Florida at the moment. Much of the flexibility that is provided to school principals emerges in the area of Instructional Leadership, where the skills required within that leadership standard focus more on curriculum implementation and assessment. It needs to be pointed out however, that for many principals in Florida's schools, the curriculum is becoming narrower and narrower as more and more time is being spent on learning, studying and preparing for the annual standardized test, the Florida Comprehensive Assessment Test (FCAT). For those schools where most students do quite well, this may not be such an onerous task, but for schools that are likely to be labeled failing schools, with all sorts of sanctions attached, principals who do not focus their attention on FCAT performance do so at their own peril. All this becomes the mandated 'how' of school leadership and school improvement.

The case of Florida identifies new levels of pressure and stress that come about in the nation's search for no child being left behind. In the first instance of that search, teachers were seen to be the problem for chronic student 'underperformance;' then, school leaders were identified as the way in which teacher behavior might be changed; today, university departments of educational leadership are being seen as both the problem as well as the state's solution to raise student achievement defined as test scores. Unfortunately, as the figure below shows, student performance in reading, which has been the main thrust of the *No Child Left Behind Act* and a raft of other state level legislation that follows on from it, appears to only have had marginal increases in the past 35 years and that effect only lasts while the child is at an early point in their school career.

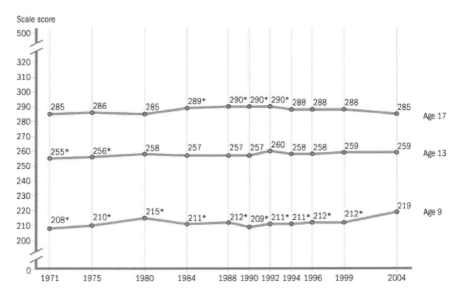

Figure 1: Trends in average reading scale scores for students ages 9, 13, and 17: 1971–2004

The scale scores for middle school students have remained static and those for high school students have actually gone backwards in the last decade.

Thus, once more, we must question the efficacy of top down managerial systems with respect to educational systems and comprehensive reforms. While such administrative actions have brought Florida notoriety in terms of meeting standards and accountability measures (see *Quality Counts),* it is quite different from the comprehensive 'what-how integration' documented in the case of Victoria. Where Victoria strives to develop leaders who are sensitive to context, to people, and school improvement through creating a statewide vision, Florida focuses almost exclusively on the 'what' of standards and accountability so as to improve student achievement. These goals, however, do not have to be mutually exclusive.

WHERE TO IN THE FUTURE?

What we have tried to demonstrate in this comparative case approach and in the book as a whole is the need for comprehensive systems' views of education that are 'complex and simple at the sample time.' In Victoria, there are 7 broad flagship strategies with 25 indicators in total; in Florida, there are 91 discrete tasks to be mastered even before one becomes a practicing school administrator. The differences in the numbers reflect different leadership theories-in-practice. In defense of Victoria, Elmore (2007) notes

> The good news is that Victoria, because of the thoughtful design of its improvement strategy, is on the leading edge of policy and practice in the world. There are few improvement strategies close to or as well developed, and probably none that are focused with such depth and complexity on the basic human capital problems associated with school improvement at scale. Unfortunately, this is also the bad news. What it means is that there are relatively few places Victoria can look to find the answers to the kinds of problems that will surface through the middle and later stages of the strategy. The special affliction of the precursor is to have to make the mistakes that others will learn from. (p. 5)

Many of us remember how in the mid-1980s, similar praise was directed toward Miami-Dade. The fourth largest school district was the *cause celebre, the whow!* for studying shared-decision-making [sdm], site-based management [sbm], and merit schools. Changes in superintendency and union leadership brought an ignominious end to these reforms. By the mid 1990's school reformers turned northward to Saskatchewan, Canada to study school-level governance. It, too, became, temporarily, the whow! Sadly, however, school reforms come and go, and so we cannot know the future of either case, Victoria or Florida. Both are using leadership to make changes and improve schools. One or both may be successful. How can we say this when the differences between Victoria and Florida are so striking?
- First, all school reforms are fragile and fleeting.
- Second, no educational researcher, neither we nor Elmore, knows what the ideal educational system looks like from top to bottom.

– Third, wherever there are educational reformers who know-what and know-how, there is hope for positive changes-even today in Florida.

Therefore, as leaders in action and in research, we must continue to study differences as found here. For example, do we begin with a few big ideas [e.g., culture, community, rebuilding, definitions of success] and then develop specific processes and skills? Or, do we begin with the nitty-gritty of daily life of a school administrator [e.g., given an internal audit report, the administrator will ....] and work to make the big picture come alive with years of experiences? Whatever the contexts, we, as educators, must have strategies, even contradictory strategies, in order to move systems forward. A good leader not only learns the rules, but also how to design systems and devise strategies that create new learning opportunities that work within and around the rules, across contexts. And, as MacBeath concludes, leaders make "the existential leap from the 'what' to the 'how'" and when it fails it learns from failure and has another go.

Is there a bottom-line message? We think so. In the case of Florida, the authors are working with their educational leadership colleagues both within the university and the surrounding school districts. We have chosen not to make expedient changes in our leadership preparation program. That is, although the state authorities have mandated the 'what' of school leadership, we, at the receiving end, can respect the fact that governments have some right to control the 'what', or at least a large part of it, but WE also can create new learning opportunities for ourselves and our students by ensuring that time and energy are spent focusing on the 'how'. Would we prefer to work collaboratively in building leadership capacities with the authorities? Of course we would, if asked. But there is nothing stopping us from being "enmeshed in the work" (Bogotch, 2002) and reforming educational leadership even without resources and support other than from our colleagues. If we were to adapt the 'core-plus approach' in schools used by Townsend (1994), we could identify the core-plus curriculum for leadership education where the 'core' is what is mandated by the state, and the 'plus' is what is determined locally as being important for the development of leaders in general. Analogously, the core-plus Department of Educational Leadership might have, as its *core business*, the preparation of leaders for local school systems, but its *plus business* would be to engage in research and teaching that promotes a better understanding of leadership itself. Thus simultaneously we are preparing school leaders for Florida, or Victoria or somewhere else (core), but also preparing them with the world of knowledge (plus). It is somewhere in this knowledge base that the 'whow' exists.

REFERENCES

Bogotch, I. (2002). 'Enmeshed in the work?' The educative power of developing standards. *Journal of School Leadership, 12*(5), 503–525.

Cairns, L. (1998). 'The capable teacher: The challenge for the 21st Century'. Paper presented at the 28th Annual Conference, Australian Teacher Education Association, Melbourne, Australia.

Council of Chief State School Officers (CCSSO) (1996). Interstate school leaders' licensure consortium: Standards for school leaders. Washington, DC: Author

DEECD (2003). *Blueprint for Government Schools: Future Directions for Education in the Victorian School System*, Melbourne: Department of Education and Early Childhood Development: State of Victoria.

Education Week, (2008). *Quality Counts.*

Elmore, R. (2007). *Educational Improvement in Victoria.* Melbourne, Victoria: Office for Government School Education, Department of Education.

Florida School Leaders. (2006). The William Cecil Golden School Leadership Development Program. https://www.floridaschoolleaders.org/

Fraser D., & Petch J. (2007). *School Improvement: A Theory of Action,* Office of School Education, Department of Education and Early Childhood Development: State of Victoria.

Levine, A. (2005). *Educating school leaders.* Washington, DC: The Education Schools Project.

Matthews, P., Moorman, H., & Nusche, D. (2007). *School leadership development strategies: Building leadership capacity in Victoria, Australia: A case study report for the OECD activity Improving school leadership,* OECD Directorate of Education: Paris

Sammons P., Hillman J., & Mortimore, P. (1995). *Key Characteristics of Effective Schools: A Review of School Effectiveness Research,* London: Office for Standards in Education and Institute of Education.

Sergiovanni, T. J. (1984). *Handbook for Effective Department Leadership: Concepts and practices in today's secondary schools.* Boston: Allyn & Bacon.

Sergiovanni, T. J. (2005). *The Principalship: A Reflective Practice Perspective,* 5th ed. Boston: Allyn & Bacon.

Stephenson, J. (1994). 'Capability and competence: Are they the same and does it matter?' *Capability,* 1

Townsend, T. (1994). *Core Plus Education: Effective Schooling for the Community.* London: Routledge.

Tony Townsend is a Professor and has just completed a four year term as Chair of the Department of Educational Leadership in the College of Education at Florida Atlantic University. Previously he was an Associate Professor in the Faculty of Education at Monash University in Australia. His research interests include school effectiveness and improvement, school restructuring with a particular emphasis on public education, educational leadership, student engagement, strategic planning, global education and community education and development. Tony has given numerous lectures, workshops, conference papers and presentations in the areas of school effectiveness and improvement, leadership, community education, policy development and school and community administration in over 35 developed, and developing, countries and has published extensively in the areas of school effectiveness, school improvement and community education and development, in Australia, Europe and North America

Ira Bogotch is a Professor of Educational Leadership at Florida Atlantic University. He serves as the Associate Editor of the *International Journal of Leadership in Education* and is on numerous editorial boards including *Educational Administration Quarterly* and *Urban Education.* His research focuses on school-based management, leadership discourses, socio-cultural differences in and around schools, and social justice as an educational construct.

THE AUTHORS

Gert Biesta is Professor of Education at The Stirling Institute of Education, University of Stirling, Scotland, UK. He conducts theoretical and empirical research on the relationships between education and democracy in formal and informal educational settings and takes inspiration from pragmatism and continental philosophy.

Sharmistha Das is a Research Fellow in the School of Education of the University of Aberdeen, in Scotland. She has worked as a practitioner and a researcher within the field of education in Bangladesh, England and Scotland. Recent years' experience has developed her keen interest in the areas of organisational culture, values promoting teachers' professional identities and classroom cultures.

Charles Dukes is an assistant professor in the department of Exceptional Student Education at Florida Atlantic University in Boca Raton, Florida, USA where he teaches courses in special education. His research interests include linking multicultural and special education, positive behavioral interventions, and urban school reform.

Alma Harris is Professor of Educational Leadership at London Centre for Leadership in Learning, at the Institute of Education, University of London. Her research work has focused upon organizational change and leadership, especially school improvement, focusing particularly on ways in which leadership can contribute to school development and change.

Klaus Kasper Kofod is an Assistant Professor in the Department of Educational Sociology at the Danish University of Education, Copenhagen, Denmark, and he is a member of the Research Programme on Professional Development and Leadership. His research interests included leadership and management in educational institutions, organising, organisational culture and change, and the professions.

John Krejsler is an Associate professor in the Department of Educational Anthropology in the Danish School of Education, University of Aarhus, Copenhagen and he is a member of the Research Programme on Professional Development and Leadership. His research interests are higher education, teacher education and epistemology (poststructural and critical theory), as well as professional subjectivities and power relations in education.

John MacBeath is Emeritus Professor of Educational Leadership in the Faculty of Education at the University of Cambridge. His research interests encompass leadership at every level within a school from classroom to school and beyond school. Student leadership is of particular interest, which links closely to self-evaluation in which students can pay a leading role.

Kavin Ming is an assistant professor at the Donald and Helen Ross College of Education at Lynn University in Boca Raton, Florida, USA where she teaches courses in literacy and special education. Her research interests include linking multicultural and special education, at risk populations, and literacy development.

Luis Mirón is Dean of the College of Social Sciences and Distinguished Professor of Social Sciences at Loyola University in New Orleans. His research has focused on the social construction of urban schooling, performative methodologies and, most recently, on the school rebuilding policies and "experiments" in post-Katrina New Orleans.

Lejf Moos is an Associate professor in the Department of Educational Anthropology in the Danish School of Education, University of Aarhus, Copenhagen and he is a member of the Research Programme on Professional Development and Leadership. His research interests include school leadership at multiple levels, school development and assessment, evaluation and accountability in schools and educational systems.

Pat Thomson is a Professor and Director of Research in the School of Education at the University of Nottingham. Her current research focuses on the changing work of school administrators; postgraduate writing pedagogies; students who are excluded from school; democratising education and how children understand and represent their social and material place in the world.

INDEX